Library of Arabic Linguistics

The reasons behind the establishment of this Series on Arabic linguistics are manifold. First: Arabic linguistics is developing into an increasingly interesting and important subject within the broad field of modern linguistic studies. The subject is now fully recognized in the Universities of the Arabic speaking world and in international linguistic circles, as a subject of great theoretical and descriptive interest and importance.

Second: Arabic linguistics is reaching a mature stage in its development benefiting from both the early Arabic linguistic scholarship and modern techniques of general linguistics and related disciplines.

Third: The scope of this discipline is wide and varied, covering diverse areas such as Arabic phonetics, phonology and grammar, Arabic psycholinguistics, Arabic dialectology, Arabic lexicography and lexicology, Arabic sociolinguistics, teaching and learning of Arabic as a first, second, or foreign language, communications, semiotics, terminology, translation, machine translation, Arabic computational linguistics, history of Arabic linguistics, etc.

Viewed against this background, Arabic linguistics may be defined as: the scientific investigation and study of the Arabic language in all its aspects. This embraces the descriptive, comparative and historical aspects of the language. It also concerns itself with the classical form as well as the modern and contemporary standard forms and their dialects. Moreover, it attempts to study the language in the appropriate regional, social and cultural settings.

It is hoped that the Series will devote itself to all issues of Arabic linguistics in all its manifestations both on the theoretical and applied levels. The results of these studies will also be of use in the field of linguistics in general, as well as related subjects.

Although a number of works have appeared independently or within Series, yet there is no platform designed specifically for this subject. This Series is being started to fill this gap in the linguistic field. It will be devoted to Monographs written in either English or Arabic, or both, for the benefit of wider circles of readership.

All these reasons justify the establishment of a new forum which is devoted to all areas of Arabic linguistic studies. It is also hoped that this Series will be of interest not only to students and researchers in Arabic linguistics but also to students and scholars of other disciplines who are looking for information of both theoretical, practical or pragmatic interest.

The Series Editor

Transitivity, causation and passivization

Library of Arabic Linguistics

Series editor
Muhammad Hasan Bakalla
King Saud University, Riyadh, Kingdom of Saudi Arabia

Advisory editorial board
Peter F. Abboud *University of Texas at Austin*
M. H. Abdulaziz *University of Nairobi*
Yousif El-Khalifa Abu Bakr *University of Khartoum*
Salih J. Altoma *Indiana University*
Arne Ambros *University of Vienna*
El Said M. Badawi *American University in Cairo*
Michael G. Carter *University of Sydney*
Ahmad al-Dhubaib *King Saud University* (formerly, University of Riyadh)
Martin Forstner *Johannes Gutenberg University at Mainz*
Bruce Ingham *University of London*
Otto Jastrow *University of Erlangen-Nurnberg*
Raja T. Nasr *University College of Beirut*
C. H. M. Versteegh *Catholic University at Nijmegen*
Bougslaw R. Zagorski *University of Warsaw*

George Nehmeh Saad
University of Massachusetts, at Amherst

Transitivity, causation and passivization

A semantic-syntactic study of the verb in classical Arabic

Monograph No. 4

Routledge
Taylor & Francis Group
LONDON AND NEW YORK

First published 1982 by Kegan Paul International Ltd

2 Park Square, Milton Park, Abingdon, Oxfordshire OX14 4RN
52 Vanderbilt Avenue, New York, NY 10017

Routledge is an imprint of the Taylor & Francis Group, an informa business

First issued in paperback 2019

ISBN 13: 978-0-7103-0037-9 (hbk)
ISBN 13: 978-1-138-98604-6 (pbk)

This book is dedicated to the memory of my brother, Nabil

Editor's note

Syntax is the study of the sentences of a language and their interrelationships; Case Grammar is a theory about the functions of the semantico-syntactic concepts of cases in the construction of sentences. This theory was devised by the American linguist Charles Fillmore in the late 1960's within the general orientation of Generative Grammar.

The present monograph deals with certain aspects of the syntax of the Arabic language which includes both Classical Arabic and Modern Standard Arabic. In particular, it treats the concepts and processes of transitivity and causativization and their relationship to the question of passivization. It is true that such concepts and processes have been dealt with in early Arabic linguistic scholarship since Sibawayhi. However this monograph attempts to formalize the rules which govern the syntactic processes mentioned above using the Case Grammar theory and technique together with the appropriate notions from early Arabic grammatical sources. In addition, this study does not spare the effort to draw on, and make use of, other linguistic notions and techniques. The reader will find that the present study draws from linguistic notions developed and advanced by W. P. Lehmann and M. A. K. Halliday and other modern linguists.

This monograph consists of six chapters. While the first chapter is an introduction, the last one contains the conclusions of this work. Chapter 2 lays down the theoretical foundation and the framework upon which this study is based. The language-universal and language-specific matters which are related to Case Grammar theory are discussed here, and illustrative examples are given not only from Arabic but also from other languages including Turkish, Japanese and English. All the cases which are relevant to the present work are introduced here and described in full detail.

Chapter 3 treats the passive/active construction in Arabic both within the early Arabic grammatical theories and the modern techniques of Transformational Generative Grammar in general and Case Grammar in particular. It also gives a detailed classification of the verbs in Arabic and indicates the appropriate case frame of each class and its sub-classes.

Chapter 4 presents a detailed analysis of the causative verbs in Arabic. It also deals with the morphological and inflectional derivation of the causatives. Both the syntactic and semantic properties of causatives are given a special consideration here, and the formal rules for their derivation are also given.

Chapter 5 is on transitivity and ergativity in Arabic. It claims that passivization in Arabic is best defined in terms of these two notions. Again, the Arabic verbs are further classified and sub-classified on the basis of these concepts.

A word about the author is now in order. George Saad's work represents a synthesis of the theories of the Arab Grammarians of the 8th-10th centuries with those of contemporary linguists. His insights flow from the preparation he received as a scholar in the Middle East and in the United States. Born in 1940, in Haifa, Palestine, he received his early education in Arabic, French and English language schools in Palestine and Lebanon. He obtained two Licence d'Enseignement degrees, one in Arabic Literature and Language in 1966, and another in English Literature and Language in 1969, both from the Lebanese University. He was awarded his Ph.D. in Linguistics from the University of Texas at Austin, in 1975.

The author is a principal contributor to the emerging field of contemporary linguistics in the Arab world. His scholarly work encompasses both theoretical and applied linguistics. His research focuses on syntax, and his writings include several articles about Arabic syntax and Universal Grammar. His special interest in syntax of the Arabic tradition, particularly syntax of the Qur'an, has led him to study the work of the eighth-century scholar, Sibawayhi, the most prominent Arab Grammarian. Dr. Saad has been one of the pioneers in bringing to the attention of American linguists the Arab Muslim grammarians, especially Sibawayhi, some of whose insights about language remain unsurpassed.

In addition to his specialization in syntax, Dr. Saad has also developed a theoretical framework for the study of the relationship between language and culture. He has actively participated in conferences on Arabic syntax, morphology, and lexicography, and has contributed frequently to Pan-Arab and international symposia, colloquia, and forums.

Dr. Saad's career as an educator began in 1961, as a high school teacher of English and Arabic language and literature. He has taught continuously since, at the University of Texas while a graduate student, later at the University of Riyadh, and currently at the University of Massachusetts at Amherst, in the United States. In addition to teaching courses in linguistic theory, linguistic methodology, and the teaching of Arabic as a second language, he has published textbooks and source materials. He assisted the authors in the writing of *Intermediate Modern Standard Arabic*, and co-authored *Elementary Modern Standard Arabic*, both textbooks by Abboud, et al., University of Michigan, 1971, and 1975, respectively. He is the author of an innovative text for teaching *Arabic Sounds and Letters*, University of

Massachusetts, 1979. He also co-authored *A Dictionary of Modern Linguistic Terms*, Librairie du Liban, Longmans, 1981.

Finally, the present monograph is an original research work which lays down the foundation of a modern scientific interpretation of some aspects of Arabic syntax. It is therefore a must for students and researchers in Arabic linguistics in particular, as well as to researchers in the fields of linguistics and adjacent sciences in general. Dr. Saad is well-qualified to bring out this present study as a source of information and illumination on this little-known but very interesting area of the Arabic syntax.

M. H. Bakalla
King Saud University, Riyadh
1 January 1982

Contents

List of Tables xiv
List of Proposed Arabic Case Roles xiv
List of Symbols and Abbreviations xv
ACKNOWLEDGEMENTS xviii

1 INTRODUCTION 1
1.1 Purpose and Justification 1
1.2 Preliminaries 3
1.2.1 The Language 3
1.2.2 Verb Classification 4
1.2.3 Transliteration 4
1.2.4 Word Order: Arabic, a VSO Language 8
1.3 Outline 12

2 THEORETICAL FRAMEWORK 13
2.1 Introductory Remarks 13
2.2 The Q Component 14
2.3 The P Component 16
2.3.1 Background 16
2.3.2 Case Roles 20
2.4 Surface Phenomena 27
2.4.1 Residual Problems 27
2.4.2 Transformations 28

3 THE PASSIVE 31
3.1 The Early Arab Grammarians Account of Passivization 31
3.2 A Survey of the Arabic Passive in Transformational Grammar 32
3.3 The Nature of the Arabic Passive Construction 34
3.4 Passivizability 38
3.4.1 Nonpassivizable Verbs 39
3.4.1.1 One-place Verbs 39
3.4.1.2 Defective Verbs and the Verb *Kana* 'To Be' 42

3.4.1.3 The *Kallafa* 'To Cost' Type Verbs 45
3.4.1.4 The *sabaha* 'To Resemble' Type Verbs 46
3.4.2 Passivizable Verbs 49
3.4.2.1 Implemental Verbs 49
3.4.2.2 Physical Perception Verbs 51
3.4.2.3 Reciprocal Form III FaMaLa Verbs 52
3.4.2.4 Resultative Verbs 52
3.4.2.5 Emotive and Cognitive Verbs 53
3.4.2.6 Verbs of Transforming 55
3.4.2.7 Verbs of Acquiring 55
3.4.2.8 Causative Verbs 56
3.4.2.9 Verbs of Certainty and Doubt 56
3.4.2.10 Miscellanea 58
3.4.3 Problems and Solutions 59
3.4.3.1 Range as Subject of the Passive Verb 59
3.4.3.2 Time and Place as Subjects of the Passive Verb 61
3.4.3.3 Subjectivization 61

4 CAUSATIVE VERBS 65
4.1 Introduction 65
4.2 Covert Causatives 66
4.2.1 Derivation of Covert Causatives 66
4.2.1.1 Morphologically Derived Causatives 66
4.2.1.2 Prepositionally Derived Causatives 67
4.2.2 Causativization 68
4.2.3 Syntactic and Semantic Properties of Covert Causatives 72
4.2.4 Syntactic Derivation of Covert Causative Constructions 76
4.3 Overt Causatives 81
4.3.1 Differences between O.C.C. and C.C.C. 81
4.3.2 Hypercausatives 83

5 TRANSITIVITY, ERGATIVITY, AND THE DERIVATION OF PASSIVES 87
5.1 Introduction 87
5.2 Transitivity and Ergativity 87
5.2.1 Transitivity 87
5.2.2 Ergativity 89
5.2.3 A Verb Typology in Terms of Transitivity and Ergativity 91
5.2.4 Transitivity, Ergativity and the Case Roles 94
5.3 Syntactic Derivation of Passives 94
5.4 Three Place Nonmiddle Verbs 95

5.5 Reflexives 97
5.5.1 Two Place Reflexive Verbs 97
5.5.2 Reflexivity 98

6 CONCLUSION 102

BIBLIOGRAPHY 105

GLOSSARY OF TECHNICAL TERMS: ENGLISH-ARABIC 109

GENERAL INDEX 115

THE ARABIC SECTION 122

LIST OF TABLES

TABLE — Page

1 TRANSLITERATION OF THE ARABIC WRITING SYSTEM 5

2 ARABIC CONSONANTS AND VOWELS 6

3 SYSTEM OF CLASSIFICATION FOR THE FIRST TEN MOST COMMON FORMS 7

LIST OF PROPOSED ARABIC CASE ROLES (i.e. Arabic Deep Structure Cases)

CASE ROLE — Page

1. Agent 20
2. Instrument 21
3. Patient 21
4. Target 22
5. Range 22
6. Source 23
7. Goal 24
8. Place 24
9. Time 24
10. Manner 24
11. Beneficiary 25
12. Comitative 25

LIST OF SYMBOLS AND ABBREVIATIONS

$\rightarrow$	Single Arrow. It signifies a linguistic rule and is to be read "rewrite as"
$\Rightarrow$	Double Arrow. It signifies a semantic rule and is to be read "is further specified as"
$\sim$	Wavy Line. It indicates that no order is implied between the elements on both ends of such a line. Thus, for example, $x \sim y$ is equivalent to $y \sim x$
Δ	The Greek letter *delta*. It signifies an unspecified meaningful Agent case role in an "agentless" passive construction
Σ	The Greek letter *sigma*. It stands for "Sentence"
A	Adjectival expression
CA	Classical Arabic
Causat.	Causative
CAUSE	A nonlexicalized semantic predicate that signifies causation
Desid.	Desiderative. This is a verbal modifier that signifies "wish" or "desire"
F	A Q–component Syntactic feature
G	Genitival expression
Imperf.	Imperfect
Intens.	Intensive. This is a verbal modifier that signifies intensive frequentative or extensive action
Inter.	Interrogative
Itr	Intransitive
K	Case Role or Deep Structure Case
MSA	Modern Standard Arabic
Masc.	Masculine
M.S.	Masculine Singular

Necess.	Necessative. This is a verbal modifier that signifies necessity
Neg.	Negative
O	Object
OV	Object-Verb. This is a word order according to which the object precedes the verb
OV language	A language in which the unmarked word order is OV (see OV above)
P	P–component or Proposition component. This is a deep structure that consists of an unmodified verb and one or more case roles or deep structure cases
Pl	Plural
Perf.	Perfect
Poten.	Potential. This is a verbal modifier that signifies ability
Q	Q–component or Qualifier component. This is a categorial element through which verbal modifiers affecting the entire sentence are introduced into setences
Recip.	Reciprocal. This is a verbal modifier that signifies reciprocity
Rel	Relative construction or Relative clause
S	Subject
SOV	Subject–Object–Verb. This is a word order according to which the object precedes the verb, and the subject precedes the object
SOV language	A language in which the unmarked word order is SOV(see SOV above)
SVO	Subject–Verb–Object. This is a word order according to which the verb precedes the object and the subject precedes the verb
SVO language	A language in the which the unmarked word order is SVO (see SVO above)
Subj.	Subjunctive
Tr	Transitive
V	Verb
VO	Verb–Object. This is a word order according to which the verb precedes the object

VO language	A language in which the unmarked word order is VO(see VO above)
VSO	Verb–Subject–Object. This is a word order according to which the subject precedes the object, and the verb precedes the subject.
VSO language	A language in which the unmarked word order is VSO(see VSO above)

ACKNOWLEDGEMENTS

I am deeply indebted to W.P. Lehmann who took special interest in this work from its very inception. Without the guidance of this great scholar, this book might never have been completed.

I thank Peter Abboud, who gave generously of his valuable time and knowledge, for his constructive criticism and evaluation.

To the late Najm Bezirgan, C.L. Baker, Solveig Pfleuger and Ali Kasimi, I am grateful for their contributions to this work, each from his or her own scholarly perspective.

Any linguist will recognize the influence of Charles Fillmore on the hypotheses presented in this work. I am, in more than one way, a student of his. His work in linguistics was most inspiring to me, and for that I thank him.

The influence of the Muslim Arab grammarians is evident in every chapter of this book. My conclusions are inspired by their theories and by their tireless devotion to linguistic detail as well as linguistic generalization. In particular, I can characterize myself as a disciple of Sibawayhi, al-Zamakhshari and Ibn Ya'ish.

Finally, I wish to express my special gratitude to Muhammad Hasan Bakalla, a scholar who has the rare quality of possessing both the depth of insight and the breadth of knowledge about traditional, modern and contemporary linguistic theory. He contributed significantly to enhancing my knowledge of Arabic and Qur'anic syntax. His encouragement, and his scholarly and moral support are most highly appreciated.

G.N.S.
Amherst, June 30, 1981

1 Introduction

1.1 Purpose and Justification

The purpose of this study is to investigate the relationship of transitivity and causation to the process of passivization in Arabic, to describe in as concise a form as possible the syntactic nature of Arabic passive constructions, and to explore the syntactic and semantic properties of passivizable verbs and those of verbs that cannot be passivized.

It is generally assumed that languages have two major classes of verbs distinguished primarily by whether or not they take a direct object. Transitive verbs take direct objects and may undergo passivization; intransitives lack objects and may not be passivized. In accordance with this definition of transitivity, every passive sentence has an underlying active sentence. A verb like *qatala* 'to kill' is a transitive verb which takes an object and which may be passivized:

(1)	a. *qatala zaydun ᶜamran.*	'Zayd killed 'Amr'
	b. *qutila ᶜamrun.*	' 'Amr was killed'

To derive a passive construction like b from an active construction like a, it is traditionally assumed that a passivization process takes place in which the subject *zaydun* is deleted, the object *ᶜamran* becomes subject and is assigned the nominative case ending thus becoming *ᶜamrun*, and a change in the internal vowels of the verb is brought about.

This traditional approach to transitivity and passivization fails to account for the following facts:

(i) Active constructions like a and passive constructions like b are not synonymous. Since passive sentences are syntactically derivable from active sentences, according to the traditional approach, the passivization process mentioned above may be considered a passive transformation or series of transformations. A very important problem that immediately poses itself for such a treatment of the passives pertains to the hypothesis, adopted in this work, that transformations are meaning preserving. The putative passive transformation is not meaning preserving because whereas the agent is explicitly specified in a, it is not in b. One might hypothesize the existence of a passive transformation and a truncation transformation similar to those suggested in the literature for English. Derivation (2) below illustrates the point:

(2) Someone killed Bill . . . . .Underlying Form
Bill was killed by someone . . . . .Passive Transformation
Bill was killed .Truncation Transformation

This would seem plausible except that Arabic passives are agentless and there is no agentive particle corresponding to the English by or the French par, for example, in Arabic. *Min* 'from' is the closest Arabic preposition to by semantically, but even so it cannot occur in passives. Thus one encounters *qutila zaydun* 'Zayd was killed,' but not **qutila zaydun min ᶜamrin* 'Zayd was killed by 'Amr' or **qutila zaydun min ʔaḥadi al-nāsi* 'Zayd was killed by someone.'

(ii) Certain transitive verbs in Arabic take a direct object but they do not passivize:

(3) 1a.	*tazawwaja zaydun hindan*	'Zayd married Hind'
b.	**tuzuwwijat hindun*	'*Hind was married'[1]
2a.	*jāʔanī xabarun*	'a (piece of) news came (to) me'
b.	**jiʔtu*	'*I was come'
3a.	*waṣalathā risālatun*	'a letter reached her'
b.	**wuṣilat*	'she was reached'
4a.	*balaġanā annahu istaqāla*	'It reached us that he resigned'
b.	**buliġnā*	'we were reached'
5a.	*ḥaḍarū al-ʔijtimāᶜa*	'They attended the meeting'
b.	**ḥuḍira al-ʔijtimāᶜu*	'The meeting was attended'
6a.	*yušbihu zaydun ᶜamran*	'Zayd resembles 'Amr'
b.	**yušbahu ᶜamrun*	'*'Amr is resembled'

(iii) Certain intransitive verbs do not take a direct object but they passivize. Such passives are known as impersonal passives, and the passive verb takes the third person singular form:

(4) 1a.	*nāma zaydun fī al-dāri*	'Zayd slept in the house'
b.	*nīma fī al-dāri*	'It was slept in the house'
2a.	*ḏahabtu ʔilā al-qudsi*	'I went to Jerusalem'
b.	*ḏuhiba ʔilā al-qudsi*	'It was gone to Jerusalem'
3a.	*jāʔa zaydun bi hindin*	'Zayd came with (i.e. brought) Hind'
b.	*jīʔa bi hindin*	'It was come with Hind'

(iv) Certain passive sentences in Arabic do not have corresponding active sentences:

(5) a.	*junna zaydun*	'Zayd was possessed; maddened'
b.	*zukimat hindun*	'Hind caught a cold'
c.	*sulla al-rajulu*	'The man was afflicted with tuberculosis'
d.	*duhišū*	'They were amazed, astonished'
e.	*ḏuhilat al-nisāʔu*	'The women were emaciated'
f.	*ʔūlīᶜa bihā*	'he was enamored (fond) of her'
g.	*fulija walas*	'Wallace was paralyzed'
h.	*zuhiya ᶜamrun*	' 'Amr was conceited'

It might be argued that these verbs are nothing but stative verbs and that they happen to be passive only in form especially when one looks at the English translations of the sentences of these verbs. These verbs must not be treated as stative because their derived verbals do not have the form of stative adjectives but rather the form of passive participles. Moreover, the stative meaning of the above English sentences can be expressed by using the passive participle, with the verb *kāna* 'to be' in the past tense:

(6)	a.	*kāna zaydun majnūnan*	'Zayd was mad'
	b.	*kāna al-rajulu maslūlan*	'The man was afflicted with T.B.'
	c.	*kānat al-nisāʔu mašdūhātin*	'The women were emaciated'
	d.	*kāna mūlaᶜan bihā*	'He was fond of her'

It should be mentioned here that these verbs imply understood agency; in order to understand this agency we have to look into the beliefs of the people who used these verbs. Some of these verbs have been used for over 1400 years now. To the people who used them, the agent is some force they can't understand. This force can be God, the devil, evil spirits, angels, etc.

In view of what has preceded, it is obvious that the traditional definition of transitivity has to be reconsidered, and that a study afresh of the passivization process is needed; and this is what this book will attempt to do.

1.2 Preliminaries

1.2.1 The Language

The language described in this work has been in use for more than fourteen centuries. We will use the term Arabic to refer to its two well-known varieties: Classical Arabic and Modern Standard Arabic.

Classical Arabic (henceforth CA) is the revered language of the Holy Koran, and the language of pre-Islamic poetry and post-Islamic poetry, literature, philosophy, theology, mathematics, sciences, etc.

Modern Standard Arabic (henceforth MSA), also known as Modern Written Arabic and Modern Literary Arabic, is the uniform variety of Arabic which is used all over the Arabic speaking world as the usual medium of written communication in books, periodicals, journals, magazines, newspapers, signs, business and personal letters. MSA is also used as the medium of oral communication on the stage, in radio and television broadcasts, in formal speeches, public and university lectures, learned debates, conferences, in some songs, and in general on occasions accompanied by some degree of formality and solemnity.

The colloquial Arabic dialects, on the other hand, which differ considerably among themselves and from place to place are used for everyday oral communication by all the people of the dialect area.

MSA differs from CA mainly in lexicon and style and to a much lesser extent in grammar; both differ from the colloquials in lexicon, style, phonology, syntax and sociolinguistic function.

Arabic, as defined above (i.e., MSA and/or CA), is a literary language learned by literate Arabs after their initial acquisition of a modern dialect of spoken Arabic. Control of Arabic varies considerably among individuals. This poses a problem for the linguist because there can be no direct appeal to "native intuition." As a result, informants of Arabic whose judgements can be safely trusted are few in number; they are those who are highly educated and specialized in Arabic. "Native intuition" about Arabic is difficult to separate from intuition about grammatical structures in the informant's spoken language.

Phonologically one can easily discern the influence of the phonological system of the speaker's native dialect on literary Arabic. In an Arabic word like *madrasah,* for example, a Syrian places the primary stress on the first syllable while an Egyptian places it on the second. Syntactically it is more difficult to discern the influence of the colloquial on Arabic.

At least one instance of syntactic change or development in Arabic from CA to MSA will be discussed in this book. Where a difference between the two varieties of Arabic is discernible, the term CA or MSA will be used, otherwise the term Arabic will refer to both varieties.

1.2.2. Verb Classification

Grammars of Arabic have emphasized morphological structure as a basis for verb classification. There are fifteen forms of Arabic verbs derived from the basic triliteral root.[2] These forms are known in the west by their corresponding Roman numerals I-XV. No Arabic root can take all fifteen forms, although there is no phonological basis for explaining why all forms should not be possible or for predicting which forms a root may take. Rather, one finds that the various verb forms are related by syntactic and semantic constraints and that all verbs are ultimatley derived from the roots of simple form I verbs or from the roots of nouns. Ten of the fifteen forms (I-X) are the most common, the rest being concerned with rare or obsolete classical occurrences. Table 3 (below (p. 7) shows this system of classification for the first ten most common forms. F, M, and L in this table stand for first, middle, and last consonant of the root. All forms may occur in the passive except for forms VII and IX, for which no passive exists. The parenthesized (?i) is not part of the morphological derivation and is predictable.

1.2.3 Transliteration

A transliteration of the Arabic writing system is given in Table 1 (p. 5). The definite article will be always transliterated as al- in spite of the fact that it has a *hamza* ? in the Arabic system of writing. An articulatory phonetic chart of Arabic consonants and vowels is given in Table 2 (p. 6).

TABLE 1

TRANSLITERATION OF THE ARABIC WRITING SYSTEM

Arabic Letter	Translit-eration		Phonetic Value	Arabic Letter	Translit-eration		Phonetic Value
			Consonants				
ء	?	'	ʔ	ض	ḍ		đ
ب	b		b	ط	ṭ		ŧ
ت	t		t	ظ	ẓ		ð̶
ث	ṯ	th	θ	ع	c	'	ʕ
ج	j		j	غ	ġ;	gh	ɣ
ح	ḥ		ħ	ف	f		f
خ	x	kh	x	ق	q		q
د	d		d	ك	k		k
ذ	ḏ	dh	ð	ل	l		l
ر	r		r	م	m		m
ز	z		z	ن	n		n
س	s		s	ه	h		h
ش	š	sh	ʃ	و	w		w
ص	ṣ		ṣ	ي	y		y
			Vowels				
ـَ	a		a	ـَا	ā		a:
ـُ	u		u	ـُو	ū		u:
ـِ	i		i	ـِي	ī		i:

Under Transliteration, the symbols on the left hand column are used here for the transliteration of the Arabic texts;the symbols on the right hand column are also used in transliterating Arabic names and titles, as commonly used.

TABLE 2
ARABIC CONSONANTS AND VOWELS

	Labial	Dental	Alveolar	Velarized	Palatal	Velar	Uvular	Pharyngeal	Glottal
Stops	b	t d		ṭ ḍ		k	q		ʔ
Fricatives	f	ṯ ḏ	s z	ṣ ẓ	š		x ġ	ḥ c	h
Affricate					j				
Nasals	m		n						
Lateral			l						
Vibrant			r						
Semivowels	w				y				

		Front	Back
High	Short	i	u
	Long	ī	ū
Low	Short	a	
	Long	ā	

TABLE 3

SYSTEM OF CLASSIFICATION FOR THE FIRST TEN MOST COMMON FORMS

	Form	Perfect	Imperfect
I.	Active	FaM$\begin{Bmatrix}a\\u\\i\end{Bmatrix}$La	yaFM$\begin{Bmatrix}a\\u\\i\end{Bmatrix}$Lu
	Passive	FuMiLa	yuFMaLu
II.	Active	FaMMaLa	yuFaMMiLu
	Passive	FuMMiLa	yuFaMMaLu
III.	Active	FāMaLa	yuFāMiLu
	Passive	FūMiLa	yuFāMaLu
IV.	Active	?aFMaLa	yuFMiLu
	Passive	?uFMiLa	yuFMaLu
V.	Active	taFaMMaLa	yataFaMMaLu
	Passive	tuFuMMiLa	yutaFaMMaLu
VI.	Active	taFāMaLa	yataFāMaLu
	Passive	tuFūMiLa	yutaFāMaLu
VII.	Active	(?i) nFaMaLa	yanFaMiLu
	Passive	*(?u)nFuMiLa	*yunFaMaLu
VIII.	Active	(?i)FtaMaLa	yaFtaMiLu
	Passive	(?u)FtuMiLa	yuFtaMaLu
IX.	Active	(?i)FmaLLa	yaFMaLLu
	Passive	*(?u)FMuLLa	*yuFMaLLu
X.	Active	(?i)staFMaLa	yastaFMiLu
	Passive	(?u)stuFMiLa	yustaFMaLu

1.2.4 Word Order: Arabic, a VSO Language

In the very small body of linguistic literature that has been written about Arabic in transformational grammar, Arabic has been treated as an SVO language. Such treatment is found in works like Snow's dissertation (1965), Killean's dissertation (1966), and Lewkowicz' dissertation (1967). This has been done under the influence of Noam Chomsky (1957) and (1965). Noam Chomsky did not specify in these works whether the base he proposed was for English only or for all languages. This has misled people into believing that the base he proposed was a universal base.

In this section it will be shown that Arabic is a VSO language by examining its basic order typology in light of W. P. Lehmann's typological study (1973) and Joseph H. Greenberg's linguistic universals (1961).

Consistent VO languages are inflectional rather than agglutinative in their morphology. Arabic is inflectional in its morphological structure, and this can be illustrated by comparing the simple form of the verb with the Arabic causative and the Arabic reciprocal, or with any derived form:

(7) a. *kataba risālatan* — 'he wrote a letter'
b. *kattabahu risālatan* — 'he made him write a letter'
c. *kātabahu* — 'he corresponded (with) him'

In inflectional languages, entities marking morphological categories may merge with the root, affect elements in the root, or be affected by elements in the root, in contrast with agglutinative languages in which entities marking categories are affixed and maintained distinct from the root. In the above examples the lengthening of the vowel in *kātaba* and the gemination of *t* in *kattaba* are instances of the inflectional character of Arabic.

Lehmann (1973) proposed a fundamental principle of placement for categorial entities which represent modifiers. By this principle, modifiers are placed on the opposite side of a basic syntactic element from its primary concomitant. The verb is the primary concomitant of the object, which is a noun. Therefore modifiers that modify the object which is a noun occupy the position opposite to the verb which is the primary concomitant of the object. According to this principle, nominal modifiers must follow the noun in VO languages, the order must be as follows: V O Nominal modifier(s).

This placement of nominal modifiers is characteristic of Arabic which is a consistent VO language. In Arabic, nominal modifers—such as relative constructions adjectival and genitival expressions—follow nouns:

(8) a. N Rel — *šāhada zaydun al-kalba ʔallaḏī ʔakala qiṭᶜata al-laḥmi*
'Zayd saw the dog that ate the piece of meat'

b. N A — *šāhada zaydun al-kalba al-kabīra*
'Zayd saw the big dog'

c. N G — *šāhada zaydun kalba jārihi*
'Zayd saw the dog of his neighbor'

By the same principle of placement of categorial entities, verbal modifiers such as negation, interrogation, causation, reciprocity, reflexivization etc., must be placed on the opposite side of the object. Thus, in VO languages the order is as follows:

Verbal modifier(s) V O

Again this is consistent with Arabic which is a consistent VO language:

(9)	a. *kasara*			'He broke'
	b. *mā kasara*	Neg.	V	'He did not break'
	c. *?inkasara*	Reflex.	V	'It got broken'
	d. *?akasara*	Inter.	V	'did he break?'
	e. *kassara*	Intensive	V	'He broke into many pieces'
	f. *takassara*	Reflex. Intens.	V	'it got broken into many pieces'

Let us examine Arabic now taking into consideration the universals proposed by Greenberg (1961). His universal number three says: "Languages with dominant VSO order are always prepositional." Arabic is prepositional:

(10) a. *fī al-bayti* 'in the house'
b. *ᶜalā al-ṭā?irati* 'on the airplane'

His universal number nine says: "With well more than chance frequency, when question particles or affixes are specified in position by reference to the sentence as a whole, if initial such elements are found in prepositional languages and, if final, in postpositional." In Arabic such particles are initial in position; this can be illustrated from the position of the question particles *?a* and *hal* in the following two sentences:

(11) a. *?aqara?ta al-qaṣīdata?* 'did you read the poem?'
b. *hal al-ṭullābu fī al-ṣaffi?* 'are the students in the classroom?'

The two declarative sentences corresponding to these two interrogative sentences are:

(12) a. *qara?ta al-qaṣīdata* 'you read the poem'
b. *al-ṭullābu fī al-ṣaffi* 'the students are in the classroom'

Greenberg's universal number twelve reads: "If a language has dominant order VSO in declarative sentences, it always puts interrogative words or phrases first in interrogative word questions." This is true of Arabic and it can be illustrated by the following pair of sentences:

(13) a. *hāḏā zaydun* 'This is Zayd'
b. *man hāḏā?* 'Who is this?'

Universal number sixteen says: "In languages with dominant order VSO, an inflected auxiliary always precedes the main verb" In Arabic, inflected auxiliaries always precede the main verb:

(14) a. *yajibu ?an ?aḏhaba* 'I must go'
b. *?astaṭī^{c}u ?an ?aḏhaba* 'I can go'

Universal seventeen reads: "With overwhelmingly more than chance frequency, languages with dominant order VSO have the adjective after the noun." In Arabic adjectives always follow nouns:

(15) a. *al-kalbu al-kabīru* 'The big dog'
b. *rajulun šujā^{c}un* 'A courageous man'

Greenberg's universal number six reads as follows: "All languages with dominant VSO order have SVO as an alternative or as the only alternative basic order." This universal can be illustrated by the following sentences in Arabic:

(16) a. *ḍaraba zaydun ^{c}amran* VSO 'Zayd hit 'Amr'
b. *zaydun ḍaraba ^{c}amran* SVO 'Zayd hit 'Amr'
c. *ḍaraba ^{c}amran zaydun* VOS 'Zayd hit 'Amr'
d. *^{c}amran ḍaraba zaydun* OVS 'Zayd hit 'Amr'

Although these sentences look like they support Greenberg's universal number six, however there are counter examples to this universal in Arabic. If the subject is indefinite, then the order SVO is not allowed:

(17) a. *ḍaraba rajulun ^{c}amran* VSO 'A man hit 'Amr'
b. **rajulun ḍaraba ^{c}amran* SVO 'A man hit 'Amr'
c. *ḍaraba ^{c}amran rajulun* VOS 'A man hit 'Amr'
d. *^{c}amran ḍaraba rajulun* OVS 'A man hit 'Amr'

Sentences (16) and (17) suggest a distinction between subject and topic. The head noun phrase is the topic of the sentence; however, it need not be the subject. As a matter of fact, the subject and the topic are the same only in (16b). In (16d) and (17d) the topic is object rather than subject.

We have been using the term "subject" without defining it. Because of the influence of western logic on linguistics, sentences have been assumed to consist in the first place of subject and predicate. Chomsky (1965: 71–74) defines "subject of a sentence" in terms of a sequence of rules like the following:

(18) a. $\Sigma \longrightarrow$ NP VP
b. VP $\longrightarrow$ V NP

This supposedly basic configuration identifies the subject, which is the noun phrase in (18a). In accordance with Chomsky's configuration (18), every sentence contains a verb phrase. Influenced by Chomsky's analysis of English, Snow (1965), Killean (1966) and Lewkowicz (1967) analyzed Arabic as an SVO language. Arabic distinguishes unambiguously between subject and topic. Every topic is the head noun of the sentence in which it occurs; the subject is not the head noun of the sentence in which it occurs. Thus one can topicalize a subject or a nonsubject. Consider the following sentences:

(19) a. *ḥaḍara al-rijālu* 'The men came'
b. *šāhadtu al-binta* 'I saw the girl'

c. *fataḥtu al-bāba bi al-miftāḥi* — 'I opened the door with the key'
d. *qābaltu mudīra al-mathafi* — 'I met the director of the museum'

The underlined noun phrases which are subject, object, the object of a preposition, and the second term of the possessive construct (i.e., *Iḍāfa* construction) in a, b, c, and d, respectively, may be brought to the beginning of the sentence whereby they are assigned the nominative case ending:

(20) a. *al-rijālu ḥaḍarū* — 'The men came'
b. *al-bintu šahadtuhā* — 'The girl I saw her'
c. *al-miftāḥu fataḥtu al-bāba bihi* — 'The key I opened the door with it'
d. *al-matḥafu qābaltu mudīrahu* — 'The museum I met its director'

In certain cases topicalization does not have to be accompanied by assignment of the nominative case. The following pair of sentences illustrates the point:

(21) a. *qatala zaydun ^{c}amran* — 'Zayd killed 'Amr'
b. *^{c}amran qatala zaydun* — ' 'Amr, Zayd killed'

The underlined noun phrases in (20) are topics, not subjects. The underlined noun phrase in (19a), only, is subject. Notice that topicalization that gives (20) from (19) involves three transformations: a copying transformation, pronominalization, and nominativization. Sentence (20b), for example, can be derived from (19b) as follows:

(22) a. *šāhadtu al-binta* . . . .(19b)
b. *al-bint šāhadtu al-binta* . . . . .Copying
c. *al-bint šāhadtuhā* . . . . .Pronominalization
d. *al-bintu šāhadtuhā (20b)* . . . . .Nominativization

The other sentences of (20) can be derived in the same manner. We will call the topicalization process that gives sentences like (20 from (19) primary topicalization. Topicalization in (21b) on the other hand, simply involves a movement transformation which moves the object in a to the beginning of the sentence. We will call this latter type of topicalization secondary topicalization (the terms are borrowed from Fillmore (1968)). This analysis is consistent with the early Arab grammarians' terminology. They call what has been called subject here *fā^{c}il* 'actor,' and what has been called topic in primary topicalization *al-mubtada?u bihi* 'that which is begun with.' In secondary topicalization no copying or nominativization is involved. Thus in (21b) the topic is in the accusative case, while in (20), where primary topicalization is involved, the topic is in the nominative case. The important point is that while in (19b), for example, we have a VSO order, in (20b) we do not have an SVO order; rather the order in (20b) is SΣ or SVSO. A VP in a transitive sentence consists of a verb followed by an object in accordance with Chomsky's phrase structure rules. Notice that in Arabic the verb is followed by the subject in both the VSO order and the SΣ (i.e., SVSO) order. Therefore Arabic has no VP. On the other hand, "subject" as identified by the phrase structure rule (18a) must be followed by a VP and as such does not exist in Arabic. Therefore there is valid evidence for treating Arabic as a VSO language.

1.3 Outline

The outline of the work is as follows. In Chapter II the theoretical framework will be presented and discussed. In Chapter III an investigation of passivizability in Arabic will be attempted with the objective of identifying verbs that can and cannot passivize. In Chapter IV Arabic causative verbs will be analyzed, and the syntactic and semantic properties of verbs that may be causativized will be examined. In Chapter V the notion of transitivity will be discussed and modified and a proposal for the derivation of Arabic passive constructions will be made. A conclusion will be made in Chapter VI.

NOTES

1. 'Hind was married' is grammatical in English if married is a stative adjective or if the understood agent is someone who performed the marriage, a priest for example, rather than the bridegroom or the husband.
2. Quadriliteral roots (roots containing four consonants) do also occur in Arabic: Example *daḥraja* 'to roll' from the root *d-ḥ-r-j*.

2 Theoretical framework

2.1 Introductory Remarks

This study will be conducted within the framework of the case grammar theory. In accordance with this theory, the Arabic sentence consists of two initial components: Qualifier (Q) and Proposition (P). The earliest rule in the phrase-structure grammar is (1).[1]

$$(1) \quad \Sigma \longrightarrow Q \quad \sim \quad P$$

The wavy line between Q and P indicates that no order is implied between the two components; in other words, the deep structure is not ordered. Order between the two components is introduced by a transformation. Since Arabic is a VO language (in contrast to OV languages like Japanese and Turkish), its earliest ordering transformation would be (2):

$$(2) \quad Q \quad \sim \quad P \longrightarrow Q \quad P$$

The Q component is a categorial element through which verbal qualifiers affecting the entire sentence are introduced into sentences. These verbal qualifiers, which are generally marked on the verb component of the proposition, are a group of syntactic features that modify not only the verb but the entire proposition. The P component in its basic structure consists of a verb and one or more deep structure cases or case roles, each associated with the verb in a particular case relationship. These deep structure cases are distinct from, and do not correspond to, the three Arabic surface structure cases nominative, accusative and genitive. Twelve deep structure cases will be proposed for Arabic in contrast to the three surface structure cases that exist in the language. Using the symbol K for a P component case role and the symbol F for a Q component syntactic feature, we may rewrite rule (1) as follows:

$$(3) \quad \Sigma \longrightarrow F_1 \sim F_2 \sim \cdots Fn \sim V \sim K_1 \sim K_2 \cdots K_n$$

Rule (3) shows that not only no order is implied between the two components P and Q but also that no order is implied within each of the two components. The ordering transformation (2) may be rewritten as (4).

$$(4) \quad F_1 \sim F_2 \sim \ldots F_n \sim V \sim K_1 \sim K_2 \ldots K_n \longrightarrow F_1 \; F_2 \ldots F_n \; V \; K_1 \; K_2 \ldots K_n$$

Elements of the Q component are features like Interrogative, Negative, Causative, Reflexive, etc. Elements of the P component are case roles like Agent, Patient, Target, Goal, etc. Rule (4) applies to an unordered string consisting of sentence qualifiers, a verb, and one or more case roles. It provides order (i) between the Q component and the P component, (ii) among elements of the Q components, and (iii) among elements of the P component by placing the verb before the rest of the case roles.

2.2 The Q Component

Rule (4) discussed above provides order among the elements of the Q component in accordance with Lehmann's placement principle which places sentence qualifiers before verb roots in VO languages (Lehmann 1973). Arabic introduces questions with an interrogative particle or an interrogative pronoun. This interrogative particle or pronoun precedes verbs which occupy initial position in the same sentence. Negation particles, on the other hand, precede the verb but follow the interrogative particle or pronoun. The other categorial markers or modality features, such as Causative, Reflexive, Reciprocal, Intensive, etc., are prefixed to, or infixed in, the verb; all of them follow the interrogative and negative markers. Thus a hierarchy is provided by the application of rule (4) in accordance with Lehmann's principle. According to this hierarchy, modality features are placed closest to the verb root and features like Negative and Interrogative are placed further away from the verb root on the opposite side of the case roles (i.e., further to the left in rule (4)). We stated that according to this hierarchy, Interrogative precedes Negative. When two or more modality markers coexist in a sentence, a hierarchy is also provided among them. The following sentences clearly illustrate the hierarchy that exists among elements of the Q component as a result of the application of rule (4) in accordance with Lehmann's principle:

(5)	a. *kataba risālatan*	V (Perfect)	'He wrote a letter'
	b. *yaktubu risālatan*	V (Imperfect)	'He writes, or is writing a letter'
	c. *man kataba risālatan?*	Inter. V.	'Who wrote a letter?'
	d. *[hal, ?a] kataba risālatan?*	Inter. V	'Did he write a letter?'
	e. *mā kataba risālatan*	Neg. V	'He did not write a letter'
	f. *?amā kataba risālatan?*	Inter. Neg. V	'Didn't he write a letter?'
	g. *kattaba zaydan risālatan*	Caus. V	'He made Zayd write a letter'
	h. *?amā kattaba zaydan risālatan?*	Inter. Neg. Caus.	'Didn't he make Zayd write a letter?'
	i. *?amā kātaba zaydan?*	Inter. Neg. Reciprocal V	'Didn't he correspond (with) Zayd?'
	j. *?amā takātaba al-ra?īsāni?*	Inter. Neg. Reflex. Reciprocal V	'Didn't the two presidents correspond (with each other)?'

We may note that, for the statement of a potential, a desiderative, or a necessative, Arabic uses verbal phrases consisting of an auxiliary to express these sentence qualifiers preceding the verb which is in the subjunctive. These sentence qualifiers follow the negative and interrogative markers and precede the modality affix markers:

(6)	a. *?amā ?istaṭā^{c}a ?an yata^{c}allama al-^{c}arabiyyata*	Inter. Neg. Potential Reflex. Caus. V (Imp., Subj.)	'Couldn't he learn Arabic?'
	b. *?alā turīdu ?an taḏhaba*	Inter. Neg. Desiderative V (Imp., Subj.)	'Don't you want to go'
	c. *yajibu ?an ?arji^{c}a*	Necessative V (Imp., Subj.)	'I must go back'

Thus the order of verbal qualifiers is as follows:

(7) Inter —— Neg —— Periphrastic Qualifiers —— Modal Qualifiers

One shortcoming of (7) is the fact that it is possible to have the Negative follow the Periphrastic Qualifer:

(8)	*yajibu ?an lā taḏhaba*	Necessative Neg. Verb	'you must not go'

(9) Inter —— Neg ∿ Periphrastic Qualifiers —— Modal Qualifiers

In other words there is no hierarchy between Negative and Periphrastic Qualifiers.

The sentence qualifiers discussed above must be sharply distinguished from congruence markers. Markers for number and gender do not observe Lehmann's placement principle. In Arabic these are suffixes to the verbal in the perfect, and they are a combination of suffixes and prefixes in the imperfect:

(10)	a. *daras+at*	'She studied'	Perfect
	b. *daras+tum*	'you masc. pl. studied'	
	c. *ta+drus+u*	'She studies'	Imperfect
	d. *ta+drus+ūna*	'you masc. pl. study'	

Mood markers also must be distinguished from sentence qualifiers. These are also suffixed to the verb rather than infixed or prefixed. The following sentences illustrate these points:

(11)	a. *yadrus+u al-^{c}arabiyyata*	'He studies Arabic'
	b. yurīdu ?an *yadrus+a al-^{c}arabiyyata*	'He wants to study Arabic'
	c. *lā taḏhab+ϕ*	'Do not go (singular)'

The u in the underlined verb in (11a) is the indicative mood suffix; the a in the underlined verb in (11b) is the subjunctive mood suffix; and the nill (i.e., the absence of a suffix) in the underlined verb in (11c) is the jussive mood marker.

Tense, in this grammatical framework, does not belong to the Q component *either*. It is proposed that tense is a part of the P component. It is part of the case role Time. This treatment of tense is highly tentative and requires further study.

2.3 The P Component

2.3.1 Background

The concept of deep and surface structure cases was, as far as we know, *first* dealt with by the Sanskrit grammarian Panini, who distinguished between kāraka and vibhakti cases. Kāraka refers to the underlying semantic function of a noun phrase, while vibhakti cases are the surface structure morphological forms of the elements in question. The derivation of a particular sentence would determine the correspondence between the two case types. For example, the kartā, or deep structure agent, could be expressed as a nominative or an instrumental depending upon whether the sentence was active or passive.

This distinction between deep and surface structure cases was precisely what Fillmore (1968) wanted to suggest as a modification for transformational grammar. Fillmore uses the term case "to identify the underlying syntactic-semantic relationship" and case form "to mean the expression of a case relationship in a particular language—whether through affixation, suppletion, use of clitic particles, or constraints on word order" (1968: 21). In the underlying structure of a sentence Fillmore distinguishes between proposition, which he conceives as a "tenseless set of relationships involving verbs and nouns (and embedded sentences if there are any)," and the modality constituent, which "will include such modalities, on the sentence-as-a-whole as negation, tense, mood and aspect" (1968: 23). Thus Fillmore's initial phrase structure rule is:

$$\text{Sentence} \longrightarrow \text{Modality} + \text{Proposition}$$

As in Fillmore, the P constituent in this book is to be expanded with one or more cases, with no case appearing more than once. Unlike Fillmore, the Modality constituent which is called here the Q component does not include tense, mood or aspect. Our proposition is not tenseless.

Rule (4) creates the earliest hierarchy among the elements of the P component. The verb precedes all cases; case K_1 follows the verb and it precedes case K_2 which precedes case K_3, etc.

As noted above, the deep structure cases must be clearly distinguished from the surface structure cases. In Arabic there are three, and only three, surface structure cases: nominative, accusative and genitive. More than three deep structure cases are proposed for Arabic. The surface structure cases are language specific and they are relevant to Arabic only. The deep structure cases are universal in character.

In all the case grammars proposed so far, there is as yet no agreement as to the number or semantic and functional characterization of the deep structure cases. Any list of these cases has been no more than an approximation and at best partially arbitrary. Our best guide to the deep structure cases is not the surface structure cases but the semantic interpretation of the surface structure of a language or languages. Thus an understanding of the surface structure of a language is a must. The deep structure cases that will be suggested in this book are no more than a rough approximation in number as well as in character. Unlike Fillmore's deep structure cases (1968), those suggested here do not contain any affixes, prepositions or postpositions, etc. In other words, the deep structure does not contain, for example, something like an "underlying element, say K (for Kasus)" (Fillmore 1968: 33). Prepositions are introduced transformationally and they trigger the surface genitive case endings. Surface case endings are also introduced transformationally by late shallow structure rules.

Before listing and defining the cases that will be suggested for the deep structure of

Arabic, we will discuss in some detail two controversial concepts, namely Agent (A) and Instrument (I).

Fillmore (1968: 24) suggests an Agentive deep structure case and defines it as "the case of the typically animate perceived instigator of the action identified by the verb." In his article "Some Problems for Case Grammar" (1971), he refrains from committing himself to a precise definition of this case; yet there is nothing in this more recent paper which contradicts his earlier definition except for the removal of by from the deep structure. He defines Instrument as "the case of the inanimate force or object causally involved in the action or state identified by the verb (1968: 24). Later he modifies this definition by stating "I take the instrument, for which I would be happy to find a better name as the case of the immediate cause of an event, or, in the case of a psychological predicator, the 'stimulus,' the thing reacted to" (1971: 42). In both articles Fillmore insists that an agent be animate and that an instrument be inanimate. He makes the assumption, which is adopted here, "that there is in a single clause at most one noun phrase serving a given case role" (1971: 38). With these premises he goes on to say that an agent can take an instrument but that an instrument cannot take an instrument because this will violate the one-instance-per-clause principle. Thus (12) is grammatical while (13) is ungrammatical:

(12) John broke the window with a hammer

(13) *Air pollution killed my petunias with cyanide

Fillmore gives the following sentence as an "apparent exception" to his generalization:

(14) The car broke the window with its fender

He says that sentence (14) looks like an exception but by attending to the effect of the word its, the essential difference between (14) and (15) becomes apparent:

(15) *The car broke the window with a fender

Sentence (15) violates the one-instance-per-clause principle, but "sentence (14) is a paraphrase of sentence (16) and may be interpreted as having the same deep structure as sentence (16)" (Fillmore 1968: 23):

(16) The car's fender broke the window

Thus, according to Fillmore, sentences (14) and (16) are agentless sentences containing a "possessed noun" as Instrument the car's fender: either the entire instrument phrase may appear as the subject (as in 16) or the "possessor" alone may be made the subject, the remainder of the instrument appearing with the preposition with (as in 14) (Fillmore 1968: 22–3).

It is important to note here that the facts brought up by Fillmore are pragmatic facts about cars rather than facts about syntax. It so happens that, unless otherwise specified, cars can break windows with their own fenders, bumpers, etc. Thus if we tie a fender to the front bumper of a car, then the following sentence will have the same degree of grammaticalness as Fillmore's sentence (14):

(17) The car broke the window with a fender that was tied to its front bumper.

Consider, also, the following sentence:

(18) When I was on Padre Island last spring I saw a sand-storm pull up a tree, carry it for about 200 feet, and break the glass wall of the restaurant with it.

About ten native speakers of English have labelled sentence (18) and Fillmore's sentence (14) "equally awkward." Therefore (14) and (18) have the same degree of grammaticalness. This shows that "possession" is not the decisive factor in the grammaticalness of (14) if it is grammatical. Moreover, (14) and (16) do not necessarily have the same underlying structure. In conclusion, if sentence (14) is grammatical then the subject noun-phrase the car is not "part of the instrument" but is the agent.

The point is that the agent is not necessarily animate; to further clarify this point we can invoke the English passive constructions (the Arabic passives being agentless won't help us). Consider the following pair of sentences:

(19) a. Mary was hit with a rock
b. Mary was hit by a rock

Within the framework of Fillmore's definition of Agent and Instrument, there is no way by which we can tell the difference between these two sentences. All of the native speakers of English who were asked about these two sentences said something to the effect that in (19a) "someone hit Mary with a rock" while in (19b) "a rock hit Mary accidentally." This simply means that the noun-phrase a rock is instrumental in (19a) while it is agentive in (19b).

Consider now the following sentences:

(20)	a. *fataḥat al-rīḥu al-bāba*	'The wind opened the door'
	b. *qaḏafat al-ʔamwāju al-safīnata ʔilā al-šāṭiʔi*	'The waves pushed the ship to the beach'
	c. *ʔiqtalaᶜa al-ʔiᶜṣāru al-šajarata*	'The hurricane pulled out the tree'

Fillmore (1971: 44) says that in general it is possible for sentences having agents as subjects to contain Instrument phrases. Since it is not possible for the subject in sentences like (20) to take an instrument, as can be seen from the ungrammaticalness of a sentence like **fataḥat al-rīḥu al-bāba bi al-miftāḥi* '*The wind opened the door with the key,' the subject in sentences like (20) must not be assigned the Agent case role according to Fillmore. Consequently he considers these subjects as Instruments in the deep structure. If we follow Fillmore's argument to its logical conclusion, we have to distinguish between two types of Agent and possibly posit two Agent case roles. In general, animal animate subjects may take only inalienable (i.e., obligatorily possessed) Instruments while human animate subjects may take inalienable Instruments as well as alienable (i.e., optionally possessed) Instruments. Thus most dogs for example cannot open doors with keys while they can tear a piece of meat with their teeth.

Consider the following two sentences:

(21)	a. *mazzaqa al-kalbu al-ṯawba bi ʔasnānihi*	'The dog tore the dress with its teeth'

b. *fataḥa al-kalbu al-bāba bi al-miftāḥi* 'The dog opened the door with the key'

According to Fillmore, (21a) would be grammatical while (21b) would not; moreover the subject in (21a) would be Agent, but in (21b) it would not, because the sentence may not take an alienable Instrument. All of these observations are pragmatic facts rather than linguistically significant properties of deep structure Agents versus Instruments. Agency should not be defined in terms of humanness or intentionality because one can think of a situation in which, for example, a dog is trained somehow to open doors with keys. Moreover agency should not be defined in terms of animateness; it is conceivable that a machine be invented that would open doors with keys; in this situation a sentence like *fataḥat al-ʔālatu al-bāba bi almiftāḥi* 'the machine opened the door with the key' would be perfectly grammatical. Therefore in accordance with the theoretical framework proposed in this chapter, the subject noun phrases in sentences (21) should be assigned the case role Agent rather than the case role Instrument.

Let us now consider the following sentences:

(22) a. *fataḥa zaydun al-bāba* 'Zayd opened the door'
b. *fataḥa al-miftāḥu al-bāba* 'The key opened the door'
c. *fataḥa zaydun al-bāba bi al-miftāḥi* 'Zayd opened the door with the key'

In most case grammars, the subject in (22a) is given the role Agent while the subject in (22b) and the object of the preposition in (22c) are given the same case role, namely Instrument. This case role assignment presupposes that the relation between the verb and the subject in (22b) is the same as the relation between the verb and the object of the preposition in (22c). Rodney Huddleston (1970: 503–4) argues that whereas The wind in the sentence The wind opened the door does not presuppose "some unexpressed agentive participant," The key in the English gloss of sentence (22b) does presuppose some unexpressed agentive participant. Thus he assigns instrumenthood to The Key but not to The Wind. Huddleston's distinction is again only pragmatically motivated; the confusion on his part is due to the fact that he equates agency with human intervention in the action, in this situation the openeing of the door. We have shown earlier that the Agent of a verb like *fataḥa* 'to open' can be a human being, a trained dog, or a machine; thus agency does not have to be human agency. In many a mystery or science fiction movie we may see a key turning inside a knob of a door without any external agency. Thus the fact that external agency is usually presupposed in a sentence like (22b) does not mean that external agency is necessarily implicit in the sentence, and therefore there is no syntactic motivation for assigning instrumenthood to *al-miftāḥu* 'The key' in sentence (22b).

On the other hand, the relationship between the verb and *al-miftāḥ* in (22b) is different from the relationship between the verb and *al-miftāḥ* in (22c). In (22c) the function of the object of the preposition is purely instrumental, *al-miftāḥ*. The key is the tool or instrument used by Zayd to open the door. In (22b) the subject, though it is a tool, it is not necessarily used by anyone or anything. Sentence (22b) means that the key fits the door enough to unlock it. The most important function of the subject in this sentence is that it succeeded in opening the door. Consider the following sentences, from different languages, equivalent to sentence (22b):

(23) a. English: The key opened the door
b. German: Der Schlussel offnette die tur

c. French: La clé a ouvert la porte
d. Persian: Kelīd dæro bāz kǣrd

In these languages the sentence indicates exactly what is indicated by the Arabic sentence equivalent to sentences (23). It is also important to note here that the verb *fataḥa* 'to open' is ambiguous in Arabic, it means either 'to unlock' or 'to open,' a door for example, wide open. In (22a) Zayd could have either unlocked the door or pushed the door wide open or both. In (22b) all that *al-miftāḥ* 'The key' can do is unlock the door and make it possible for someone or something to push the door open. Some languages do not permit the verb 'to open' in (22b); rather, in these languages, the verb in sentences equivalent to (22b) has to be something like the verb 'to unlock.' The following two pairs of sentences from Iraqi Arabic and Libyan Arabic, respectively, are illustrative:

(24) 1a.	**lmiftāḥ fataḥ ilbāb*	'The key opened the door'
b.	*lmiftāḥ fakk ilbāb*	'The key unlocked the door'
2a.	*lmiftāḥ ftaḥ ilbāb*	'The key opened the door'
b.	*lmiftāḥ ḥall ilbāb*	'The key unfastened the door'

The above discussed differences between the function and the semantic import of *al-miftāḥ* in (22b) and (22c) justifies assigning the subject in (22b) and the object of the preposition in (22c) two different case roles in the deep structure.

In conclusion, the following statements can be made: (i) Agency should not be determined in terms of humanness, intentionality or animateness and Agents do not have to be necessarily animate; (ii) Inanimate Agents may take Instruments if the appropriate pragmatic situation presents itself; and (iii) Instruments occur in sentences which contain Agents and in only such sentences; the Agent can be either specified or unspecified in these sentences depending on whether the sentence is active or passive.

2.3.2 Case Roles

In this section we define the inventory of case roles (i.e., deep structure cases) which we find useful. This inventory is built on the work of Fillmore in case grammar with ideas from Chafe (1970) and M. A. K. Halliday (1967–68). This case system, however, is different from the case systems proposed by these linguists in number of case roles as well as in the characterization and definition of these case roles.

Agent. The case of the entity which acts or which is causally involved in the bringing about of an activity, a process or a state identified by the verb. This entity may be animate or inanimate; an inanimate entity that acts is an object like an astronomical body or a semi-autonomous machine. The action identified by the verb may be deliberate or nondeliberate. Agency in this case system is defined in terms of causality rather than in terms of humanness, animateness or volition. Entities which deliberately instigate or initiate an activity, or process, or a state are unambiguously Agents but these are not the only Agents in Arabic.

The underlined noun phrases are Agents in the deep structure of the following sentences:

(25) a.	*jā?a zaydun*	'Zayd came'
b.	*ḍaraba zaydun hindan*	'Zayd beat Hind'
c.	*qatalathu raṣāṣatun ṭā?išatun*	'A stray bullet killed him'
d.	*yadūru al-qamaru ḥawla al-?arḍi*	'The moon revolves around the earth'

e. *ṭayyara al-waladu al-^{c}uṣfūra* — 'The boy flew the bird'
f. *?aqla^{c}at al-ṭā?iratu min al-maṭāri fī al-sā^{c}ati al-^{c}āširati* — 'The plane took off from the airport at ten o'clock'
g. *fataḥa al-miftāḥu al-bāba* — 'The key opened the door'

The Agent can also be a sentential complement as can be seen from the following:

(26) a. *?aḥzanahu mawtu ?ibnihi* — 'His son's death saddened him'
b. *sarranī najāḥuka* — 'Your success pleased me'

Instrument. The case of the object used as tool or instrument involved in the action identified by the verb. This tool is usually inanimate.[2]

The underlined nouns phrases are Instruments in the deep structure of the following sentences:

(27) a. *fataḥtu al-bāba bi al-miftāḥi* — 'I opened the door with the key'
b. *qaṭṭa^{c}at al-laḥma bi sikkīnin* — 'She cut the meat with a knife'
c. *qutila ramyan bi al-raṣāṣi* — 'He was shot down with gunfire'
d. *kasara al-ṭiflu al-nāfiḏata bi ḥajarin* — 'The child broke the window with a stone'
e. *mala?a al-ka?sa mā?an* — 'He filled the glass with water'

The instrument can also be a clause as in the following sentences:

(28) a. *tuḥāwilu al-dawlatu raf^{c}a mustawā al-ta^{c}līmi bi binā?i madārisa ḥadīṯatin* — 'The state is trying to raise the standard of education by building new schools'
b. *?aẓhara al-muwāṭinūna taqdīrahum li ra?īsi al-jumhūriyyati bi ?an ?a^{c}ādū ?intixābahu* — 'The citizens showed their appreciation to the president of the republic by re-electing him'

Patient. The case of the entity that necessarily undergoes a change of state identified by the verb. The change of state can be a change from one state into another, a change from a state into no state, or a change from no state into a state. The underlined noun phrases are Patients in the deep structure of the following sentences:

(29) a. *ḏāba al-ṯalju* — 'The snow melted'
b. *mātat al-zahratu* — 'The flower died'
c. *kasara al-waladu al-nāfiḏata* — 'The boy broke the window'
d. *ṣāra ?axī muḥāmiyan* — 'My brother became a lawyer'
e. *hadamū al-madīnata* — 'They destroyed the city'
f. *banaw al-madīnata* — 'They built the city'
g. *qaṣṣarat al-ṯawba* — 'She shortened the dress'

Patient is also the case of the experiencer of a psychological event or of a mental, physiological or emotional state or process. The underlined noun phrases in the following sentences are Patients:

(30)	a. *ya ^{c}rifu zaydun al-faransiyyata*	'Zayd knows French'
	b. *yuḥibbu ^{c}amrun hindan*	' 'Amr loves Hind'
	c. *taḥtarimu al-bintu wālidahā*	'The girl respects her father'
	d. *xāfa al-waladu*	'The boy got frightened'
	e. *ʔaġḍaba zaydun ^{c}amran*	'Zayd angered 'Amr'
	f. *šāhadnā filman qadīman*	'We saw an old movie'
	g. *sami^{c}tu ṣawtan*	'I heard a voice'

In addition Patient is the case of the entity that comes to possess an object as a result of someone else's activity, it is also the case of the animate entity which acts but whose action is initiated by an external Agent. In the following sentences the underlined noun phrases are Patients:

(31)	a. *ʔa^{c}ṭaytu zaydan kitāban*	'I gave Zayd a book'
	b. *ʔaġzā al-rasūlu xālidan al-^{c}aduwwa*	'The prophet made Khālid invade the enemy'
	c. *ʔazāra hindan ^{c}ammāna*	'He made Hind visit Amman'
	d. *ʔajlastuhā*	'I made her sit down'

Target. The case of the entity identified by a state or location. It is also the case of the entity which undergoes a change in position or location. The entity in question receives the effects of the activity, state or process identified by the verb without necessarily undergoing a change of state. Moving objects that are not causally involved in bringing about their own movement are Targets. In a sentence like *rafasa zaydun al-bāba* 'Zayd kicked the door' although *al-bāba* 'The door' receives the effects of the activity identified by the verb it does not necessarily undergo a change of state. In a sentence like *kasara zaydun al-zujāja* 'Zayd broke the glass,' on the other hand, *al-zujāja* 'The glass' necessarily undergoes a change of state. Thus the case role of *al-bāba* 'The door' is Target while the case role of *al-zujāja* 'The glass' is Patient.

The underlined noun phrases are Targets in the deep structure of the following sentences:

(32)	a. *waqa^{c}a al-waladu ^{c}an al-saṭḥi*	'The boy fell from the roof'
	b. *hindun jamīlatun*	'Hind is pretty'
	c. *qabbala zaydun zawjatahu*	'Zayd kissed his wife'
	d. *al-rajulu fī al-bayti*	'The man is in the house'

Target is also the deep structure case of the content of a psychological, mental or emotional experience. The subjects in the following sentences are Patients while the objects are Targets:

(33)	a. *yuḥibbu zaydun hindan*	'Zayd loves Hind'
	b. *taḥtarimu hindun wālidahā*	'Hind respects her father'
	c. *yurīdu zaydun ʔan yusāfira ʔilā al-qudsi*	'Zayd wants to travel to Jerusalem'

In (33c) the Target is the sentential complement *ʔan yusāfira ʔilā al-qudsi.*

Range. This term, borrowed from Halliday (April, 1967), refers to the case of the noun phrase that completes or further specifies the verb; the nearest equivalent surface structure term for Range is 'Cognate Accusative.' A cognate accusative, which is known in Arabic as *maf^{c}ūl muṭlaq,* is a surface structure object built on the same root as its corresponding verb. But noun phrases semantically associated with particular verbs need not be cognate with the verb. Range can be a highly generic noncount noun phrase as can be seen from the underlined noun phrases in the following sentences:

(34) a. *?aḥabbahā ḥubban ^{c}aẓīman* — 'He loved her a great love'
b. *nāma nawman hādi?an* — 'He slept a calm sleep'

Range can also be a count noun phrase or a specified entity as in the following examples:

(35) a. *ġannat ?uġniyatan jamīlatan* — 'She sang a beautiful song'
b. *ġannat "al-?aṭlāl"* — 'She sang "al-?aṭlāl" (name of a song)'
c. *ḍarabtu al-liṣṣa ḍarbatayni* — 'I beat the thief two beatings'
d. *nāḍalū niḍāla al-?abṭāli* — 'They struggled the struggle of heroes'

Range can be further specified by being concretized while remaining semantically relatable to a highly generic noun phrase which is a nominal prolongation of the verb. The underlined noun phrases in the deep structure of the following sentences are Ranges:

(36) a. *?akala ṭa^{c}āman kaṯīran* — 'He ate lots of food'
b. *?akala tuffāḥatan* — 'He ate an apple'
c. *šariba mā?an* — 'He drank water'
d. *ta^{c}allama ^{c}ilman kaṯīran* — 'He learned lots of education'
e. *ta^{c}allama al-faransiyyata* — 'He learned French'
f. *la^{c}ibnā al-šaṭaranja* — 'We played chess'
g. *zara^{c}a qamḥan* — 'He sowed wheat'

Source. This is the case of the object, state, time or place from which a change, transformation, experience, action or motion identified by the verb is started or initiated. With verbs of transformation we can specify an original object or an earlier state. With verbs of motion, we can specify a starting point in a certain place, and for verbs of temporal lapse, we can specify a starting point of a time period.

The underlined words come from a Source in the deep structure of the following sentences:

(37) a. *hāḏā al-mi^{c}ṭafu maṣnū^{c}un min al-quṭni* — 'This coat is made from cotton'
b. *hāḏā ridā?un quṭniyyun* — 'This is a cotton(y) coat'
c. *jubnatun dānimarkiyyatun* — 'Danish cheese'
d. *^{c}āda min bayrūt* — 'He came back from Beirut'
e. *hiya min faransā* — 'She is from France'
f. *^{c}ištu fī dimašq min ?āḏār ?ilā ?aylūl* — 'I lived in Damascus from March till September'
g. *sāra ^{c}amrun min al-bayti ?ilā al-sūqi* — ' 'Amr walked from the house to the market'
h. *taḥawwala min rajulin wari^{c}in taqiyyin ?ilā muqāmirin sikkīrin* — 'He changed from a godfearing pious man into a gambler and a drunkard'
i. *huwa min qabīlati banī ?asadin* — 'He is from the tribe of Bani Asad'

Goal. This is the case of the object, state, time or place which is the destination of the action, change, transformation, experience or motion identified by the verb. If the Source represents an earlier object, state, place, or point in time, the Goal represents a later object, state, place or point in time. Goal is the antithesis of Source; however, Goal and Source do not have to coexist in every sentence. We have seen in (37) sentences that contain only Source and sentences that contain both Source and Goal. There are also sentences that contain only Goal without Source.

The underlined noun phrases are Goals in the deep structure of the following sentences:

(38)	a. *ṣāra zaydun muḥāmiyan*	'Zayd became a lawyer'
	b. *ʔaṣbaḥa al-ṭiflu šābban*	'The child became a young man'
	c. ^{c}*āda ʔilā bayrūt*	'He went back to Beirut'
	d. ^{c}*ištu fī dimašq min ʔāḏār ʔilā ʔaylūl*	'I lived in Damascus from March till September'
	e. *darasat ḥattā al-sā*^{c}*ati al-*^{c}*āširati*	'She studied till ten o'clock'
	f. *taḥawwala min rajulin wari*^{c}*in taqiyyin ʔilā muqāmirin sikkīrin*	'He changed from a godfearing pious man into a gambler and drunkard
	g. *sāra* ^{c}*amrun min albayti ʔilā al-sūqi*	'Amr walked from the house to the market'

Place. The case of the place in which an object is located or in which an activity or a process takes place. The underlined noun phrases in the following sentences have the Place case role:

(39)	a. *al-rajulu fī al-bayti*	'The man is in the house'
	b. *al-kitābu* ^{c}*ala al-ṭāwilati*	'The book is on the table'
	c. *al-sayyāratu hunāka*	'The car is (over) there'
	d. *al-miftāḥu fī al-jārūri*	'The key is in the drawer'
	e. *hindun* ^{c}*inda* ^{c}*amrin*	'Hind is at 'Amr's'
	f. *ʔakalnā fī maṭ*^{c}*amin* ^{c}*arabiyyin*	'We ate at an Arab restaurant'

Time. The case of the time in which or at which an action or a process identified by the verb takes place. The following sentences are illustrative:

(40)	a. *šāhadtuhu ʔamsi*	'I saw him yesterday'
	b. *saʔuqābiluhu ġadan*	'I will meet with him tomorrow'
	c. *māta fī al-*^{c}*āmi al-māḍī*	'He died last year'
	d. *darastu sā*^{c}*atayni*	'I studied two hours'

Manner. The case of the manner in which the action or process identified by the verb takes place:

(41)	a. *ḏābat al-šam*^{c}*atu bi sur*^{c}*atin*	'The candle melted quickly'
	b. *yu*^{c}*āmilu zaydun ʔabāhu bi ʔiḥtirāmin*	'Zayd treats his father with respect'
	c. *xadama bilādahu bi ʔixlāṣin*	'He served his country sincerely'

d. *naẓarat ?ilayhi mubtasimatan* 'She looked at him smiling'

Beneficiary. This is the case of the entity for the sake of whom or for the sake of which the action, process, or experience identified by the verb is carried out. This case role is distinct from the Goal case role discussed above. The underlined noun phrases in the following pair of sentences are ambiguous as to whether they are Goals or Beneficiaries:

(42) a. *kataba lahā risālatan*
b. *?arsala lahā risālatan*

Sentence (42a) means either 'He wrote a letter to her' or 'He wrote a letter for her'; sentence (42b) means either 'He sent a letter to her' or 'He sent a letter for her, i.e., he mailed a letter for her.' Assigning the Goal case role to Beneficiaries violates Fillmore's one-instance-per-clause principle which states that there is in a single clause at most one noun phrase serving a case role. If we consider Beneficiaries as Goals, then in the following sentence we would have TWO noun phrases serving ONE case role, namely Goal:

(43) *kataba lahā risālatan li ?ibnihā* 'He wrote a letter to her son for her'

The underlined noun phrases in the following sentences are Beneficiaries in the deep structure of these sentences:

(44) a. *taḥammala al-kaṯīra min al-^{c}aḏābi fī sabīli mabādi?ihi* 'He endured lots of torture for the sake of his principles'
b. *?ištarā zaydun ṯawban li hindin* 'Zayd bought a dress for Hind'
c. *naẓẓafat hindun al-ġurfata li zaydin* 'Hind cleaned the room for Zayd'
d. *?ištarat ?uṭuran jadīdatan li sayyāratihā* 'She bought new tires for her car'

Comitative. The surface structure term that corresponds to this case role is *al-maf^{c}ūl ma^{c}ahu* 'Accusative of accompaniment.' Consider the following pair of sentences:

(45) a. *ḏahabat hindun wa zaydan* 'Hind went with Zayd'
b. *ḏahabat hindun ma^{c}a zaydin* 'Hind went with Zayd'

In sentence (45a) *wa* is a particle of accompaniment but it is not a preposition; *zaydan* is an accusative of accompaniment and it has the accusative surface case ending *-an*. On the other hand *ma^{c}a* in sentence (45b), though it indicates accompaniment, is a preposition, and *zaydin* is its object and has the genitive surface case ending *-in*. Thus the two sentences of (45) have two different structures on the surface. But the two sentences are synonymous; the particle *wa* and the preposition *ma^{c}a* both indicate accompaniment and the semantic role of *zayd* in both sentences is the same. It is proposed here that the accusative noun phrase in (45a) and the genitive noun phrase in (45b) be assigned the same deep structure case which we label Comitative. Compare new sentences (45) with sentence (46).

(46) *ḏahaba hindun wa zaydun* 'Hind and Zayd went (away)'

The particle *wa* in this sentence is a conjunction equivalent to English <u>And</u>. The Agent in (46) is a conjunct and *zayd* has the nominative case ending *-un*. It might be argued that (46) is a result of sentence conjunction. Whether the deep structure of (46) is two conjoined sentences or one sentence with a phrasally conjoined noun phrase is irrelevant to the question at hand. Either analysis predicts that *zaydun* is agentive in (46). It might be argued that there is agency on the part of *zayd* in (45). This, however, is not necessarily true. In (45) *zayd* can very well be an unconscious person accompanied by *hind* in an ambulance on the way to a hospital. Thus agency is not a necessary function of the Comitative; the following sentence illustrates the point:

(47) *ḏahaba zaydun ma^{c}a al-biḍā^{c}ati*	'Zayd went with the merchandise'

It is clear that there is no agency indicated by the Comitative in (47). Another difference between sentences like (45) and sentences like (46) is that whereas accompaniment is explicitly expressed in (45), there is no indication of it in (46).

The important point to make here is that in a comitative construction there are two participants involved in the action, process, or state indicated by the verb, in similar or different ways. The Comitative is the more important of the two participants whether there is agency on its part or not. The other participant is secondary and it can be an Agent, a Patient or a Target. The following sentences illustrate the point:

(48) a. *makaṯat ma^{c}a ṭiflihā fī al-mustašfā*	'She stayed with her child in the hospital'
b. *šaribtu al-ḥalība ma^{c}a al-qahwati*	'I drank milk with coffee'
c. *taskunu hindun ma^{c}a wālidayhā*	'Hind lives with her parents'

If one of the two participants in (48a) is sick, we identify the child rather than the mother as the sick person; and the child is the more important situationally. In (48b) it is mainly coffee rather than milk that the person involved drinks. In (48c) if the house in which Hind lives belonged to one of the participants, it would be Hind's parents who own it rather than Hind herself. Interchanging the two participants in (48) gives sentences which are not synonymous with the sentences in (48). The following pair of sentences illustrates the point:

(49) a. *al-miftāḥu ma^{c}a zaydin*	'The key is with Zayd'
b. *zaydun ma^{c}a al-miftāḥi*	'Zayd is with the key'

Comitative therefore is the case role of the more important or primary participant in a comitative construction. The underlined noun phrases in the following sentences are Comitatives in the deep structure of these sentences:

(50) a. *zaydun ma^{c}a <u>hindin</u>*	'Zayd is with <u>Hind</u>'
b. *nāmat wa <u>?iyyāhu</u>*	'She slept with <u>him</u>'
c. *šāhadtu al-masraḥiyyata ma^{c}a <u>^{c}amrin</u>*	'I saw the play with <u>'Amr</u>'
d. *qātala ma^{c}a <u>rasūli allāhi</u>*	'He fought with <u>the Prophet of Allah</u>'
e. *?akala al-fijla ma^{c}a <u>al-kubbati</u>*	'He ate radishes with <u>Kubbah</u>'

2.4 Surface Phenomena

2.4.1 Residual Problems

The case system proposed in this chapter accounts for almost all the surface structure noun phrases in Arabic. Thus, the surface structure entity known as *al-tamyīz* 'Accusative of Specification' can be accounted for in a simple and natural manner within this framework. The underlined noun phrases are surface accusatives of specification in the following sentences:

(51) a. *ʔištaraytu raṭlan zaytan* — 'I bought a pound of oil'
b. *malaʔtu al-kaʔsa māʔan* — 'I filled the glass with water'

Sentences (51) may be paraphrased by sentences (52), respectively:

(52) a. *ʔištaraytu raṭlan min al-zayti* — 'I bought a pound of oil'
b. *malaʔtu al-kaʔsa bi al-māʔi* — 'I filled the glass with water'

In accordance with the definitions given above, the case role of the underlined noun phrases in (51a) and (52a) is Source, that of the underlined noun phrases in (51b) and (52b) is Instrument.

Two other surface accusatives are known as accusative of purpose and accusative of cause. Sentences (53) illustrate the two types of accusatives respectively:

(53) a. *waqafa al-nāsu tarḥīban bi al-raʔīsi* — 'The people stood up in welcome to the president'
b. *haraba zaydun xawfan min al-sajni* — 'Zayd fled for fear of imprisonment'

Sentences (53) may be paraphrased by sentences (54), respectively:

(54) a. *waqafa al-nāsu li kay yuraḥḥibū bi al-raʔīsi* — 'The people stood up in order to welcome the president'
b. *haraba zaydun li ʔannahu xāfa min al-sajni* — 'Zayd fled because he feared imprisonment'

Accusatives of purpose and of cause may thus be considered sentential complements. The deep structure case of the accusative of purpose in (53a) and the complement sentence in (54a) is Goal; the deep structure case of the accusative of cause in (53b) and the complement sentence in (54b) is Source.

Certain surface objects seem to be difficult to account for in terms of the proposed case roles. Consider the following sentences:

(55) a. *ʔurīduka ʔan taḥtarima wālidayka* — 'I want you to respect your parents'
b. *ḥaramū hindan min al-mīrāṯi* — 'They deprived Hind of inheritance'

In (55a) *ʔurīduka*– 'I want you' – may be paraphrased by *ʔurīdu minka*–'I want from you.' Thus the case role of the suffix accusative pronoun in (55a) is Source and the case role of the sentential object is Target. Also *hindan* in (55b) has the case role Patient and *al-mīrāṯi* the case role Source.

Nothing so far has been said about accusatives like the underlined noun phrases in the following sentences:

(56). a. *darastu sā^c^atan* — 'I studied one hour'
b. *mašaytu mīlayni* — 'I walked two miles'

The underlined noun phrases in (56) are known as accusatives of duration and distance, respectively. Fillmore (1971: 52) raises the possibility that such accusatives might be considered as combining the Source and Goal notions into a single unit, that is, (56) may be replaced by (57), respectively:

(57) a. *darastu min al-sā^c^ati al-sābi^c^ati ḥattā al-sā^c^ati al-ṯāminati* — 'I studied from seven o'clock till eight o'clock'
b. *mašaytu min al-bayti ʔilā al-sūqi* — 'I walked from the house to the market'

(whereby the distance from the house to the market is two miles.) This could be, except that there is no specification of the starting point or the destination in sentences (56) as they stand. No solution to the problem of assigning the case roles for the underlined noun phrases in (56) can be suggested here; for the purposes of this book, the case roles Time and Place are assigned to them respectively.

A number of problems remain unsolved and the positing of more case roles, like for example, Path may be necessary. Path may be the case role of noun phrases like the one underlined in the following sentence:

(58) *ḏahaba min al-maġribi ʔilā ʔisbānyā ^c^abra maḍīqi jabali ṭāriqin* — 'He went from Morocco to Spain across the Strait of Gibraltar'

It is, however, necessary to keep the inventory of cases as small as possible and that the case roles be defined in a consistent manner. Both of these points have been taken into consideration in this chapter. Though many problems remain unresolved the above case system accounts for most of the data in a natural and simple manner.

2.4.2 Transformations

The transformations that map deep structures into surface structures within the framework of case grammar are far from clear. Fillmore, for example, has given a formalization of the transformational component in (1968), only to reject it in (1971) in favor of a still vaguer but more semantically–oriented transformational component. The remarks given in this section are no more than a general idea about some of the ways in which deep structures are converted into surface representations of sentences.

We now consider some of the ways in which deep structures of the type proposed and discussed in this chapter are converted into surface structure. We have proposed earlier that order among the elements of a sentence (including elements within the Q component as well as elements within the P component) be introduced transformationally. Rule (4), given earlier, creates a hierarchy among elements of the P component. The verb is placed first by this hierarchy followed by an array of cases. The Agent is placed after the verb and is followed by the Patient which is followed by the Target which is followed by the other cases.

(59) Verb Agent Patient Target

By virtue of this hierarchy, the Agent is the most eligible candidate for becoming the surface subject of the sentence. In a sentence like *al-rijālu ḏahabū* 'The men went (away)' the noun phrase has the Agent case role. The following is an informal derivation of this simple sentence (the Q component is disregarded).

(60) *ḏahaba* ∿ *al-rijāl*	
ḏahaba al-rijāl	Rule (4)
ḏahaba al-rijālu	Subjectivization
al-rijālu ḏahaba al-rijālu	A Copying Transformation
al-rijālu ḏahabū	Pronominalization

Rule (4) provides order; subjectivization assigns the noun phrase the nominative surface case ending, thus making it subject. The last two transformations constitute the topicalization process.

In the absence of an Agent, the Patient becomes the surface subject; in the absence of a Patient, the Target becomes the subject and so on.

In a manner similar to subjectivization, objectivization assigns the accusative case ending to surface objects and to the different surface accusatives. In this case system prepositions are introduced transformationally. Prepositions in many instances are surface structure indicators of the semantic functions of noun phrases. They, however, do not determine what the case role of a certain noun phrase is. Rather the differences among the case roles on the level of the deep structure are what determine the selection of individual prepositions. In general, no preposition is selected for the Agent. Prepositions are generally transformationally selected for different case roles as follows:

(61) *bi* 'With (instrumental)'	Instrument, Manner
min 'From'	Source
?ilā, li 'To'	Beneficiary, Goal
{ ^{c}*alā* 'On,' *fī* 'In' / *fawqa* 'Above,' *taḥta* 'Under' / *ḥawla* 'Around' etc. }	Place
fī 'At,' *?aṯnā?a* 'During' etc.	Time
ma^{c}a, with'	Comitative

It is important to note here that not every case role given in (61) has to be associated with a preposition on the surface. It is also important to note that case roles that do not occur in (61), like Patient and Target, may be preceded by prepositions in the surface structure.

The introduction of prepositions transformationally triggers a genetivization process. Thus assignment of the genitive case ending to noun phrases is preceded by a transformation that introduces prepositions before noun phrases.

NOTES

1. The arrow notation is used throughout, but this should not be interpreted as meaning that the proposal for case grammar requires an assumption of a left-to-right orientation of the constituent of the rewriting rules. Arabic is written from right to left; writing these rules in accordance with the Arabic script would necessitate a right-to-left representation.

2. The word "usually" is used in the definition of Instrument because the Instrument does not have to be always inanimate as can be seen from the following sentences:

(i) *ramā zawjatahu bi ?ibnihi al-ṣaġīri*
'He threw (i.e., hit) his wife with his little son'

(ii) *?axāfahā bi al-ḥayyati*
'He frightened her with the snake'

3 The passive

3.1 The Early Arab Grammarians Account of Passivization

The passive construction, according to the Arab early grammarians, is syntactically derived from a corresponding active construction. The process of passivization involves the deletion of the subject of the verb in an active construction; consequently the verb takes the passive form and what used to be the object becomes subject in the passive sentence and is assigned the nominative surface case ending. The Arab grammarians, in addition, described passivization in terms of the entities that may become subject of the passive verb. The following are the grammatical categories, with illustrative sentences, that may become subjects of passive verbs:

(i) Object

(1)	1a.	*ḍaraba zaydun* ^{c}*amran*	'Zayd beat 'Amr'
	b.	*ḍuriba* ^{c}*amrun*	' 'Amr was beaten'
	2a.	^{c}*arafnā ?annahā min lubnāna*	'We knew that she is from Lebanon'
	b.	^{c}*urifa ?annahā min lubnāna*	'It was known that she is from Lebanon'

(ii) The first or second object of certain verbs that may take two accusative objects:

(2)	a.	*?a*^{c}*ṭaytu zaydan kitāban*	'I gave Zayd a book'
	b.	*?u*^{c}*ṭiya zaydun kitāban*	'Zayd was given a book'
	c.	*?u*^{c}*ṭiya kitābun zaydan*	'A book was given to Zayd'

(iii) Accusatives of time, duration, place or distance under certain conditions:

(3)	1a.	*ṣāma zaydun ramaḍāna*	'Zayd fasted Ramadan'
	b.	*ṣīma ramaḍānu*	'Ramadan was fasted'
	2a.	*sāra zaydun sā*^{c}*atayni*	'Zayd walked two hours'
	b.	*sīrat sā*^{c}*atāni*	'Two hours were walked'

(4)	1a.	*jalastu ?amāma al-?amiri*	'I sat in front of the prince'
	b.	*julisa ?amamu al-?amiri*	'In front of the prince was sat'
	2a.	*sāra zaydun mīlayni*	'Zayd walked two miles'
	b.	*sīra mīlāni*	'Two miles were walked'

(iv) Cognate accusative when modified or specified:

(5)	1a.	*jalasa Zaydun julūsan ḥasanan*	'Zayd sat down nice sitting down'
	b.	*julisa julūsun ḥasanun*	'Nice sitting down was sat'
	2a.	*ġannat hindun ?uġniyatan*	'Hind sang a song'
	b.	*ġunniyat ?uġniyatun*	'A song was sung'

(v) Prepositional phrase:

(6)	1a.	*marartu bi zaydin*	'I passed by Zayd'
	b.	*murra bi zaydin*	'Zayd was passed by'
	2a.	*nāma zaydun fī al-bayti*	'Zayd slept in the house'
	b.	*nīma fī al-bayti*	'It was slept in the house'

It is important to mention here that when the subject of a passive construction is a sentential complement or a prepositional phrase, the verb is in the 3 m.s. This is illustrated in sentences (1.2.b) and (6b) above. Such passive constructions are called "impersonal passives." Passive constructions like (3b), (4b) and (5.1.b) are common in CA, but they hardly exist in MSA.

3.2 A Survey of the Arabic Passive in Transformational Grammar

James A. Snow (1965) provides the first treatment of Arabic passives in transformational grammar. He proposes two separate optional transformations, one for the derivation of ordinary passives, the other for the derivation of impersonal passives. Both transformations operate on deep structures identical to the structures underlying the active constructions. Snow posits surface case endings in the deep structure. The first transformation, call it T-1, has the effect of deriving, for example, (7b) from (7a) below.

(7)	a.	*al-rijālu yafhamūna al-kutuba*	'The men understand the books'
	b.	*al-kutubu tufhamu*	'The books are understood'

T-1 deletes the subject nominal *al-rijāl* leaving behind the nominative case ending u, deletes the accusative case ending a of *al-kutuba,* assigns the passive form to the verb, and crosses the object over the verb. The second transformation, call it T-2, has the effect of deriving, for example, (8b) from (8a) below:

(8)	a.	*al-rijālu yusāfirūna ?ilā al-qāhirati*	'The men are travelling to Cairo'
	b.	*yusāfaru ?ilā al-qāhirati*	'It is being travelled to Cairo'

T-2 deletes the subject nominal *al-rijālu* and assigns the third person masculine singular passive form to the verb.

Snow's transformations do too many things at the same time; they, arbitrarily, do whatever it takes to change the structure underlying active sentences into passive sentences. Fillmore and other case grammarians have shown that there is no need or justification for representing surface case affixes at the level of the deep structure. Since Arabic is a VSO language, the statement of the passive transformation would not require the cross-over movement proposed by Snow. Also, although there might be some justification for assigning the passive form to the verb by the application of a passive transformation, there is no justification for assigning person, number, and gender by this passive transformation. Agreement transformations are very late rules in Arabic. Snow's analysis tells us nothing about the verbs that may be passivized in Arabic; he says they are transitive without really explaining what he means by the term transitive. Verbs like *kallafa* 'to cost' and *šābaha* 'to resemble' which may not be passivized in Arabic are predicted to passivize by Snow's T-1. For the above reasons Snow's passive transformations fail to account for the passivization process in Arabic.

Nancy Kennedy Lewkowicz (1967) assigns the passive voice to verbs at the level of the deep structure by phrase structure rules. Intransitive verbs which are assigned the feature [+ Active] do not occur passive. Transitive verbs are assigned the feature [±Active] and they can occur either active or passive. Lewkowicz is aware of the existence of certain transitive verbs like *šābaha* 'to resemble' which do not passivize. To solve this problem she suggests: "probably these verbs also should be marked [+ Active] " (p. 44). Her deep structure passive construction is identical to the corresponding active construction except for the fact that the subject is an unspecified dummy Δ and that the verb has the feature [– Active] (i.e., has the passive form). Lewkowicz' passive transformation simply involves "deletion of original subject of passive verb." Where the verb is prepositionally transitive, the subject is merely deleted leaving behind the impersonal passive sentence; where it is directly transitive, the object crosses over the verb and replaces the subject which gets deleted. Thus her transformation has two structural changes, and in this respect it is no different from Snow's two separate transformations.

Lewkowicz' account of passivization in Arabic is completely ad hoc, and fails even more than Snow's analysis to account for passivization and passivizability in Arabic. Her analysis does not predict anything about the nature of the verbs that can or cannot occur in the passive form. Thus the notion of transitivity and the process of passivization remain unexplained. Furthermore, there is no justification for crossing the object over the verb because Arabic is a VSO language.

Another linguist who had something to say about Arabic passive within the framework of the transformational theory is Samir Abu Absi (1972) who discussed the passive in Lebanese Arabic (LA). He proposes an optional passive transformation for the derivation of passives in LA, which he considers an SVO language. The deep structure of the passive construction is identical to the corresponding active surface construction except that the subject is the indefinite LA noun phrase *ḥada* 'someone.' The passive transformation has the effect of deriving, for example, the LA sentence (9b) from the corresponding active sentence (9a) below:

(9)	a.	*ḥada ḍarab il-walad*	'Someone hit the boy'
	b.	*il-walad nḍarab*	'The boy was hit'

This transformation moves the object to the beginning of the sentence, moves the subject to the end of the sentence, provides number, person, and gender agreement, accounts for the third person masculine singular form of the verb when the subject is a sentential complement, adds a feature [+ Passive] to the verb, and on top of all that, by a second structural change, deletes the original subject. In other words, this transformation does whatever is necessary to derive passives from actives in accordance with the hypothesis that LA is an SVO language. It is doubtful that a transformation as powerful as this one exists in a natural language. The most obvious shortcoming of Abu Absi's derivation of the passives is that the structure underlying the passive, claimed to be an appropriate surface structure in LA, is ungrammatical. In LA as well as in Arabic the head noun phrase of a sentence cannot be an absolute indefinite noun phrase:

(10) a. LA. **walad ?ijā*
b. Arabic. **waladun jā?a* } 'A boy came'

The same transformation is involved in deriving impersonal passives. Abu Absi noticed that when a cognate object is modified by an adjective, the sentence in which it occurs is grammatical, otherwise such a sentence is ungrammatical. The following pair of sentences illustrates the point:

(11) a.	*l-bint nḥaka ^{c}alayha ḥaki ḥilu*	Lit. 'Nice talk was talked about the girl'
b.	**l-bint nḥaka ^{c}alayha ḥaki*	Lit. 'Talk was talked about the girl'[1]

Abu Absi posits a cognate object in the deep structure of active sentences underlying impersonal passive sentences. The following is his derivation of an impersonal passive sentence:

(12). a.	**ḥada ḥaka ḥaki ^{c}ala l-bint* Lit. 'Someone talked talk about the girl'	Underlying Form
b.	**ḥaki nḥaka ^{c}ala l-bint* Lit. 'Talk was talked about the girl'	Abu Absi's Passive Rule
c.	*nḥaka ^{c}ala l-bint* 'It was talked about the girl'	Cognate Object Deletion Rule
d.	*l-bint nḥaka ^{c}alayha* 'The girl was talked about'	Secondary Topicalization

Derivation (12) shows a misunderstanding of the nature of topicalization processes on Abu Absi's part. In Chapter I it was shown that the rule that gives a sentence like (12d) from a sentence like (12c) is a primary, rather than secondary, topicalization rule. The arguments presented in Chapter I in connection with topicalization hold for LA as well as Arabic. Abu Absi analyzes LA as an SVO language which forces him to arbitrarily propose movement operations within the framework of his passive rule. In spite of all the shortcomings of Abu Absi's analysis, he has shown awareness of the important role that cognate accusatives play in the passivization process in LA. The importance of cognate objects with respect to passivization in Arabic will be investigated later in this chapter.

In conclusion, the above analyses which are proposed within the framework of the transformational theory fail to account for the process of passivization in Arabic (and in LA) not only in terms of descriptive adequacy but even in terms of observational adequacy. In other words, not only do these analyses assign an inappropriate basic order typology and an inappropriate phrase structure grammar to Arabic on the deep structure level, but they also fail to generate grammatical, and to prevent the generation of ungrammatical, Arabic passive sentences.

3.3 The Nature of the Arabic Passive Construction

It was shown in Chapter I that the Arabic passive construction contains no agent. It is important at this point to clarify what is meant by agent. The term agent must not be confused with the deep structure case Agent discussed in Chapter II. The agent in English, for example, is the noun phrase that follows the agentive particle by in a passive construction like John was killed by Bill; such a construction may be called full passive in contrast to an agentless passive like John was killed. Arabic has no full passives and no agentive particle equivalent to English by. This, however, is a surface phenomenon. The languages of the world can be divided into two groups with respect to what type of passive construction they have in their surface structure: languages like Arabic that have only agentless passives and languages like English that have agentless as well as full passives. Some linguists have investigated this question and have come out with the conclusion that there is no language that has full passives without having agentless passives. Although the Arabic passive construction is agentless on the surface, it indicates implicit or understood external agency. To illustrate the point let us compare sentences a and b below:

(13) a.	*futiḥa al-bābu*	'The door was opened'
b.	*?infataḥa al-bābu*	'The door opened'

Sentence a is an agentless passive on the surface because it does not explicitly contain an agent; however the verb has the passive form and the sentence implies external agency. The verb in b, on the other hand, has the reflexive form and the sentence does not imply any external agency. The differences between sentences like a and sentences like b will be further explored in Chapter V. In light of these facts, it would be appropriate to claim that the Arabic passive construction is not agentless semantically and on the deep structure level. The agent of the Arabic passive construction is unspecified. The character of this unspecified agent is determined by co-occurrence restrictions dictated by the nature of the verb. This unspecified agent, in other words, is a member of a set of noun phrases (including sentential complements) that may occur as agent in the active construction which corresponds to the passive construction in question. The following are illustrative sentences:

(14) a.	*qutila zaydun*	'Zayd was killed'
b.	*?ukilat al-tuffāḥatu*	'The apple was eaten'
c.	*?ufturisa al-ḥamalu*	'The lamb was killed (by a wild animal)'
d.	*ḥusida ^{c}amrun*	' 'Amr was envied'
e.	*quri?at al-risālatu*	'The letter was read'
f.	*ḥukima ^{c}alā zaydin bi al-?i^{c}dāmi*	'Zayd was sentenced to death'
g.	*tuwuffiya al-?amīru*	'The prince was taken unto Him (i.e., died)'

In a the agent can be person, animal or thing, in b it can be only animate, in c only wild animal, in d only human, in e only literate human, in f only someone like a judge, and in g it can be only God. As can be seen from these sentences, the degree of specificity or nonspecifity of the agent depends on the semantic and pragmatic nature of the verb. In g the agent is completely recoverable and is hardly unspecified. The character of the unspecified agent may depend on other pragmatic facts. The verb in a has been shown to accept humans, animals, or things as agents. In the following sentence which indicates a calamity the agent can be an inanimate object only:

(15)	*qutila zaydun fī ḥādiṯi sayyāratin*	'Zayd was killed in a car accident'

It has been argued up to this point that Arabic passives are agentless in the surface structure. Ahmed Kamal El-Din Abdel-Hamid (1972: 150), like many others before him, claims "that in contemporary practice one frequently meets, especially in newspapers and translations from European languages with constructions such as *min qibali* 'on the part of,' *^{c}alā yadi* 'at the hand of,' *bi-wāsiṭati* 'by means of' or *bi-* 'by' which are used to express the agent after a verb in the passive." In addition to these "agentive" constructions which are claimed to be equivalent to the English agentive particle <u>by</u> or the French agentive particle <u>par</u>, others are known to exist in Arabic such as *min jānibi* 'from the side of' [*min ^{c}indi, min ladun*] ' on the part of' *bi sababi* 'because' etc. The following are Arabic passive sentences which seem to be counterexamples to the claim that Arabic passives are agentless on the surface:

(16)	a.	*dummirat al-madīnatu bi al-nābālm*	'The city was destroyed by napalm'
	b.	*qutila zaydun ^{c}alā yadi ^{c}aduwwihi*	'Zayd was killed on the hand of his enemy'
	c.	*?ursila mab^{c}ūṯun min qibali al-ra?īsi al-?amrīkiyyi ?ilā al-šarqi al-?awsaṭi*	'An envoy was sent, on the part of the American president to the Middle East'
	d.	*quddima ?iqtirāḥun ?ilā al-?umami al-muttaḥidati min jānibi safīri lubnāna*	'A proposal was submitted to the United Nations from the side of the ambassador of Lebanon'
	e.	*kusira al-zujāju bi sababi ?ihmālihā*	'The glass was broken because of her negligence'

It is claimed that passive constructions with indirect agents like those in (16) are a contemporary innovation especially in newspapers and translations from European languages and purists have gone as far as rejecting constructions like those in (16) because they consider them nonindigenous constructions imposed on the Arabic language by the influence of western languages, especially English and French. This usage of the passive, however, is very old. The following verses from the Holy Koran, where the preposition *min* plays the role of the agentive passive particle (except in (17a) below where the construction *min ladun* plays that role), prove the point:

(17)	a.	*kitābun ?uḥkimat ?āyātuhu ṯumma fuṣṣilat min ladun ḥakīmin xabīr* (XI.1)	'A Book with verses basic or fundamental, further explained in detail, - from One Who is Wise and Well-Acquainted (with all things)!
	b.	*. . . ?unzila ^{c}alayhi ?āyatun min rabbihi* (XXX.27)	'. . . a Sign sent down to him from his Lord'
	c.	*?ittabi^{c} mā ?ūḥiya ?ilayka min rabbika* (VI. 106)	'Follow what thou art taught by inspiration from thy Lord!'
	d.	*. . . wa mā ?ūtiya al-nabiyyūna min rabbihim* (II.136)	'. . . and that given to (all) Prophets from their Lord'

Passives like these occur in CA as well as in MSA though they are more common in the latter.

The indirect agentive phrases in (16) and (17) are not real passive agentive phrases.

The passive English agentive phrase, for example, cannot occur in active constructions:

(18) a. Mary was hurt by John
b. *Mary hurt by John

The putative Arabic passive agentive phrases in (16) and (17) can occur in active constructions:

(19) a.	*rabbanā . . . hab lanā min ladunka raḥmatan* (III.8)	'Our Lord . . . grant us mercy from thine own Presence'
b.	*wa mā al-naṣru ?illā min ᶜindi allāh* (III.126)	'There is no help except from God'
c.	*al-ḥaqqu min rabbika* (III. 60)	'The Truth (comes) from God'
d.	*dammara al-ᶜaduwwu al-madīnata bi al-nābālm*	'The enemy destroyed the city with napalm'
e.	*tamma ḥallu al-muškilati bi wāsiṭatihim*	'The solution of the problem got achieved by means of them'
f.	*zāra al-ra?īsa al-?amrīkiyya wafdun min qibali al-ḥukūmati al-miṣriyyati*	'A delegation on the part of the Egyptian government visited the American president'
g.	*takabbadū xasā?ira fādiḥatan ᶜalā ?aydī al-ṯuwwāri*	'They suffered heavy losses on the hands of the rebels'

In accordance with the case system proposed and discussed in Chapter II, the agent in a passive construction can only be either Agent or Patient in the deep structure. The following are illustrative full passives from English:

(20) a. John was killed by Bill
b. A voice was heard by Bill

The case role of the specified explicit passive agent Bill is Agent in a, Patient in b. The case role of the unspecified implicit passive agent in the following Arabic passive sentences is Agent in a, Patient in b, respectively:

(21) a.	*qutila zaydun*	'Zayd was killed'
b.	*sumiᶜa ṣawtun*	'A voice was heard'

Let us identify now the case roles of the putative Arabic agents in (16) and (17). It was shown in Chapter II that prepositions are in general surface structure indicators of the semantic function of the noun phrases that follow them and therefore of the case roles of those noun phrases. The preposition *min* is the Source preposition; therefore the case role of the noun phrases following *min* in (16c, d) and (17) is Source. The preposition *bi* is generally associated with the Instrument case, thus the case of the noun phrase following *bi* in (16a) is Instrument. Although in general prepositions are surface indicators of case roles, they do not always indicate the case roles; the preposition *ᶜalā*, for example, is generally associated with the Place case role yet in (16b) the noun phrase following *ᶜalā* is an inalienally possessed instrument: it would be appropriate to assign the noun phrase *yadi ᶜaduwwihi* 'the hand of his enemy' the case role Instrument. This case role assignment is consistent with the semantic function of the noun phrase that follows *ᶜalā* in (16b). But the phrase *ᶜalā yadi* 'on the hand of' or *ᶜalā ?aydī* 'on the hands of' may not always be interpreted as having the instrumental semantic function; in Hans Wehr's dictionary it is translated into English by "with the help of" and the Arabic word *yad* 'hand' has the following semantic range in addition to the literal meaning: 'power, control, influence, authority, assistance, help, aid.' The following sentence illustrates the semantic indication of the phrase *^{c}alā yadi* 'on the hand of.'

(22) *tamma faṣlu al-quwwāti ^{c}alā yadi hinrī kisinjir* — 'The disengagement got achieved with the help (or by the influence) of Henry Kissinger'

Semantically "Henry Kissinger" is the source of the coming about of "the disengagement" in (22). Thus we assign noun phrases that follow the expression *^{c}alā yadi* 'on the hand of or *^{c}alā ʔaydī* 'on the hands of' the Source case role; we do not, however, exclude the possibility of assigning the instrumental noun phrase that follows the preposition *^{c}alā* in sentences like (16b) the Instrument case role. A cause of an activity that is inactively involved in the bringing about of that activity is semantically and pragmatically no more than the source of that activity; therefore we assign the noun phrase following *bi sababi* 'because' in (16e) the case role Source. The phrase *bi-wāsiṭati* 'by means of' is a means adverbial; noun phrases following this means adverbial are assigned the Instrument case role in accordance with the case system discussed in Chapter II.

It was stated earlier that the agent of a passive construction can only have either the Agent or the Patient case role. It has been shown in the above discussion that the expressions considered traditionally as equivalent to English by or French par are not really agentive expressions. We have also shown that none of the noun phrases following these expressions, which we label as "pseudo-agentive particles," are either Agents or Patients in the deep structure; they have been shown to have either the Instrument or the Source case role.

In summary, the following points were made in this section:

(i) Arabic passive constructions are agentless in the surface structure.
(ii) Arabic passive constructions indicate an implicit or understood unspecified external passive agent and therefore they are not agentless on the deep structure level.
(iii) The unspecified passive agent can be either Agent or Patient in the deep structure.
(iv) There is no genuine agentive particle in Arabic.
(v) Sentences like those of (16) and (17) above are not surface structure full passives and do not syntactically and/or semantically correspond to, for example, English or French full passives that contain the agentive particle by or par, respectively, and
(vi) passive constructions that "indirectly express the agent" are not modern innovations brought about by the influence of the western languages; instances of such passives have been given from the Holy Koran.

3.4 Passivizability

It has been shown that passivization does not depend solely on whether the verb is transitive or intransitive within the framework of the traditional definition of transitivity. Certain transitive verbs that take a direct object have been shown not to passivize; on the other hand, certain intransitive verbs that do not take a direct object have been shown to passivize. Therefore, a new verb classification with respect to passivizability is necessary. The simplest and most revealing classification is one according to which all verbs are divided into two major classes: passivizable and nonpassivizable. Such a classification, however, would not be useful unless it is clearly shown which verb types fall naturally under which of the two classes. Consequently it is necessary to specify syntactic and semantic features of passivizable verbs in contradistinction to those of nonpassivizable verbs. This means that, among other things, the case frames of the verbs of each of the two classes must be determined.

3.4.1 Nonpassivizable Verbs

The term "nonpassivizable verbs" is used here to refer to verbs that cannot occur in the passive form. They include the following:

3.4.1.1 One-place Verbs.

These are verbs that require only one noun phrase in order to complete a sentence or concept. They can be stative, inchoative, or active verbs as shown in (23) below respectively:

(23)	a.	*qabuḥat hindun*	'Hind was ugly'
	b.	*ḏāba al-ṯalju*	'The snow melted'
	c.	*jāʔa zaydun*	'Zayd came'

The case frames of the verbs in (23) are [________ Target], [________ Patient], and [________ Agent], respectively. Regardless of which case occurs with which verb, these one-place verbs are nonpassivizable. Therefore, the following generalization can be made:

Verbs with the case frame [______ K] are nonpassivizable.
(where K stands for any case)

Although these verbs require only one noun phrase to complete a meaning or thought, they can have more than one noun phrase in their case frames, as in the following sentences:

(24)	a.	*māta xālidun fī bayrūta*	'Khalid died in Beirut'
	b.	*ᶜāda zaydun min dimašqa*	'Zayd came back from Damascus'
	c.	*ġannat fayrūz ḥattā al-ṣabāḥi*	'Fairuz sang till the morning'
	d.	*fariḥtu laka*	'I was happy for you'
	e.	*sāfarat ʔilā al-qāhirati*	'She travelled to Cairo'
	f.	*ʔistayaqẓa fī al-sāᶜati al-ᶜāširati*	'He woke up at ten o'clock'
	g.	*ḥaḍara wa ʔaxāhu*	'He came with his brother'
	h.	*rajaᶜa bisurᶜatin*	'He came back quickly'

These sentences do not passivize; the following are the case frames of their verbs:

(25)	a.	[——— Patient	Place]
	b.	[——— Agent	Source]
	c.	[——— Agent	Goal]
	d.	[——— Patient	Benefactive]

e.	[_____ Agent	Goal	]
f.	[_____ Patient	Time	]
g.	[_____ Agent	Comitative	]
h.	[_____ Agent	Manner	]

It was stated in Chapter II that an earlier transformation provides order among the elements of the P component whereby the verb is placed first followed by the different cases; this transformation also provides hierarchy among the cases. The order of the elements of the P component of sentences (24) is shown in (25) which is thus a result of such a transformation. Later topicalization transformations introduce various orders among the elements of the P component.

The verb types given in (25) are, of course, not the only nonpassivizable types of verbs: all verbs whose case frames consist of either an Agent or a Patient followed by any of the cases in the second column of (25) are also nonpassivizable. Therefore, if in (25) K_1 stands for Agent or Patient and K_2 stands for any other case, we can make the following generalization: verbs with case frames [_____ K_1 K_2] are nonpassivizable. But one-place verbs can occur with more than two cases in their case frame as can be seen in (26):

(26) *raja^c^a zaydun ?amsi ma^c^a ?axīhi bisur^c^atin min bayrūta ?ilā dimašqa.* — 'Zayd went back yesterday with his brother quickly from Beirut to Damascus'

The verb in (26) has the case frame [_____ Agent Time Comitative Manner Source Goal]. Therefore, the generalization given above has to be modified to read:

Verbs with case frames [_____ K_1 K_2 – – – Kn] are nonpassivizable
(where Kn stands for any number of cases and where n is a finite number)

In sentences (24) the case that immediately follows the verb (i.e., the subject of the verb in these sentences) is either Agent or Patient. Although many one-place stative verbs resist co-occurrence with more than one case, there are some that may take a Target as a subject followed by other cases:

(27) a. *saqaṭat al-tuffāḥatu min al-šajarati* — 'The apple fell from the tree'
[_____ Target Source]

b. *tadaḥraja al-ḥajaru ?ilā qā^c^i al-hadabati* — 'The stone rolled to the bottom of the hill'
[_____ Target Goal]

Therefore K_1, given above, stands not only for Patient and Agent, but for Target as well.

Two cases that may occur in the case frames of one-place verbs have not been mentioned yet: Instrument and Range. The following one-place verbs may have an Instrument in their case frames:

(28) a. *ya?kulu zaydun bi yadayhi* — 'Zayd eats with his hands'
b. *ḥalaqtu bi šafratin jadīdatin* — 'I shaved with a new blade'

Sentences like (28) do not undergo passivization. The two verbs in (28) can be described as pseudo-intransitive, and the two sentences may have Targets in their deep structures which can be thought of as "something edible" and "something shavable." An optional Target-Deletion transformation deletes the Target from an active sentence which contains a verb, like *?akala* 'eat' and *ḥalaqa* 'shave,' whose frame is [____ Agent Target Kn]. Consequently, whatever the passivization process may be if it precedes Target-Deletion, it bleeds it; if it follows Target-Deletion, it is bled by it. Therefore, in targetless sentences, verbs whose case frames are [____ Agent Instrument] are nonpassivizable.

The Range case is roughly the deep structure equivalent to the cognate accusative as was stated in Chapter II. The Range case may occur in the case frames of all verbs in Arabic except in those of defective verbs which will be discussed later. Thus one-place verbs may have the Range case in their case frames:

(29) a. *māta zaydun mawtan ?abyaḍa* 'Zayd died a natural death'
b. *ḥazinat hindun ḥuznan šadīdan* 'Hind was sad an intense sadness'
c. *^{c}adā al-waladu ^{c}adwan sarī^{c}an* 'The boy ran a fast race'
d. *habaṭat al-?as^{c}āru hubūṭan mufāji?an* 'The prices dropped suddenly'

Sentences (29) are nonpassivizable and the case frames of their verbs are [____ Patient Range], [____ Patient Range], [____ Agent Range] and [____ Target Range], respectively.

The generalization about nonpassivizable verbs can now be given in its final form:

Verbs with case frames [____ K_1 K_2 K_3 – – – – – Kn] are nonpassivizable where

(i) K_1 stands for Agent, Patient or Target
(ii) K_2 K_3 – – – Kn stand for any other cases, and
(iii) Fillmore's one-instance-per-clause principle is not violated, that is, the same case cannot occur in a single sentence more than once however complex that sentence may be.

All the one-place verbs mentioned so far are intransitive verbs in accordance with the traditional definition of transitivity. There is a group of one-place verbs, however, which seem to be transitive. These verbs take direct objects in the accusative surface case. Examples of verbs belonging to this group are: *waṣala* 'arrive,' *ḥaḍara* 'attend,' [*jā?a, ?atā*] 'come,' *daxala* 'enter,' and *ṣa^{c}ida* 'go up, ascend.' These verbs are nonpassivizable as shown in (30):

(30) 1a. *ṣa^{c}ida al-minbara* 'He ascended the pulpit'
b. **ṣu^{c}ida al-minbaru* 'The pulpit was ascended'
2a. *daxalat al-bayta* 'She entered the house'
b. **duxila al-baytu* 'The house was entered'

The objects in (30) can be preceded by the preposition *?ilā* 'to' which would make the verbs *ṣa^{c}ida* and *daxala* overtly intransitive:

(31) a. *ṣa^{c}ida ?ilā al-minbari*
b. *daxalat ?ilā al-bayti*

The sentences of (30a) are synonymous with those of (31); the only difference between them is that whereas the noun phrases in (30a) are direct objects and have the accusative case ending *-a*, the noun phrases in (31) are objects of the preposition *?ilā* and have the genitive case ending *-i*. It will be further noted that the verbal noun derived from verbs like *ṣa^{c}ida* and *daxala* has the pattern FuMŪL. This is a verbal noun pattern of intransitive verbs. The early Arab grammarians called objects like those in (30a) *al-manṣūb ^{c}alā naz^{c} al-xāfiḍ* 'accusativized by deletion of the genetivizer.' Thus, in the shallow structure sentences like (30a) contain prepositions which get deleted by a surface structure transformation. Verbs of this group have the deep structure case frame [_____ Agent Goal]; such verbs have been shown to be nonpassivizable.

3.4.1.2 Defective verbs and the Verb *kāna* 'To Be.' These are two-place verbs in the surface structure. They require a noun phrase, as subject and a noun phrase, sentence, adjective or prepositional phrase as predicate. The early Arab grammarians called these verbs *nāqiṣah* 'defective' because they require more than simply a noun phrase to complete a sentence or thought. But transitive verbs are two-place verbs as well. The Arab grammarians consider defective verbs nontransitive, (that is, neither transitive nor intransitive), in the sense that the concept of transitivity does not apply to them. The following two sentences, whose verbs are *kāna* 'to be' and *kāda* 'to almost be, undergo, or do' are illustrative of this group of verbs:

(32)	a.	*kāna zaydun šujā^{c}an*	'Zayd was brave'
	b.	*kāda al-fārisu yaqa^{c}u ^{c}an jawādihi*	'The knight almost fell from his horse'

There is at least one syntactic argument for distinguishing these verbs from transitive and intransitive verbs; whereas all transitive and intransitive verbs may take the Range case, these verbs may not:

(33)	a.	*ḥazina zaydun ḥuznan šadīdan*	'Zayd was sad an intense sadness'
	b.	*ḍaraba zaydun ^{c}amran ḍarban šadīdan*	'Zayd beat 'Amr intense beating'
	c.	**kāna zaydun šujā^{c}an kawnan ^{c}aẓīman*	*'Zayd was brave a great being'
	d.	**kāda al-fārisu yaqa^{c}u ^{c}an jawādihi kawdan qarīban*	*'The knight almost fell from his horse a close almostness'

(There is no verbal noun of the verb *kāda* in the language;
if it existed it would have the form *kawd*.)

All defective verbs are nonpassivizable. In the remaining part of this section only one defective verb will be discussed and explored, the verb *kāna* 'to be.'

In addition to its function as a defective verb, *kāna* is used in Arabic as an intransitive one-place verb. As a defective verb *kāna* is a copula; as a one-place verb it means 'to exist' or 'to happen.' The nondefective use of *kāna* can be seen in the following sentences:

(34)	a.	*wa kāna allāhu mundu al-?azali*	'And Allah existed since the beginning'
	b.	*wa kāna ?an ^{c}uyyina safīran*	'And it happened that he was appointed ambassador'

Thus the nondefective *kāna* is no different from any of the one-place nonpassivizable verbs discussed above.

The defective verb *kāna* looks like ordinary two-place transitive verbs in the surface structure:

(35)	a.	*kāna zaydun ṭabīban*	'Zayd was a doctor'
	b.	*qatala zaydun ṭabīban*	'Zayd killed a doctor'

The first noun phrase in (35) has the nominative surface case ending *-un* while the second noun phrase has the accusative surface case ending *-an*. The early Arab grammarians called the predicate noun phrases in (15a) *ᶜumdah* 'shore, prop' in contrast to the object noun phrase in (15b) which they called *faḍlah* 'residue.' A *ᶜumdah* is essential for a sentence containing a defective verb and may not be deleted; without it the sentence is either ungrammatical or interpretable as containing a nondefective verb. A *faḍlah*, on the other hand, is not essential for the grammaticalness of a sentence containing a passivizable verb because in certain contexts it may be deleted leaving behind a complete sentence. Thus sentences like *ʔuqtul!* 'kill!' *lā taqtul* 'don't kill,' and *qatala marratan wāḥidatan faqaṭ* 'He only killed one time' are grammatical while sentences like *kun!* 'be!' *lā takun* 'don't be' are not unless *kāna* is interpreted as a nondefective one-place verb.

Ibn Ya'īsh, describing the difference between *kāna* and non-defective verbs, writes: "*kāna* is considered a verb because it can be conjugated in the present, past, future, imperative and negative-imperative like other verbs. It is considered defective because whereas a real verb denotes meaning and time as in *ḍaraba* which denotes the past time and the activity of beating, *kāna* denotes only time . . . . Activity is what makes a verb; *kāna* does not denote activity therefore it is not a real verb. When it occurs with a predicate, the predicate is the substitute of activity." (Ibn Ya'īsh 7: 89–90). It is clear that, in a sentence like *kāna zaydun ḥazīnan* 'Zayd was sad,' Ibn Ya'īsh considers the predicate *ḥazīnan* 'sad' as the verb rather than *kāna*. There is evidence in the language that supports this claim:

(i) The tense denoted by *kāna* can be incorporated into certain adjectival or nominal predicates to give a nondefective verb; that is *kāna* + predicate can be "verbalized," as shown in the following sentences:

(36)	1a.	*kānat hindun jamīlatan*	'Hind was beautiful'
	b.	*jamulat hindun*	
	2a.	*kāna zaydun ḥazīnan*	'Zayd was sad'
	b.	*ḥazina zaydun*	
	3a.	*kāna al-barmakiyy wazīran li al-rašīdi*	'Al-Barmakiyy was a minister for al-Rashid'
	b.	*wazara al-barmakiyy li al-rašīdi*	
	4a.	*kāna sībawayhi tilmīḏan li al-xalīli*	'Sībawayhi was a student of al-Khalīl's'
	b.	*tatalmaḏa sībawayhi ᶜalā al-xalīli*	
	5a.	*kāna zaydun ʔamīran*	'Zayd was a prince'
	b.	*ʔamura zaydun*	

(ii) The predicate of *kāna* sentences can be shown to be a verb when it is active participle, passive participle, or adjective. Active particples govern an object in the same manner as active verbs; passive participles govern a passive subject like passive verbs; and active particples, passive participles and adjectives can take certain manner adverbials and the cognate accusative just like ordinary verbs. Inflection of these predicates for number, gender and case are matters of the surface structure.

The situation with predicate nouns of *kāna* sentences is not this straightforward, however. Predicate nouns may not take manner adverbials or cognate accusatives; they do not govern objects or passive subjects. The reason is that they do not have incorporated in them the tense element that ordinary verbs have. This fact does not invalidate the claim that they are, at least at some level, verbs. These verbs, however, are not derived from verb roots (*drs, darasa* 'to study') or even from noun roots (*wjh, wajh* 'face;' *wajjaha* 'to direct someone'), but from entire nouns in accordance with a suggestion given by Chafe (1970: 143, 201–202) for the derivation of English predicate nouns. Chafe derives such verbs by a semantic rule equivalent to the following rule:

(37) Verb [state] $\Longrightarrow$ N + Predicativizer,

where the double arrow is to be read "is further specified." Consequently, this verb would have all the features of the noun from which it is derived. The argument given here is semantic and the fact that in the surface structure a verb can take an object while a noun can't is irrelevant. This can be seen from the synonymy of the following pair of sentences:

(38) a. *kāna zaydun ṣadīqa ^{c}amrin* 'Zayd was 'Amr's friend'
b. *ṣādaqa zaydun ^{c}amran* 'Zayd befriended (stative) 'Amr'

The semantic relationship between the predicate *ṣadīq* and the genitive noun phrase *^{c}amrin* in (38a) is the same as the semantic relationship between the verb *ṣādaqa* and the object *^{c}amran* in (38b).

This analysis of *kāna* and its predicate is consistent with Sībawayhi's claim that tense in the sentence *ḏahaba* 'he went' is separate from the verb *ḏahaba* 'to go' in the same manner as *?amsi* 'yesterday' is separate from *ḏahaba* in the sentence *ḏahaba ?amsi* 'he went yesterday' (Sībawayhi I: 11). In terms of the case system given in Chapter II, tense is part of the Time case. If the verb is obtained from a verb root like *ḍrb* 'beat' or *ḏhb* 'go' or from a noun root like *?sd* 'lion' or *ḥjr* 'stone,' tense (along with features from the Q component) will be incorporated in the verb. If all the Time case "contains" is tense, it never materializes in the surface structure; if it also "contains" a time adverbial like for example *?amsi* 'yesterday,' this time adverbial will show up in the surface structure. The following diagram illustrates the process:

(39)

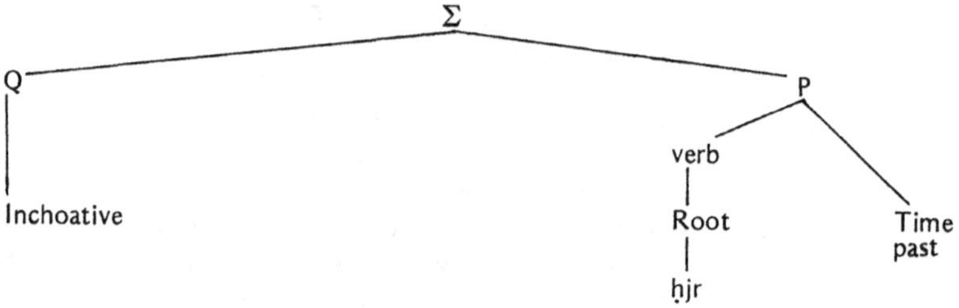

The incorporation of Past and the inchoative feature into the verb root will give *taḥajjara* 'turn to stone; become petrified.' If, on the other hand, the verb is derived from an entire noun, it cannot carry tense. In this case *kāna* is introduced to carry the tense from "under" the Time case. If the time specified in the Time case is past, *kāna* materializes in the surface structure as *kāna;* if the time is present or future, as *yakūnu, sayakūnu* or *sawfa yakūnu,* in sentences that are temporally unmarked, *kāna* never materializes and we get a "nominal sentence." The three instances can be seen in the following three sentences:

(40)	a.	*kāna zaydun ṭabīban*	'Zayd was a doctor'
	b.	{*yakūnu* / *sayakūnu* / *sawfa yakūnu*} zaydun ṭabīban	'Zayd will be a doctor'
	c.	*zaydun ṭabībun*	'Zayd is a doctor'

In short, *kāna* is nothing but a tense carrier.

3.4.1.3 The *kallafa* 'To Cost' Type Verbs. Verbs belonging to this class such as *kallafa* 'to cost,' *wazana* 'to weigh (itr),' *dāma* 'to last,' and ^{c}*alā* 'to rise (in one reading)' are two place verbs:

(41)	a.	*kallafa hāḏā al-kitābu xamsa līrātin*	'This book cost five pounds'
	b.	*yazinu hāḏā al-ṣundūqu kīluġrāmayni*	'This box weighs two kilograms'
	c.	*dāma al- ijtimā^{c}u ṯalāṯa sā^{c}ātin*	'The meeting lasted three hours'
	d.	*ya^{c}lū al-maṣīfu ?alfa qadamin ^{c}an saṭḥi al-baḥri*	'The summer residence rises a thousand feet above sea level'

Though according to the traditional definition of transitivity, these verbs are transitive because they take a subject in the nominative case and an object in the accusative, sentences (41) cannot be passivized.

A syntactic property of the verbs in (41) is that they may not take the Range case role:

(42)	a.	**kallafa hāḏā al-kitābu xamsa līrātin taklīfan kabīran*	'This book cost five pounds a great cost'
	b.	**yazinu hāḏā al-ṣundūqu kīluġramayni waznan ṯaqīlan*	'This box weighs two kilograms heavy weight'
	c.	**dāma al- ijtimā^{c}u ṯalāṯa sā^{c}ātin dawāman ṭawīlan*	'The meeting lasted three hours long lasting'
	d.	*ya^{c}lū al-maṣīfu ?alfa qadamin ^{c}an saṭḥi al-baḥri ^{c}uluwwan šāhiqan*	'The summer residence rises a thousand feet above sea level a (very) high rising'

Halliday (1967: 59) distinguishes two types of what was termed the Range case role: quality Ranges and quantity Ranges. The Range discussed in Chapter II may be labelled quality Range because it completes or further specifies the verb by modifying or qualifying it. Quantity Range, on the other hand, completes or further specifies the verb by quantifying it. In accordance with Halliday's distinction which is adopted here, the objects in (41) are assigned the Range case role (quantity Range). The case frames of the verbs in (42) violate Fillmore's one-instance-per-clause principle because each of these case frames now contains two Range case roles (a quantity Range and a quality Range); this explains the ungrammaticalness of sentences (42). The verbs in (41) are clearly stative; therefore the case role of the subjects in these sentences is Target, and the case frame of the verbs in (41) is [____ Target Range]. Verbs that have such a case frame are nonpassivizable.

3.4.1.4 The *šābaha* 'To Resemble' Type Verbs. This class of verbs whose meaning ranges from 'to resemble' to 'to be equal to' can be divided into two subclasses, the *šābaha* subclass and the *^{c}ādala* subclass. The following verbs are the most common of the two subclasses:

(i) *šābaha, ?ašbaha, maṯala, māṯala, ḍāra^{c}a, ḥākā* to resemble, to be similar to, to be like'
(ii) *^{c}ādala, ^{c}adala, sawiya, sāwā, ḍāhā* 'to be equal, to equal, to tie (i.e., to have an equal score with)'

The following are illustrative sentences:

(43)	a.	*yušābihu zaydun ^{c}amran*	'Zayd resembles 'Amr'
	b.	*^{c}ādala farīqukum farīqanā*	'Your team tied with our team'

Like the *kallafa* 'to cost' type verbs, these verbs are transitive according to the traditional definition of transitivity because they take a nominative subject and an accusative object

This class of verbs seems to violate Fillmore's one-instance-per-clause principle. In (43), for example, there is good reason to assign the two noun phrases accompanying the verb the same case role, because if Zayd resembles 'Amr (as in (43a)) then 'Amr resembles Zayd, and if your team tied with our team (as in (43b)) then our team must have tied with your team. Thus (43) can be thought of as being synonymous with (44) below, respectively:

(44)	a.	*yušābihu ^{c}amrun zaydan*	' 'Amr resembles Zayd'
	b.	*^{c}ādala farīqunā farīqakum*	'Our team tied with your team'

Fillmore (1971: 39) argued that the two noun phrases in sentences like (43)—and (44)—do not have the same case roles. The gist of his argument is that sentences like (43) involve a comparison between two entities and that the object rather than the subject is the standard of the comparison. The early Arab rhetoricians called the subject, in sentences like (43), *al-mušabbah* 'the compared' and the object *al-mušabbah bihi* 'the compared with;' they called the process *al-tašbīh* 'Comparison, Simile.' 'The compared with' is always "greater than" or "meaner than" 'the compared' depending on whether the quality involved in the comparison is a good quality or a bad quality, as in the following:

(45)	a.	*hindun ka al-qamari*	'Hind is like the moon'
	b.	*zaydun ka al-ḥimāri*	'Zayd is like a donkey'

To compare a woman to the moon in Arabic is to say that she is very beautiful, and to compare a person to a donkey is to say that he is an ignoramus. In (45) the moon is presupposed to be more beautiful than Hind and the donkey is presupposed to be more stupid than Zayd. If the noun phrases in (45) are interchanged, we get (46), respectively:

(46)	a.	*al-qamaru ka hindin*	'The moon is like Hind'
	b.	*al-ḥimāru ka zaydin*	'The donkey is like Zayd'

Sentences (45) and (46) are not synonymous. In the same manner sentences (43) and (45) are not synonymous. To further illustrate the point let us consider the following sentences:

(47)	a.	*yuḍāri^{c}u ?anwaru al-ṯu^{c}bāna xubṯan*	'Anwar resembles the snake in malice'
	b.	*māṯala ġassānu tši fī nukrāni al-ḏāti*	'Ghassan was like Che in self-denial'
	c.	*yušbihu zaydun jaddahu al-?akbara al-mašhūra*	'Zayd resembles his famous ancestor'

The subject and object cannot be interchanged in the sentences of (47) without changing the meanings of these sentences. In light of Fillmore's observations and the early Arab rhetorician's analysis, we note the following facts about sentences (47). In a the standard of comparison is *al-ṯu^{c}bān* 'the snake;' the property observable in *al-ṯu^{c}bān* is *al-xubṯ* 'malice;' this property is attributable to the subject of the sentence Anwar. In b the standard of comparison is Che; the property observable in Che (self-denial) is attributable to Ghassan. In c the property (or properties) observable in the object noun phrase is (or are) not explicitly mentioned; still the object rather than the subject is the standard of comparison. On the basis of the above arguments, the noun phrases that occur with *šābaha* 'to resemble' type verbs must not be assigned the same case role.

All the *šābaha* type verbs discussed above are stative verbs. There are active verbs in Arabic that indicate comparison. The property observable in the standard of comparison is incorporated in these verbs, as can be seen in the following sentences:

(48)	a.	*qāwā zaydun ^{c}amran*	'Zayd tried to be like 'Amr in strength'
	b.	*ṭāwala zaydun ^{c}amran*	'Zayd tried to be like 'Amr in height (i.e., stature)'

and in the following line from al-Mutanabbī (1964, 2:91):

(49) *?afī kulli yawmin taḥta ḍibnī šuway^{c}irun ḍa^{c}īfun yuqāwinī qaṣīrun yuṭāwilu*

'Why do I have to contend everyday with a worthless poet who is weak and strives to be as strong as I am and who is short and strives to be as tall as I am (i.e., to be of my stature)'

The underlined words in (49) are the verbs in question.

Other verbs like *qāwā* and *ṭāwala* are: *šārafa* 'to strive to surpass someone in rank,' *fāxara* 'to strive to surpass someone in glory,' and *šā^{c}ara* 'to strive to excel someone in composing poetry.'

It is important to state at this point that all of the verbs discussed in this section, except for *?ašbaha*, *ᶜādala*, *māṯala* and *sawiya*, are form III FāMaLa verbs. In Chapter II the feature reciprocal was touched upon. Reciprocity is the basic feature of form III FāMaLa verbs though some form III verbs such as *ᶜāqaba* 'to punish' and *sāfara* 'to travel' are not reciprocal. Sībawayhi (II: 253) writes "know that when you say *fāᶜaltuhu* there is an action coming towards you from someone (or something) else in as much as the same action is going from you towards someone (or something) else." Reciprocity is discernible in the following sentences:

(50)	a.	*šābaha zaydun ᶜamran*	'Zayd resembled 'Amr'
	b.	*šāᶜara zaydun ᶜamran*	'Zayd competed with 'Amr in composing poetry'
	c.	*sāyara zaydun ᶜamran*	'Zayd walked with 'Amr'
	d.	*qātala zaydun ᶜamran*	'Zayd fought against 'Amr'

In spite of the fact that reciprocity is an inherent feature in form III FāMaLa verbs, it is important to emphasize that the noun phrases that occur with these verbs need not be assigned the same deep structure case.

There is another group of verbs in Arabic whose basic feature is reciprocity, the form VI taFāMaLa verbs. The following sentences, with taFāMaLa verbs, correspond to sentences (50), respectively:

(51)	a.	*tašābaha zaydun wa ᶜamrun*	'Zayd and 'Amr resembled (each other)'
	b.	*tašāᶜara zaydun wa ᶜamrun*	'Zayd and 'Amr competed (with each other in composing poetry)'
	c.	*tasāyara zaydun wa ᶜamrun*	'Zayd and 'Amr walked (with each other)'
	d.	*taqātala zaydun wa ᶜamrun*	'Zayd and 'Amr fought (against each other)'

The verbs in both (50) and (51) have the feature reciprocal which belongs to the Q component in terms of the case system proposed in Chapter II. But whereas the verbs in (51) are one-place verbs, those in (50) are two-place verbs. Thus only one deep structure case occurs in the case frame of the verbs in (51). This deep structure case is Target in (51a) and it is the case role of the conjoined noun phrases *zaydun wa ᶜamrun* 'Zayd and 'Amr.' The case role of the conjoined noun phrases in the other sentences of (51) is Agent. This accounts for the nonpassivizability of the verbs in (51). The case frame of the verbs of the last three sentences in (50) is [_____ Agent Target]; as we shall see later this is a case frame of passivizable verbs. The difference between the *šābaha* 'to resemble' type verbs and other form III FāMaLa verbs like those in the last three sentences of (50) is that whereas the former are stative, the latter are active. Thus the case role of the subject in sentences like (43), (44), (45), (46), (47) and (50a) is Target. As for the object in these sentences, it is as we have argued earlier the standard of comparison, or "the compared with" if one wishes to use the terminology of the early Arab rhetoricians. This standard of comparison is the goal or destination in terms of which the Target (i.e., the subject of the sentences under discussion) is identified. Therefore, the case frame of the *šābaha* 'to resemble' type verbs is [_______ Target Goal] which is a case frame of nonpassivizable verbs. Verbs like *qāwā* 'to strive to be like someone' discussed above are no different from other form III active verbs in terms of their case frame.

In certain contexts some *šābaha* type verbs may be passivized:

(52) *tāyd lā yuḍāhā* 'Tide is unequalled'

The passive verb in (52) is not stative; it is rather causative. Sentence (52) can be paraphrased as follows: "No detergent can be made to equal Tide in its strength of washing clothes." Another meaning of the verb in (52) is 'to imitate' which is clearly not stative. Therefore (52) is not a counterexample.

The above analysis shows that verbs like *šābaha* 'to resemble' should be treated as reciprocal rather than equative verbs, which has been the practice in analyzing the English verb "resemble" in transformational grammars. Thus, the data from Arabic and an analysis within the framework of case grammar help us understand the syntactic and semantic nature of verbs like *šābaha* 'to resemble,' not only in Arabic, but in all languages.

3.4.2 Passivizable Verbs

These include the following:

3.4.2.1 Implemental Verbs. This term is borrowed from Ibn Ya'īsh, who divides transitive verbs into *al-fi^{c}l al-^{c}ilāj wa ġayr al-^{c}ilāj* 'Implemental and nonimplemental verb.' Ibn Ya'īsh (7: 62) writes"[2] . . . *wa al-muta^{c}addī yakūnu ^{c}ilājan wa ġayra ^{c}ilāj. fa al-^{c}ilāju mā yaftaqiru fī ?ījādihi ?ilā ?isti^{c}māli jāriḥatin ?aw naḥwihā, naḥwa: ḍarabtu zaydan wa qataltu ^{c}amran. wa ġayru al-^{c}ilāji mā lam yaftaqiru ?ilā ḏālika, naḥwa: ḏakartu zaydan wa fahimtu al-ḥadīṯ.*" 'and the transitive is *^{c}ilāj* and *non ^{c}ilāj*. The *^{c}ilāj* is that which needs, for it to exist, the utilization of a limb or the like. For example: I hit Zayd and I killed 'Amr. The *non^{c}ilāj* does not need that. For example: I mentioned Zayd and I understood the conversation.' The key phrase in this quotation is *jāriḥatin ?aw naḥwihā* 'a body part or the like.' What Ibn Ya'īsh is referring to is obligatorily possessed implements (inalienable implements) and optionally possessed implements (alienable implements). Implemental verbs are verbs that require an implement, which may be either alienable or inalienable depending on the individual verb. This implement is in the case frame of every implemental verb regardless of whether it shows in the surface structure or not. If the Agent is animate, then the implement has the Instrument case role in the deep structure; if the Agent is inanimate, then the implement has the Agent case role itself in the deep structure. In the case of inanimate Agents, such as semi-autonomous machines, which may require an instrument as in (53):

(53) *fataḥat al-?ālatu al-bāba bi miftāḥin xāṣṣin* 'The machine opened the door with a special key'

The implement has the Instrument role in the case frame of the verb. Impingement verbs like *ḍaraba* 'to hit' and *rafasa* 'to kick' fall under this category; however implemental verbs are not necessarily impingement verbs. For example the implemental verb *ġamaza* 'to wink at' is not an impingement verb. Thus there are three types of implemental verbs:

(i) verbs that require an implement which can be either alienable or inalienable. Examples are: *ḍaraba* 'to hit,' *qatala* 'to kill,' *kasara* 'to break,' *dafa^{c}a* 'to push,' [*qaḏafa, ramā*] 'to throw.'

(54) a. *ḍaraba zaydun hindan bi yadihi* 'Zayd hit Hind with his hand'

b. *ḍaraba zaydun hindan bi ^{c}aṣan* 'Zayd hit Hind with a stick'

(ii) Verbs that require an inalienable implement. The following are examples of such verbs with the implements they require, respectively:

(55)

^{c}aḍḍa; ?asnān	'to bite; teeth'
qabbala; fam, šafatāni	'to kiss; mouth, lips'
laḥasa; lisān	'to lick; tongue'
lāka; ?asnān	'to chew; teeth'
maṣṣa; šafatāni	'to suck; lips'
raḍa^{c}a; šafatāni	'to suck a breast (baby); lips'
rafasa; qadam	'to kick; foot'
qaraṣa; ?anāmil	'to pinch; fingers'
ṣafa^{c}a; kaff	'to slap; palm of the hand'
lakama; qabḍat al-kaff	'to box; fist'
fāha; fam	'to utter; mouth'

The following are illustrative sentences:

(56) a.	*^{c}aḍḍahā drakyula bi asanīn ġayri bašariyyatin*	'Dracula bit her with nonhuman teeth'
b.	*qabbalathu bi famin ^{c}a͟dbin*	'She kissed him with a sweet mouth'
c.	*?anā ?ulākimu bi qabḍati muḥammadin*	'I box with Muhammad's fist'

(iii) Verbs that require an alienable implement. These are verbs derived from nouns that denote the implement. In certain instances they denote the kind of instrument used, as in *qaṭa^{c}a* 'to cut' where the implement is some kind of a sharpedged instrument like a knife, *ṭa^{c}ana* 'to stab' where the implement is some kind of a pointed, tapered instrument like a dagger. In other instances they denote the exact instrument as in *ramaḥa* 'to spear,' *qaṣṣa* 'to cut with a pair of scissors,' *nabala* 'to shoot arrows.'

In spite of the fact that the verb denotes the implement, an Instrument role may occur in the surface structure of such verbs:

(57) a.	*qaṭa^{c}a al-ḥabla bi sikkīnin*	'He cut the rope with a knife'
b.	*ramaḥa zaydan bi rumḥin kalīlin*	'He speared Zayd with a dull spear'

It is important to note that Instruments of type (ii) implemental verbs do not surface unless they are further specified (modified by an adjective or specified by genitive for example). Sentences (56) above illustrate this surface structure constraint: *bi ?asnānin ġayri bašariyyatin* 'with nonhuman teeth,' *bi famin ^{c}a͟dbin* 'with a sweet mouth,' *bi qabḍati muḥammadin* 'with Muhammad's fist.' The same is true of those verbs of type (iii) which denote the exact implement. The Instrument in (57b) above illustrates this: *bi rumḥin kalīlin* 'with a dull spear.' The case frames of the verbs in the following sentences, which illustrate implemental verbs, are given in (59):

(58) a.	*?ulqiyat ^{c}alayhi raḥan <u>fa qatalathu</u>* (al-Ṭabarī, 3: 9)	'A millstone was thrown at him <u>and it killed him</u>'
b.	*hazzat al-rīḥu ?aġṣāna al-šajarati*	'The wind swayed the branches of the tree'

1c.	*ḍaraba zaydun ᶜamran bi ᶜaṣan*	'Zayd hit 'Amr with a stick'
2c.	*ḍaraba zaydun ᶜamran*	'Zayd hit 'Amr'
1d.	*qatalathu hindun bi xanjarin masmūmin*	'Hind killed him with a poisoned dagger'
2d.	*qatalathu hindun*	'Hind killed him'

(59) a. [________ Agent Patient] (This is the case frame of the underlined conjunct in (58a)

b. [________ Agent Target]

c. [________ Agent Target Instrument]

d. [________ Agent Patient Instrument]

In (58a and b) the implement is the Agent itself, in (58c and d) the Instrument occurs in the surface structure of (58 1c) and of (58 1d); it does not in (58 2c) and (58 2d). In conclusion: all implemental verbs require implements. Verbs whose Agents are not implements have Instruments in their case frames. Instruments which are not specified in the deep structure are not lexicalizable and hence never materialize in the surface structure. Finally, verbs which have case frames like those shown in (59) are passivizable.

3.4.2.2 Physical Perception Verbs. This group of verbs consists of five subgroups, one subgroup for each of the commonly accepted human sensory modalities: sight, hearing, taste, smell, and touch. Physical perception verbs are of three types:

(i) *Stative: samiᶜa* 'to be able to hear' and *baṣura* 'to be able to see.' The adjectives corresponding to these verbs have the pattern FaMīL (the pattern of adjectives corresponding to stative verbs): *samīᶜ* 'capable of hearing,' *baṣīr* 'endowed with eyesight.' There is no morphological evidence for a stative verb of taste, smell or touch in Arabic. Such verbs are homophonous with, and morphologically nondistinguishable from, nonstative verbs of taste, smell, and touch:

(60) a.	*jaddī lā yabṣuru*	'My grandfather doesn't see'
b.	*zaydun yasmaᶜu al-ʔāna*	'Zayd can hear now'

The case frame of stative physical perception verbs is [_____Target]; they are one-place verbs and therefore they are non-passivizable.

(ii) Inchoative: *samiᶜa* 'to hear,' [*raʔā, šāhada ʔabṣara*] ' to see,' *šamma* 'to smell.' The verbal derivative corresponding to these verbs is the active participle which has the pattern FāMiL: *sāmiᶜ* 'hearing or hearer,' *rāʔin* 'seeing or seer,' etc. These verbs are inchoative in the sense that their "subjects" are undergoers of the sensory experience. The sensory experience implied in these verbs is not implied in the verbs of (i) above. In other words "to be able to see or hear" does not imply actually seeing or hearing, for example. On the other hand, the undergoer is not an actor; a verb like *samiᶜa* 'to hear' or *šamma* 'to smell' does not necessarily imply any activity, purpose or responsibility. Consider the following sentences:

(61) a. *sami^{c}a zaydun ṣawtan ġarīban* 'Zayd heard a strange voice'
b. *?abṣara zaydun ^{c}amran* 'Zayd saw 'Amr'
c. *šamma zaydun rā?iḥatan ḏakiyyatan* 'Zayd smelled a sweet smell'

The noun phrase *zayd* is the undergoer of the sensory experience in (61). According to the case system proposed in Chapter II this noun phrase is here assigned the Patient role. As for the second noun phrase in (61), it represents the content of Zayd's experience and therefore it is assigned the Target role. The case frame of sentences (61) is [______ Patient Target]. Verbs that have such a case frame are passivizable.

(iii) Active: *naẓara* 'to look,' *rāqaba* 'to watch' [*?aḏina, ?istama^{c}a, tasamma^{c}a, ṣaġā, ?aṣġā*] 'listen,' *šamma* 'to smell,' [*ḏāqa, ṭa^{c}ima*] 'to taste,' [*lamasa, massa*] 'to touch.' These verbs denote activity which is accompanied by intention, purpose or responsibility.
The verb *naẓara* 'to look' denotes directed action. In a sentence like *naẓara ?ilayhā* 'he looked at her' the person looked at is the destination of the action identified by the verb, and the subject is the Agent. Thus the case frame of *naẓara* is [______Agent Goal]. The same is true of the 'listen' verbs: *?aḏina, ?istama^{c}a, tasamma^{c}a, ṣaġā, ?aṣġā*. Verbs that have such a case frame are nonpassivizable. The verb *rāqaba* 'watch,' though an active verb, does not denote directed action towards a destination, that is, it does not require a Goal. It denotes intensive action and the object, in a sentence like *rāqaba zaydun ^{c}amran* 'Zayd watched 'Amr,' is a Target not a Goal. The case frame of *rāqaba* is [_____ Agent Target] which is a case frame of passivizable verbs. The verbs *šamma* 'to smell,' *ḏāqa, ṭa^{c}ima* 'to taste' and [*lamasa, massa*] 'to touch' have the same case frame as *rāqaba*. The verbs of taste and touch cannot be inchoative in Arabic because they are surface-contact verbs, that is one has to perform an action when he tastes or touches something.
Another verb related to the touch verbs but different from them is *?aḥassa* 'to feel' as in *?aḥassa bi al-ḥarārati* 'he felt the heat.' The case frame of this verb is [_____Patient Target] and therefore it is passivizable.

3.4.2.3 Reciprocal Form III FāMaLa Verbs. These verbs were discussed in Section 3.4.1.4 and, except for the *šābaha* 'to resemble' type verbs, they were shown to be passivizable.

3.4.2.4 Resultative Verbs. These are verbs whose activity results in the creation of an entity which did not exist until that activity was completed. Examples are: *ṣana^{c}a* 'to make,' *banā* 'to build,' *xalaqa* 'to create,' *?assasa* 'to found.' Fillmore (1968: 4) proposes two distinct deep structure cases for the objects in sentences like the following:

(62) a. *hadamū al-madīnata* 'They destroyed the city'
b. *banaw al-madīnata* 'They built the city'

The object in (62a) is understood as existing antecedently to the activity indicated by the verb, while in (62b) the existence of the object resulted from the activity indicated by the verb. Fillmore considers the distinction between the two objects not only semantic but syntactic as well. Thus, according to him, one might relate sentence (62a), but not sentence (62b), to the question given in (63).

(63)	*māḏā fa^{c}alū bi al-madīnati?* (in one reading)	'What did they do to the city?

Although this line of argument makes perfect sense, it is a pragmatic accident that sentence (62b) is not relatable to the question given in (63). In the proper context sentences like (62b) may be related to questions like (63) as can be seen in (64):

(64)	1a.	*māḏā fa^{c}ala al-sūriyyūna bi madīnati al-qunayṭirah?*	'What did the Syrians do to the city of Quneitra?'
	2a.	*ʔa^{c}ādū bināʔahā*	'They rebuilt it'
	1b.	*al-ʔāna wa qad tamma faṣlu al-quwwāti bayna sūrya wa ʔisraʔīl, māḏā sayaf^{c}alu al-sūriyyūna bi madīnati al-qunayṭirah?*	'Now that the disengagement has taken place between Syria and Israel what would the Syrians do to the city of Quneitra?'
	2b.	*sawfa yabnūnahā ^{c}alā janāḥi al-sur^{c}ati*	'They will build it with winged haste (i.e., at a very fast pace)'
		(with the understanding that Quneitra was demolished as a result of two wars: June, 1967 and October, 1973)	
	1c.	*māḏā fa^{c}alta bi al-bināʔi allaḏī ṣammamtahu?*	'What did you do with the building you designed?'
	2c.	*banaytuhu*	'I built it'

It is suggested here that the objects in sentences (64) be assigned the same deep structure case. The Patient case was defined in Chapter II as the case of the object that necessarily undergoes a change of state; the change of state was identified as change from a state into another state, change from a state into no state, or change from no state into a state. The objects in (64) are to be assigned the Patient role. The implication of assigning this case to both objects is that not only verbs like *banā* 'to build' are resultative but also verbs like *hadama* 'to destroy.' A resultative verb, therefore, is not only a verb whose activity results in the creation of an entity which did not exist until that activity was completed, but also a verb whose activity results in the destruction of an entity which existed until that activity was completed. Resultative verbs like *hadama* 'to destroy' are: *ʔabṭala* 'to rescind,' *ḥalla* 'to dissolve (an organization for example),' *ʔazāla* 'to remove' and *ʔalġā* 'to cancel.'

The case frame of resultative verbs is [____ Agent Patient]. Verbs which have such a case frame are passivizable.

3.4.2.5 Emotive and Cognitive Verbs. These verbs indicate an emotional, psychological or mental experience. Emotive verbs are verbs like: *ʔaḥabba* 'to love,' *kariha* 'to hate,' *saxira min* 'to deride,' *ʔiḥtaqara* 'to scorn,' *ʔiḥtarama* 'to respect,' *hasada* 'to envy,' *ʔašfaqa ^{c}alā* 'to pity.' Cognitive verbs are verbs like *^{c}arafa* 'to know,' *jahila* 'to not know,' *fahima* 'to understand.' The following sentences illustrate this class of verbs:

(65)	a.	*kariha zaydun hindan*	'Zayd hated Hind'
	b.	*hasada xālidun ʔaxāhu*	'Khalid envied his brother'
	c.	*ʔašfaqa ^{c}alā al-waladi*	'He pitied the boy'
	d.	*^{c}araftu al-jawāba*	'I knew the answer'
	e.	*jahilū wājibātihim*	'They did not know their duty'

The subject in sentences (65) is Patient because it undergoes an experience. The underlined genitive in (65c) and the objects in the other sentences represent the content of the patient's experience. Thus the second noun phrase in sentences (65) is assigned the Target role. The case frame of these verbs is [______ Patient Target]. Verbs with such a case frame are passivizable.

It is important at this point to note that morphological distribution can play a role in determining the syntactic and semantic properties of the Arabic verb. In particular, the verbal derivatives are surface structure indicators of the nature of the verb. We have seen earlier that the verb *sami^{c}a* 'to hear' is ambiguous as to whether it corresponds to the stative adjective *samī^{c}* 'capable of hearing' or to the verbal derivative *sāmi^{c}* 'hearing or hearer.' If it corresponds to the former, it is stative and nonpassivizable; if it corresponds to the latter, it is inchoative and passivizable. To further illustrate the point let us consider the following pair of sentences whose verbs are *ḥazina* 'to be sad' and *ġaḍiba* 'to be angry,' respectively:

(66)	a.	*ḥazina zaydun ^{c}alā ?ibnihi*	'Zayd was sad at his son'
	b.	*ġaḍiba zaydun ^{c}alā ?ibnihi*	'Zayd was angry at his son'

Sentence <u>a</u> is nonpassivizable while <u>b</u> is passivizable as can be seen from (67) below:

(67)	a.	**ḥuzina ^{c}alā ?ibnihi*	'(Someone) got sad at his son'
	b.	*ġuḍiba ^{c}alā ?ibnihi*	'(Someone) got angry at his son'

The verb *ḥazina* 'to be sad' is a stative verb in contradistinction to the verb *ḥazana* 'to make someone sad' which is a causative passivizable verb; thus (67a) would be grammatical if it corresponded, not to (66a), but to a sentence like *ḥazanahu ^{c}amrun ^{c}alā ?ibnihi* ' 'Amr made him sad at his son,' for example. The verbal derivative of *ḥazina* is *ḥazīn* 'sad' which has the pattern <u>FaMīL</u>, an adjective pattern of stative verbs. Thus, *ḥazina* is unambiguously stative. The verb *ġaḍiba* 'to be angry' on the other hand has two verbal derivatives *ġaḍib* and *ġāḍib*. *ġaḍib* has the pattern <u>FaMiL</u> which is an adjective pattern of stative verbs and *ġāḍib* has the pattern <u>FāMiL</u> which is the active participle pattern of nonstative verbs (i.e., active and inchoative verbs). The verb *ġaḍiba* is clearly not active. Its verbal derivatives indicate its semantic nature. It is like *sami^{c}a* 'to hear' in the sense that it is ambiguous with respect to inchoation and stativity. On the basis of these facts the verb *ḥazina* may be translated by 'to be sad' while the verb *ġaḍiba* has to be translated by 'to be or become angry.' In terms of the semantic import of (66), (66a) means 'Zayd was sad because of his son' while (66b) is ambiguous between the two meanings 'Zayd was angry because of his son' or 'Zayd became angry at his son.' Sentences (66) may be paraphrased by (68) below (where stative, rather than inchoative, *ġaḍiba* is taken into consideration):

(68)	a.	*ḥazina zaydun bi sababi ?ibnihi*	'Zayd was sad because of his son'
	b.	*ġaḍiba zaydun bi sababi ?ibnihi*	'Zayd was angry because of his son'

The case frame of the verbs in (67) and (68) is [______ Patient Source] which is a case frame of nonpassivizable verbs. When *ġaḍiba* is inchoative, on the other hand, Zayd's son would be the <u>content</u> rather than the cause of Zayd's experience of anger. The case frame of inchoative *ġaḍiba* in (66b) would be [______ Patient Target] which is a case frame of passivizable verbs.

3.4.2.6 Verbs of Transforming. These are three place verbs; they can take a subject and two accusatives. The most common verbs of this class are *ṣayyara* 'to make (s.o or s.th) into (s.th.),' *?ixtāra* 'to choose (s.o.) as (s.th.),' *?intaxaba* 'to elect (s.o.) as (s.th.),' *ja*^{c}*ala* 'to make (s.o. or s.th.) into (s.th.),' ^{c}*ayyana* 'to appoint (s.o.) as (s.th.),' *da*^{c}*ā* 'to call (s.o. s.th.),' and *sammā* 'to name (s.o. s.th.)

Appointative, two-place form X ?istaFMaLa verbs, are another type of Verbs of Transforming. Examples of such verbs are: *?istawzara* 'to appoint (s.o.) as (cabinet) minister,' *?istaqḍā* 'to appoint (s.o.) as judge' and *?istaktaba* 'to appoint (s.o.) as writer (i.e., clerk).'

The following two sentences illustrate the above two types of Verbs of Transforming:

(69)	a.	*ṣayyara al-xabbāzu al-*^{c}*ajīna xubzan*	'The baker made the dough into bread'
	b.	*?istawzara al-rašīdu ja*^{c}*faran*	'Al-Rashid appointed Ja'far as (cabinet) minister'

The case frame of *ṣayyara* in (69a) is [_____ Agent Patient Goal]. It is important to note that only the Patient can become the subject of the passive verb:

(70)	a.	*ṣuyyira al-*^{c}*ajīnu xubzan*	'The dough was made into bread'
	b.	**ṣuyyira xubzun al-*^{c}*ajīna*	'Bread was made the dough into'

Therefore three place Verbs of Transforming can be passivized provided the Patient, but not the Goal, becomes the subject of the passive verb. In other words, the existence of the Goal in the case frame of verbs like *ṣayyara* is irrelevant to passivization. The relevant portion of such a case frame is [_____ Agent Patient – – – –]. Therefore verbs whose case frames contain [_____ Agent Patient – – – –] are passivizable.

In sentence (69b) the Goal is incorporated in the verb. Sentence (69b) can be paraphrased by (71):

(71)	a.	^{c}*ayyana al-rašīdu ja*^{c}*faran wazīran*	'al-Rashid appointed Ja'far as (cabinet) minister'

The case frame of (71) is the same as the case frame of (69a) namely [_____ Agent Patient Goal] which is the case frame of all three-place Verbs of Transforming.

3.4.2.7 Verbs of Acquiring. "Acquiring" is a translation of Ibn al-Ḥājib's and al-Astrābādhī's (1: 108–109) term *al-?ittixāḏ*. Examples of such verbs are: *?axaḏa* 'to take,' [*?ibtā*^{c}*a, ?ištarā*] 'to buy,' *tabannā* 'to take (s.o.) as a son for oneself,' *?iftaraša* 'to take or use (s.th.) as a mattress,' *?iftarasa* 'to prey, i.e., to take a prey for oneself.' *?imtaṭā* 'to make (s.th) as a riding means for oneself.' The following sentences illustrate this type of verbs:

(72)	a.	*?iftaraša al-*^{c}*ušba*	'He took (i.e. used) the grass as a mattress'
	b.	*tabannā ṭiflan*	'He adopted a child (as a son of his)'
	c.	*?ijtarra al-ba*^{c}*īru ṭa*^{c}*āmahu*	'The camel dragged back its food for itself, i.e., the camel ruminated its food'

It is important to note that most of the verbs of acquiring are form VIII ?iFtaMaLa verbs. These verbs indicate an action performed by the Agent in the interest of the Agent. Hence the early Arab grammarians called this semantic function for form VIII *al-?ittixāḏ* which literally means 'taking something, or using something for the benefit of oneself.' Therefore it would be appropriate to assign these verbs the feature Benefactive in the Q component.

The case frames of these verbs are [_____Agent Target] and [_____ Agent Patient], both of which are case frames of passivizable verbs.

3.4.2.8 Causative Verbs. These are verbs that denote causation; they have the feature causative in the Q component. They are usually form II FaMMaLa and form IV ?aFMaLa verbs. The following sentences illustrate this type:

(73) a. *?aḏāba zaydun al-sukkara* 'Zayd melted the sugar'
b. *?aḥzanahu mawtu ?ibnihi* 'His son's death saddened him'

The case frame of the verbs in (73) is [_____Agent Target] which is a case frame of passivizable verbs. Sentences (73) imply sentences (74).

(74) a. *ḏāba al-sukkaru* 'The sugar melted'
b. *māta ?ibnuhu* 'His son died'

The case frame of the verbs in (74) is [_____ Patient]; but consider the following pair of sentences:

(75) a. *sayyara zaydun ᶜamran* 'Zayd made 'Amr walk'
b. *sāra ᶜamrun* ''Amr walked'

The case frame of (75b) is [_____Agent], Zayd has the Agent case role in (75a). Therefore the case frame of the verb in (75a) would be [_____Agent Agent]. This case frame violates Fillmore's one-instance-per-clause principle. Verbs like *sayyara* in (75a) are passivizable. To avoid violating Fillmore's principle we have either to assign the second noun phrase in (75a) a case role different from Agent, or we have to analyze sentence (75a) as being clausally complex which would compel us not to analyze *sayyara* 'to make walk' as a single discontinuous verb. But *sayyara* is a single lexical item. This problem will be discussed in the next chapter. Suffice it to say here that verbs like *sayyara* as well as other causative verbs are passivizable.

3.4.2.9 Verbs of Certainty and Doubt (*?afᶜāl al-yaqīn wa al-šakk*). These are three-place verbs; they take a subject and two accusatives. The early Arab grammarians call them *?afᶜāl al-qulūb* 'verbs of the heart, i.e., which signify an act that takes place in the mind.' The most common verbs of Certainty are: *ra?ā* 'to see (i.e., to perceive),' *ᶜalima* 'to know,' *darā* 'to know,' *wajada* 'to find, i.e., to perceive.' The most common verbs of Doubt are: *ẓanna* 'to think, to believe,' *ḥasiba* 'to think, to reckon, to suppose,' *zaᶜama* 'to think, to deem,' *ᶜadda* 'to count (i.e., to reckon),' *?iᶜtabara* 'to consider.' The following two sentences illustrate the verbs of Certainty and Doubt, respectively:

(76) a. *ᶜalimtu ?axāka karīman* 'I knew your brother (to be) generous'
b. *ḥasibtu ?axāka karīman* 'I thought your brother (to be) generous'

The early Arab grammarians considered sentences like (76) clausally complex whereby the two accusatives "originate" from an equational or 'nominal' sentence. This view is adopted here. (76) contain (77) in them as an embedded sentence:

(77) *?axūka karīmun* 'Your brother is generous'

That (76) are clausally complex can be seen from the following sentences which are synonymous with (76):

(78) a. *ᶜalimtu ?anna ?axāka karīmun* 'I knew that your brother is generous'

b. *ḥasibtu ?anna ?axāka karīmun* 'I thought that your brother is generous'

The embedded sentences in (78) indicate the <u>content</u> of an experience; hence they are assigned the Target role. The case frame of sentences (78) is [—— Patient Target] which is a case frame of passivizable verbs. Sentences (79) are the passive sentences corresponding to (78):

(79) a. *ᶜulima ?anna ?axāka karīmun* 'It was known that your brother is generous'

b. *ḥusiba ?anna ?axāka karīmun* 'It was thought that your brother is generous'

Let us compare now (79) with (80) the passive sentences corresponding to (76):

(80) a. *ᶜulima ?axūka karīman* 'Your brother was known (to be) generous'

b. *ḥusiba ?axūka karīman* 'Your brother was known (to be) generous'

Whereas the entire *?anna* clause, *?anna ?axāka karīmun,* is the subject of the passive verb in (79), only the first accusative of (76) has become the subject of the passive verb (i.e., *?axūka*) in (80). To explain the difference between (79) and (80) we might consider the deep structure of (76a) and (78a) (ignoring the <u>b</u> sentences) to be, roughly and informally, (81):

(81)

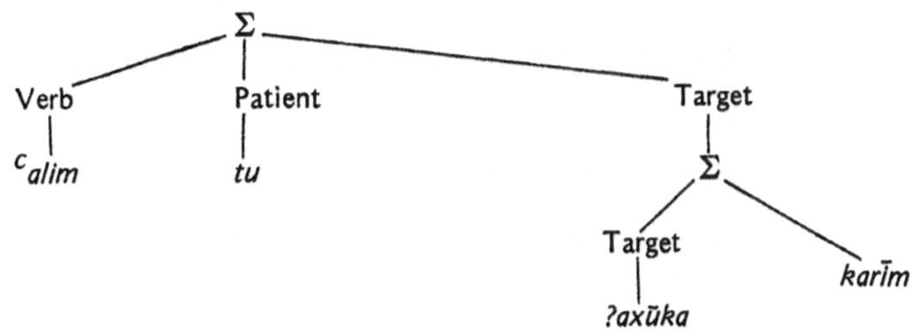

A complementizer insertion transformation would introduce a complementizer like *ʔanna* or *la* (i.e., *lām al-ʔibtidāʔ*: an emphasis particle like *ʔanna*) "in front of" the embedded sentence. When all the relevant transformations apply to (81) the surface structure (78a) or (82) would result:

(82) *ᶜalimtu la ʔaxūka karīmun* 'I knew that your brother (for sure) is generous'

The verb in (78a) and (82) has the case frame [____ Patient Target] and is passivizable as can be seen in (79a) and (83), respectively:

(83) *ᶜulima la ʔaxūka karīmun* 'It was known that your brother (for sure) is generous'

Another option would be to raise the Target of the lower sentence into the matrix sentence. This will destroy the targethood of the embedded sentence. The resulting case frame of the verb will be [____ Patient Target], a case frame of passivizable verbs. After all relevant transformations apply, sentence (76a) would result. This result necessitates that 'raising' be applied before 'complementizer placement.' If 'raising' is applied after 'complementizer placement,' we get the following sentences after all other relevant transformations have applied:

(84) a. *ᶜalimtu ʔaxāka ʔanna<u>hu</u> karīmun*
b. *ᶜalimtu ʔaxāka la<u>hwa</u> karīmun*

The underlined pronouns, <u>*hu*</u> 'him, his' and <u>*huwa*</u> 'he,' are a result of a compensatory pronominalization shallow rule which provides a pronoun, equivalent to the raised noun, to be attached to *ʔanna* and *la*. Pronominalization in (84) should not be conceived of as a result of a 'copying' transformation, first because 'copying' does not imply 'raising,' and second, because <u>*ʔanna*</u> and <u>*la*</u> independently of the question at hand cannot be immediately followed by a verb or predicate. Even when there is no referent, a pronoun is created to separate <u>*ʔanna*</u> or <u>*la*</u> from the predicate as shown in the following sentences:

(85) *ʔinnahu yajrī al-ʔāna ʔiḥtifālun ᶜaẓīmun* 'A great celebration is going on now'

Evidence against the 'raising' analysis proposed here can be found in Arabic; but discussing that evidence and an attempt to justify or disprove 'raising' is beyond the scope of this book. We simply assume that the above 'raising' analysis is correct.

3.4.2.10 <u>Miscellanea</u>. Other types of passivizable verbs, with illustrative examples, are:

(i) <u>Locative verbs</u>: *waḍaᶜa* 'to put,' *zaraᶜa* 'to plant.'

(86) *waḍaᶜa al-kitāba ᶜalā al-ṭāwilati* 'He put the book on the table'

The case frame of these verbs is [____ Agent Target . . .].

(ii) Expose verbs: *?aqtala* 'to expose someone to being killed,' *?abā^{c}a* 'to expose something for sale'

(87) *?aba^{c}tu al-farasa* 'I exposed the mare for sale'

The case frame of these verbs is [_____Agent Target].

(iii) Declare verbs: *ṣaddaqa* 'to declare someone as telling the truth, i.e., to believe (s.o.),' *kaḏḏaba* 'to declare (s.o.) as a liar,' *fassaqa* 'to declare (s.o.) as godless or sinful,' *kaffara* 'to declare (s.o.) as infidel or irreligious

(88) a. *ṣaddaqahu* 'He believed him'
b. *kaḏḏabahu* 'He accused him of being a liar'

The case frame of these verbs is [_____ Agent Target].

(iv) Remove verbs: *salaxa, jallada* 'to remove the skin, to skin,' *qarrada* 'to remove the ticks (off an animal),' *^{c}arrā* 'to remove (someone's clothes), undress,' *kašafa* 'to remove the the cover, uncover.'

(89) a. *salaxa al-xarūfa* 'He skinned the lamb'
b. *^{c}arrat zaydan* 'She undressed Zayd'

It is difficult to tell with verbs like "*^{c}arrā*" 'to undress' and "*kašafa*" 'to uncover' how much of a change of state the object acted upon by the Agent undergoes. The case role of *zaydan* in (89b) is a borderline between Patient and Target. Nevertheless, since in most Remove verbs the object is Patient, the case role assigned to this type of verb is [_____Agent Patient].

(v) Surpass verbs: *sabaqa* 'to surpass in running, outdistance,' *šarafa* 'to surpass in rank,' *faxara* 'to surpass in glory,' *baḏḏa* 'to get the better of.'

(90) *sabaqa zaydun ^{c}amran* 'Zayd outran 'Amr'

The case frame of these verbs is [_____ Agent Target].

3.4.3 Problems and Solutions

Passivizable verbs have been shown to have the case frames [_____ Agent Target], [_____ Agent Patient], and [____ Patient Target], which might give the impression that the subject of a passive verb can only be either Patient or Target. There are counter examples, however, to such a claim: verbs which have case frames, different from the above three are passivizable, and case roles different from Patient or Target become subject of the passive verb. In what follows these counter examples will be discussed and solutions proposed.

3.4.3.1 Range as Subject of the Passive Verb. One of the case roles that seems to be eligible to become subject of the passive verb is Range. Consider the following sentences:

(91) a. *sāra zaydun sayran šadīdan* 'Zayd marched intense marching'
b. *jalasa zaydun julūsa al-?umarā?i* 'Zayd sat down the sitting of princes'
c. *ġannat fayrūz ?uġniyatan jadīdatan* 'Fairuz sang a new song'
d. *raqaṣat hindun raqṣatayni* 'Hind danced two dances'

The verbs in these sentences have the case frame [____ Agent Range]. These sentences, however, are passivizable and sentences (92) below are the passive constructions corresponding to them:

(92) a. *sīra sayrun šadīdun* 'Intense marching was marched'
b. *julisa julūsu al-?umarā?i* 'The sitting of princes was sat down'
c. *ġunniyat ?uġniyatun jadīdatun* 'A new song was sung'
d. *ruqiṣat raqṣatāni* 'Two dances were danced'

It is important at this point to identify an essential difference between the Ranges in the a and b sentences and the Ranges in the c and d sentences of (91) and (92) above. In the a and b sentences the Range is a noncount, generic, cognate noun and is no more than a nominal prolongation of the verb; in the c and d sentences the Range is a count noun (i.e., noun of unity) and is not simply a nominal prolongation of the verb. Noun phrases like *sayr* 'walking' and *julūs* 'sitting down' are not entities that exist independently of the verb; they are verbal nouns and in this sense they represent the activity indicated by the verb. Noun phrases like *?uġniyah* 'song' and *raqṣah* 'dance,' on the other hand, are entities that can exist independently of the verb though they are not concrete entities.

Sentences like (92 a and b) are appropriate passives in CA but not in MSA; sentences like (90 c and d) are appropriate passives in both varieties of Arabic. Thus generic noncount Ranges may become subjects of the passive verb in CA but not in MSA. This is an instance of historical change in the syntax of Arabic from CA to MSA.

There is a restriction in CA on the passivizability of verbs whose case frame is [____ Agent Range], where the Range is a noncount generic nominal prolongation of the verb: if the Range is an absolute indefinite (i.e., an unmodified cognate), then the verb may not be passivized. In (91 a and b) the Range, though generic, is modified by an adjective and a genitive noun phrase, respectively, and is therefore not an absolute indefinite; hence the verbs in them may be passivized. The verb in sentence (93a) below, however, where Range is an absolute indefinite, is nonpassivizable as shown in (93b):

(93) a. *sāra zaydun sayran* 'Zayd marched marching'
b. **sīra sayrun* 'Marching was marched'

Ibn Yaʿīsh (7: 73) offers an explanation for the passivizability of sentences like (91 a and b) and the nonpassivizability of sentences like (93a) in CA. He writes "Verbal nouns (i.e., cognate accusatives) in sentences like (91 a and b) are of two types: a type whose function is only to emphasize the verb without adding anything to its meaning (as in (93a)) and a type which adds something to the meaning of the verb (as in (91 a and b)). The first type cannot be made AFFECTED OBJECT by EXTENDING THE MEANING OF THE EXPRESSION and may not be made SUBJECT OF THE PASSIVE."[3] According to Ibn Yaʿīsh only *al-mafʿūl (bihi)* 'Affected object' is eligible to become subject of the passive verb. The noncount generic Range becomes eligible for this function only when its meaning is extended so as to become an "Affected object." Ibn Ya'īsh's proposal is equivalent to a claim that the Range is made a Target by a transformation. This change from one semantic function to another is within the realm of the metaphorical usage in language. Such a transformation is definitely not meaning preserving, but then any transformation, or process, by which a literal meaning is changed into a figurative meaning would not preserve meaning. Thus such passives are metaphors rather than genuine passive constructions. Nevertheless, a syntactic process, namely passivization, is involved in creating such metaphorical passive constructions and it would not be appropriate to exclude them from the grammar of CA. An analysis of the syntax of metaphors is of course not possible within the limitations of this work; however, we assume that CA has a transformational rule, call it Targetization, that changes the Range case role, when the Range is generic, into the Target case role:

(94) [____ Agent Range$_{generic}$] ⟹ [____ Agent Target]

Rule (94), which is part of the grammar of CA but not MSA, feeds the passivization process.

When the Range is not a generic noncount nominal prolongation of the verb, the case frame [____ Agent Range] is assumed to be a case frame of passivizable verbs.

3.4.3.2 Time and Place as Subjects of the Passive Verb. Two other case roles that may be subjects of the passive verb in CA are Time and Place. The following are illustrative sentences:

(95)	a.	*ṣāma zaydun ramaḍāna*	'Zayd fasted Ramadan'
	b.	*jalasa zaydun ʔamāma al-ʔamīri*	'Zayd sat in front of the prince'
	c.	*sāra zaydun mīlayni*	'Zayd marched two miles'
	d.	*sāra zaydun sāᶜatayni*	'Zayd marched two hours'

The accusative noun phrases in c and d are accusatives of distance and duration, respectively, and were assigned the case roles Place and Time, respectively, in Chapter II. Thus the case frame of the verbs in a and d is [____ Agent Time] and that of the verbs in b and c is [____ Agent Place]. Why such verbs passivize, as shown in (96) below, can be explained by assuming that a targetization rule similar to (94) above applies:

(96)	a.	*ṣīma ramaḍānu*	'Ramadan was fasted'
	b.	*julisa ʔamāmu al-ʔamīri*	'It was sat in front of the prince'
	c.	*sīra mīlāni*	'Two miles were marched'
	d.	*sīrat sāᶜatāni*	'Two hours were marched'

It is of course possible to assign the accusatives of distance and duration the Range rather than the Place and Time case roles on the basis that they represent a nominal spatial and temporal prolongation of the verb; such an assignment would not necessitate any change in the analysis proposed here.

3.4.3.3 Subjectivization. Three other counter examples will be discussed in this section. It will be necessary first, however, to digress in order to discuss an important concept. One might get the impression from the discussion of passivization up till this point that the formation of the subject of the passive verb is an essential part of the process of passivization. In point of fact it is no different from the formation of the subject of the active verb, which in Arabic is in accordance with the following hypothesis:

(97) The closest noun phrase to the verb becomes subject provided the noun phrase and the verb are not separated by a preposition.

The underlined noun phrases in the following sentences are subjects:

(98)	a.	*rajaᶜa zaydun min bayrūt*	'Zayd came back from Beirut'
	b.	*qatalū ᶜamran*	'They killed 'Amr'
	c.	*bīᶜat al-farasu*	'The mare was sold'

In accordance with (97) formation of the passive subject is a surface phenomenon, the result of a shallow subjectivization transformation which is a syntactic rule that assigns the nominative case ending to the subject of a verb regardless of whether that verb is in the active or passive form. Roughly this rule would derive, for example, a sentence like *ḏahaba zaydun* 'Zayd went (away)' from a structure like *ḏahaba zayd* by adding the *-un* nominative case ending to *zayd*. It follows that what determines whether a verb is passivisable or not is its case frame and not the formation of the passive subject. Now to return to the three counter examples:

(i) Consider the following sentences:

(99)	a.	*?istaġfara zaydun ?allāha*	'Zayd asked for forgiveness from God'
	b.	*?istarḥama zaydun al-?amīra*	'Zayd asked for mercy from the prince'

The verbs in (99) seem to have the case frame [_____ Agent Source] which was shown to be a case frame of nonpassivizable verbs. Verbs which are form X ?istaFMaLa verbs and may semantically be labelled as Requestitive are passivizable as can be seen from (100) below:

(100)	a.	*?ustuġfira ?allāhu*	'God was asked for forgiveness'
	b.	*?usturḥima al-?amīru*	'The prince was asked for mercy'

Sentences (99), however, are synonymous with sentences (101):

(101)	a.	*ṭalaba zaydun al-maġfirata min ?allāhi*	'Zayd asked for forgiveness from God'
	b.	*ṭalaba zaydun al-raḥmata min al-?amīri*	'Zayd asked for mercy from the prince'

The case frame of sentences (101), [_____ Agent Target Source], is that of passivizable verbs and is the real case frame of sentences (99) rather than [_____ Agent Source]. The verbs in (99) have the syntactic feature Requestitive which belongs to the Q component. A requestitive verb is obtained by incorporating the feature Requestitive from the Q component and the Target from the P component into the underlying form of the verb:

(102)

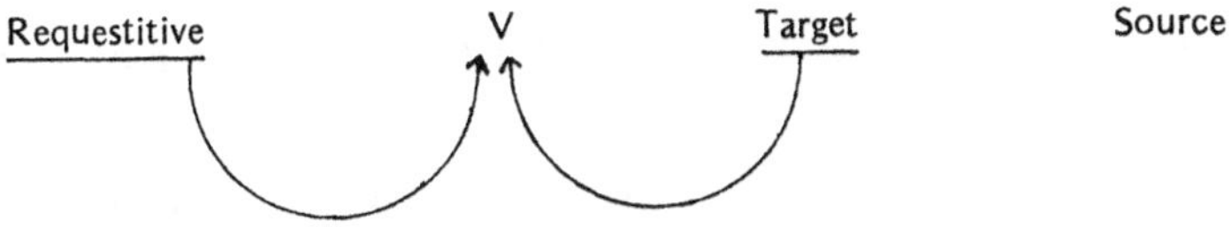

No preposition is introduced transformationally in the derivation of sentences (99) (though (99) and (101) are synonymous, they have two different surface structures) and the existence of *min* 'from' in (101) does not entail its introduction transformationally at any point in the derivation of (99). In the absence of the Target and the Agent from the P component, the Source becomes the closest noun phrase to the verb and is thus assigned the nominative case ending by subjectivization. That is how the Source comes to be the surface subject in (100):

(ii) Let us consider now the following sentence:

(103) *?intaxaba al-ša^{c}bu ra?īsan* 'The people elected a president'

The case frame of this sentence, [______Agent Goal], belongs to non-passivizable verbs. The sentence, however, is passivizable as can be seen in (104):

(104) *?untuxiba ra?īsun* 'A president was elected'

It is important to note that semantically and pragmatically a sentence like (105a) below, a corresponding passive of which is (105b), underlies (103):

(105) a. *?intaxaba al-ša^{c}bu zaydan ra?īsan* 'The people elected Zayd president'
b. *?untuxiba zaydun ra?īsan* 'Zayd was elected president'

In (105b) the Agent is unspecified and the Patient becomes subject. In (104) the Patient, as well as the Agent, is unspecified, and the Goal thus becomes subject of the verb.

(iii) Finally let us consider the following sentences:

(106) a. *nāma zaydun fī al-dāri* 'Zayd slept in the house'
b. *ḏahabtu ?ilā al-qudsi* 'I went to Jerusalem'
c. *jā?a zaydun bi hindin* 'Zayd brought Hind'
d. *?istanjada zaydun bi ^{c}amrin* 'Zayd asked for help from 'Amr'

The case frames of the verbs in (106) are (107), respectively (it should be remembered that the verb in (106d) is requestitive):

(107) a. [______Agent Place]
b. [______Agent Goal]
c. [______Agent Target]
d. [______Agent Target Source]

Sentences (106 a and b) are passivizable (in CA but not in MSA), as a result of the Targetization transformation discussed earlier. The case frames (107 c and d) were shown to be the case frames of passivizable verbs. The following are the passive sentences corresponding to (106):

(108) a. *nīma fī al-dāri* — 'It was slept in the house'
b. *duhiba ?ilā al-qudsi* — 'It was gone to Jerusalem'
c. *jī?a bi hindin* — 'Hind was brought'
d. *?ustunjida bi ᶜamrin* — ' 'Amr was asked for help'

The verb in all of these sentences is in 3.m.s. It was stated earlier that subjectivization is a shallow rule. The transformation (or transformations) that introduce (s) prepositions in sentences is (are) earlier than subjectivization and trigger(s) the genitivization of the noun phrase that follows the preposition. Thus the object of a preposition is not eligible for subjectivization. In this situation the verb is assigned an impersonal subject whereby it is in 3.m.s.

NOTES

1. Sentence (11b) would be grammatical if the cognate object *ḥaki* is heavily stressed.
2. The following is the Arabic quotation from Ibn Ya'īsh (7:62):

" والمتعدّي يكون علاجا وغير علاج . فالعلاج ما يفتقر في إيجاده إلىٰ استعمال
جارحة أو نحوها ، نحو : ضربتُ زيداً وقتلتُ عمراً . وغير العلاج ما لم يفتقر
إلىٰ ذلك ، نحو : ذكرتُ زيداً وفهمتُ الحديث . "

3. The following is the Arabic quotation from Ibn Ya'īsh (7:73):

" فالمصادر تجيء على ضربين : منها ما يُراد به تأكيد الفعل من غير زيادة
فائدة ، ومنها ما يراد به إبانة فائدة . فما أُريد به تأكيد الفعل فقط لم
تجعلْه مفعولا على سَعَةِ الكلام ، ولا يُقام مقام الفاعل ، وما كان
فيه فائدة جاز أن تجعلَه مفعولا علىٰ السَعَة ، وأن تُقيمه مقام الفاعل. "

4 Causative verbs

4.1 Introduction

Arabic, like many other languages, has more than one means for expressing causation. One can immediately distinguish several classes of Arabic causative constructions on syntactic and semantic grounds. For example, Arabic has constructions which express in one clause the cause for an action which is described in another clause:

(1)	a.	*ṭaradūhu li ?ihmālihi*	'They fired him because of his negligence
	b.	*?ujillat al-riḥlatu li ?anna al-ṭaqsa kāna mumṭiran*	'The picnic was postponed because the weather was rainy'
	c.	*kāna zaydun al-sababa fī wuqū^{c}i al-muškilati*	'Zayd was the cause of the occurrence of the problem'
	d.	*?anta mas?ūlun ^{c}an mawtihā*	'You are responsible for her death'

The surface indicator of causation is a preposition in a and b, a noun in c, and an adjective in d. Causative constructions like (1) will not be dealt with here.

Another type of causative constructions is one in which a sentence is embedded as the complement of a verb of causation whose subject is the Agent of the causation:

(2) *ja^{c}ala zaydun hindan tarquṣu* — 'Zayd made Hind dance'

Such periphrastic or explicit causatives will be referred to as overt causatives.

A construction which is syntactically distinct from overt causatives but which is semantically relatable to them is illustrated by the following sentences which are, at least on the surface, simplex sentences:

(3)	a.	*ajlasa zaydun hindan*	'Zayd made Hind sit down'
	b.	*?aṭāra al-waladu al-^{c}uṣfūra*	'The boy flew the bird'

Causative verbs like those in (3) will be referred to as covert causatives. This chapter will deal with the syntax and semantics of overt and covert causatives.

4.2 Covert Causatives

4.2.1 Derivation of Covert Causatives

4.2.1.1. Morphologically Derived Causatives. There are three classes of covert causative verbs derived from the basic triliteral form I verb:

(i) Form I Causatives Derived by Internal Vowel Modification (FaMaLa)

These are derived from FaMaLa, FaMiLa or FaMuLa pattern verbs in accordance with the following morphological rule:

(4)

$$\left\{ \begin{array}{c} \text{FaMiLa} \\ \text{FaMuLa} \\ \text{FaMaLa} \end{array} \right\} \longrightarrow \text{FaMaLa}$$

The following pairs of verbs illustrate this class:

(5)

	1a.	*ḥazina*	'to be sad'
	b.	*ḥazana*	'to make (someone) sad'
	2a.	*xafiya*	'to be hidden'
	b.	*xafā*	'to hide'
	3a.	*xabula*	'to be insane'
	b.	*xabala*	'to make insane'
	4a.	*šanu^{c}a*	'to be ugly, disgraceful'
	b.	*šana^{c}a*	'to disgrace'
	5a.	*^{c}adala*	'to be equal'
	b.	*^{c}adala*	'to make equal'
	6a.	*fatana*	'to be charmed'
	b.	*fatana*	'to charm'

Out of ninety or so verbs of this class that we have researched only one FaMuLa→FaMiLa alternation has been found:

(6)

	a.	*karuha*	'to be hateful'
	b.	*kariha*	'to hate'

It can therefore be safely assumed that rule (4) is correct and that the pattern of these covert causative verbs is FaMaLa.

(ii) Form II Causatives (FaMMaLa)

These are morpholigically derived from basic form I verbs in accordance with the following rule:

(7)

$$\text{FaM} \left\{ \begin{array}{c} \text{i} \\ \text{u} \\ \text{a} \end{array} \right\} \text{La} \longrightarrow \text{FaMMaLa}$$

The following pairs of verbs illustrate this class:

(8)	1a.	*qaṣura*	'to be short'
	b.	*qaṣṣara*	'to shorten'
	2a.	*fariḥa*	'to be glad'
	b.	*farraḥa*	'to make glad'
	3a.	*jamada*	'to freeze$_{itr}$'
	b.	*jammada*	'to freeze $_{tr}$'

Form II verbs may also be denominative, i.e., derived from the roots of nouns in accordance with the rule FML → FaMMaLa. The following illustrate the point:

(9)	1a.	*sababun*	'Cause'
	b.	*sabbaba*	'to cause'
	2a.	*lawnun*	'color'
	b.	*lawwana*	'to color'
	3a.	*ruxāmun*	'Marble'
	b.	*raxxama*	'to pave with marble'

Such verbs, as (9), express the making or doing of, or being occupied with, the thing expressed by the noun from which they are derived, and are resultative rather than causative.

(iii) Form IV Causatives (?aFMaLa)

These are morphologically derived from form I basic verbs in accordance with the following rule:

(10)

$$\text{FaM}\begin{Bmatrix}\text{i}\\ \text{u}\\ \text{a}\end{Bmatrix}\text{La} \rightarrow \text{?aFMaLa}$$

The following pairs of verbs illustrate this class:

(11)	1a.	*samiᶜa*	'to hear'
	b.	*?asmaᶜa*	'to make (someone) hear'
	2a.	*karuma*	'to be noble hearted'
	b.	*?akrama*	'to honor'
	3a.	*baṭala*	'to be void'
	b.	*?abṭala*	'to nullify'

4.2.1.2 Prepositionally Derived Causatives. These causatives are not morphologically derived; that is, the form I simple verb from which these causative verbs are derived does not undergo any change. They are simple formed by the addition of the preposition *bi* to the verb. The following pairs of verbs illustrate this class:

(12)	1a.	*jā?a*	'to come'
	b.	*jā?a bi*	'to bring'
	2a.	*ḏahaba*	'to go'
	b.	*ḏahaba bi*	'to take (someone somewhere)'

4.2.2 Causativization

In this section the syntactic and semantic properties of causativizable and noncausativizable verbs will be explored. The former are verbs that may be made causative morphologically and/or prepositionally; the latter are verbs that may not be made causative, either morphologically or prespositionally.

The syntactic effect of causativization is that it increases by one the number of objects which the causativized verb can take. Generally,[1] all intransitive verbs are causativizable. Thus, whereas a simple intransitive takes no object, a causativized intransitive verb takes one object directly or by means of a preposition.

(13)	1a.	*ḍaḥika ^{c}amrun*	' 'Amr laughed'
	b.	*?aḍḥaka zaydun ^{c}amran*	'Zayd made 'Amr laugh'
	2a.	*jā?a ^{c}amrun*	' 'Amr came'
	b.	*jā?a zaydun bi ^{c}amrin*	'Zayd brought 'Amr'

The subject of the intransitive verb in 1a becomes the direct object of the causative verb in 1b, and the subject of the intransitive verb in 2a becomes the object of the preposition bi in 2b. The direct object is in the accusative case in 1b; the object of the preposition bi is in the genitive case in 2b.

Simple intransitive causativizable verbs may be semantically divided into three groups: stative, inchoative and active. The following sentences illustrate these three groups, respectively:

(14)	a.	*ṣa^{c}uba ḥallu al-muškilati*	'Solving the problem was difficult'
	b.	*ḏāba al-ṯalju*	'The snow melted'
	c.	*ḏahaba zaydun*	'Zayd went (away)'

It is important to note that the great majority of Arabic stative verbs can be paraphrased inchoatively as well as statively; that is, such verbs can be paraphrased by the verb *kāna* 'to be' plus an adjective or by the verb *ṣāra* 'to become' plus an adjective. The following sentences illustrate the point:

(15)	1a.	*sahula al-darsu*	'The lesson was (or became) easy'
	b.	*kāna al-darsu sahlan*	'The lesson was easy'
	c.	*ṣāra al-darsu sahlan*	'The lesson became easy'
	2a.	*mariḍa zaydun*	'Zayd was (or became) sick'
	b.	*kāna zaydun marīḍan*	'Zayd was sick'
	c.	*ṣāra zaydun marīḍan*	'Zayd became sick'

Therefore, semantically, it would be appropriate to divide simple intransitive causativizable verbs into two groups, active and nonactive, where nonactive verbs can be stative and/or inchoative verbs.

Not all intransitive verbs are basic form I intransitives. Many are derived intransitive, or detransitivized, verbs, where the basic verb is the transitive rather than the intransitive. This can be seen in the sentences below:

(16)	1a.	*kasara zaydun al-ka?sa*	'Zayd broke the glass'
	b.	*?inkasara al-ka?su*	'The glass broke'
	2a.	*fataḥa zaydun al-bāba*	'Zayd opened the door'
	b.	*?infataḥa al-bābu*	'The door opened'

The verbs in a are form I FaMaLa transitive verbs; the verbs in b are form VII ?inFaMaLa detransitivized verbs. All detransitivized verbs are noncausativizable.

A transitive verb takes one object in the accusative case. When a causative affix is added to a transitive verb, the derived causative verb takes two objects in the accusative case. For example:

(17)	a.	*sami^{c}a zaydun ṣawtan*	'Zayd heard a voice'
	b.	*?asma^{c}at hindun zaydan ṣawtan*	'Hind made Zayd hear a voice'

The subject of the transitive verb in a is in the nominative case, the object in the accusative case; the subject of the derived causative verb in b is in the nominative case; the two objects both are in the accusative case.

Unlike basic form I intransitives, most basic form I transitive verbs are noncausativizable. A few, however, are:

(i) Physical Perception Inchoative Verbs

(18)	1a.	*sami^{c}a ^{c}amrun ?uġniyatan*	' 'Amr heard a song'
	b.	*?asma^{c}a zaydun ^{c}amran ?uġniyatan*	'Zayd made 'Amr hear a song'
	2a.	*ra?ā ^{c}amrun al-ṣūrata*	' 'Amr saw the picture'
	b.	*?arā zaydun ^{c}amran al-ṣūrata*	'Zayd showed 'Amr the picture'

(ii) Cognitive Inchoative Verbs

(19)	1a.	*fahima ^{c}amrun al-darsa*	' 'Amr understood the lesson'
	b.	*?afhama zaydun ^{c}amran al-darsa*	'Zayd made 'Amr understand the lesson'
	2a.	*^{c}alimtu ?anna hindan raja^{c}at ?ilā bayrūta*	'I knew that Hind went back to Beirut'
	b.	*?a^{c}lamanī zaydun ?anna hindan raja^{c}at ?ilā bayrūta*	'Zayd informed me that Hind went back to Beirut'

(iii) Cognitive Active Verbs

This class includes the verbs *darasa* 'to study,' *qara?a* 'to read,' and *kataba* 'to write.'

(20)	1a.	*darasa ?axī al-tārīxa*	'My brother studied history'
	b.	*darrastu ?axī al-tārīxa*	'I taught my brother history'
	2a.	*qara?a al-qur?āna*	'He read the Koran'
	b.	*?aqra?tuhu al-qur?āna*	'I made him read the Koran'

(iv) The verbs *?akala* 'to eat' and *šariba* 'to drink'

(21) 1a.	*šariba al-ṭiflu al-dawā?a*	'The child drank the medicine'
b.	*šarrabat al-ṭifla al-dawā?a*	'She made the child drink the medicine'
2a.	*?akala al-tuffāḥata*	'He ate the apple'
b.	*?akkalathu al-tuffāḥata*	'She fed him the apple'

In spite of the fact that the above transitive causativizable verbs have been divided into four distinct classes, they have one thing in common on the deep structure level and that is that their case frame is [——— K Range] (where K is Patient in (i) and (ii) and Agent in (iii) and (iv)). The transitivity relationship that holds between the verb and the accusative object, i.e., the Range in the above a sentences, is a weak one, and is a relationship of prolongation rather than extension. The Range is not affected by the action or experience identified by the verb; even when it is a concrete entity, it is no more than a nominal prolongation of the verb. This suggests an explanation for the causativizability of the above transitive verbs. These verbs are reminiscent of pseudo-transitive verbs like *daxala* 'to enter,' *rakiba* 'to ride' and *waṣala* 'to arrive.' The following sentences illustrate the shallow structure transitivity of such pseudo-transitives:

(22) a.	*daxala zaydun al-dāra*	'Zayd entered the house'
b.	*rakiba zaydun al-ḥiṣāna*	'Zayd rode the horse'
c.	*waṣala zaydun dimašqa*	'Zayd arrived (in) Damascus'

On the surface the verbs in (22) are transitive because they take a direct object in the accusatives case. Morphologically, however, they are intransitive because their verbal nouns have the pattern FuMūL. The transitivity of these verbs is a result of a very late rule that deletes the preposition preceding the second-place nominal. In the deep structure the verb in sentences a and c has the case frame [——— Agent Goal] and in b the case frame [——— Agent Place]. Neither the Goal noun phrase nor the Place noun phrase are affected by the action identified by the verb. All three verbs of (22) are causativizable. The verbs in (i), (ii), (iii) and (iv) like the verbs in (22) may be considered at least at some level as not genuine transitive verbs, which explains their causativizability.

Another transitive causativizable verb is:

(v) *ḥamala* 'to carry'

(23) a.	*ḥamala al-rajulu al-ṣundūqa*	'The man carried the box'
b.	*ḥammala zaydun al-rajula al-ṣundūqa*	'Zayd loaded the man with the box'

i.e., Zayd made it possible for the man to carry the box.

The case frame of *ḥamala* is [——— Agent Target]; morphologically its verbal noun has the pattern FaML, a pattern of genuine transitive verbs, and semantically the accusative object in (23a) is affected by the action identified by the verb. Thus nothing predicts the causativizability of this verb. It is important to note, nevertheless, that the meaning of the infix in the form II verb in (23b) is 'help,' 'make possible' or 'enable' rather than 'cause' or 'make'; in other words, (23b) may not be interpreted to mean 'Zayd caused the man to carry the box.' Therefore the verb *ḥammala* is not a genuine causative verb. This is not surprising because causativization is not the only function of the form II FaMMaLa pattern.

Three other verbs are of interest here:

(vi) *zāra* 'to visit'

This verb is causativizable in CA but not in MSA. The form IV verb *?azāra* derived from this verb is found in a line of poetry by al-Mutanabbī (2:296):

(24)	*wa lākinna bi al-fusṭāṭi bahran ?azartuhu ḥayātī wa nuṣḥī wa al-hawā wa al-qawāfiyā*	'But in Fustat there is a sea which I made my life, my advice, love, and poetry visit'

(vii) *ġazā* 'to invade'

This verb is also causativizable in CA but not in MSA. The form IV verb *?aġzā* derived from this verb is found in several places in al-Ṭabarī (vol. 3). The following sentence is found in (3:27):

(25)	*?aġzā rasūlu ?allāhi ?abā qatādatin ?ilā baṭni ?iḍamin*	'The prophet of God sent Abū Qatādah to invade the Iḍam tribe'

(viii) *^{c}aṭā* 'to take'

This verb exists in CA but not in MSA. The form IV verb *?a^{c}ṭā* derived from this verb exists in both CA and MSA. Thus historically the form IV verb is derived from the basic verb, but synchronically there is no evidence for causativization since the basic form does not exist in MSA. In CA the verb *^{c}aṭā* 'to take' is evidently causativizable.

I have no way of accounting for the causativizability of the above three verbs. Further investigation of the verbal system in CA may show that more verbs causativize in CA than in MSA. The above three verbs show that causativization in CA was more productive than it is in MSA. The historical change in the process of causation finds evidence also in the absence of the form IV pattern from most of the modern Arabic spoken languages.

In conclusion it would be appropriate to claim that, in general, transitive verbs are not causativizable, while intransitive verbs are.

The causativization of the transitive verbs listed above (in MSA and CA) produces three-place verbs. It is important to note that there are form I basic verbs that are double transitive as in the following example:

(26)	*wahaba zaydun hindan kitāban*	'Zayd donated a book to Hind'

The verb in (26) is a three-place verb. An interesting fact about causatives is that they themselves cannot be causativized. Thus non-causativizability is the common factor between transitives and causatives and between three-place causative verbs and doubly transitive verbs. Semantically both transitives and causatives require two participants in an action or experience where one participant is the causer or actor and the other is the undergoer or affected. These relationships and similarities between causatives and transitives will be further discussed in the next chapter and a formalization of these relationships will be proposed.

4.2.3 Syntactic and Semantic Properties of Covert Causatives

An important question that poses itself is: Why does Arabic maintain four major classes of covert causative verbs? In this section we will attempt to answer the question by exploring the syntactic and semantic properties of the four classes of covert causative verbs and the differences and similarities among them.

In many cases one cannot discern any difference in meaning between, for example, two covert causative verbs derived from the same simple form I verb. The following are illustrative sentences:

(27)	1a.	*farraḥanī najāḥuka*	'Your success pleased me'
	b.	*?afraḥanī najāḥuka*	
	2a.	*xafā al-kitāba*	'He hid the book'
	b.	*?axfā al-kitāba*	
	3a.	*ḏahaba allāhu bi ?abṣārihim*	'God took away their eyesight i.e., made them blind'
	b.	*?aḏhaba allāhu ?abṣārahum*	

The form II FaMMaLa verb and the form IV ?aFMaLa verb in 1, the form I FaMaLa causative verb and the form IV ?aFMaLa verb in 2, and the prepositional causative verb FaMaLa *bi* and the form IV ?aFMaLa verb in 3 are synonymous, respectively. It should not be understood from the above examples that it is possible to derive more than one causative from any simple form I causativizable verb.

Sībawayhi's teacher al-Khalīl Ibn Aḥmad al-Farāhīdī (Sībawayhi, II:248–9) makes a semantic distinction between the form I causative verb *ḥazana* and the form IV causative verb *?aḥzana* which are derived from the basic form I verb *ḥazina* ,to be sad.' According to him *ḥazana* means 'to create sadness in someone' while *?aḥzana* means 'to make someone sad.' The following are illustrative sentences with their Arabic paraphrases:

(28)	a.	*ḥazantuhu* *ja^{c}altu fīhi ḥuznan*	'I created sadness in him'
	b.	*?aḥzantuhu* *ja^{c}altuhu ḥazīnan*	'I made him sad.

The verb *ja^{c}ala* in (28) means 'to create or to establish' in a and 'to make become' in b. al-al-Khalīl gives the verbs *fatana* 'to infatuate,' *dahana* 'to grease,' and *kaḥala* 'to paint with kohl' as having a semantic load corresponding to that of *ḥazana*. The following sentences with their Arabic paraphrases illustrate the point:

(29)	a.	*fatantuhu* *ja^{c}altu fīhi fitnatan*	'I created infatuation in him'
	b.	*dahantuhu* *ja^{c}altu fīhi duhnan*	'I anointed (or greased) him'
	c.	*kaḥaltuhu* *ja^{c}altu fīhi kuḥlan*	'I painted it (the eyelid) with kohl'

(kohl is a preparation of pulverized antimony used for darkening the edges of the eyelids).

Al-Astrābādhī (1:87) says that the meanings of the two verbs *ḥazana* and *?aḥzana* are identical except that the former indicates *al-taṣyīr* -'the bringing about of a process' while the latter doesn't (*taṣyīr* is the verbal noun of the verb *ṣayyara* 'to make become' which is derived from *ṣāra* 'to become'). But this is exactly what al-Khalīl said the difference between the two verbs was. The semantic judgement about *ḥazana* and *?aḥzana*, made by al-Khalīl and unknowingly confirmed by al-Astrābādhī, is very subtle. That the difference in meaning between the two verbs is very slight explains why *ḥazana* has disappeared in MSA in spite of the fact that it is attested in the Holy Koran. In the absence of native intuitions about the difference in meaning between such verbs we accept as correct the judgement of al-Khalīl who was a native Arab, a syntactician, a phonologist and a lexicographer. A proper translation of the two verbs would be (30):

(30)	a.	*ḥazana*	'to cause someone to be sad'
	b.	*?aḥzana*	'to cause someone to become sad'

Pairs of causative verbs like *ḥazana* and *?aḥzana* indicate that a distinction is made in Arabic between the bringing about of a state and the bringing about of a process. An important property of form I causatives is that they are derivable from stative or inchoative form I base verbs but not from form I active base verbs. An apparent exception is the verb *rakaḍa* 'to cause to run.' It is important to note, however, that there is no change in the internal vowel of the verb in this derivation. Form I causatives are not as productive as form II or form IV causatives: some ninety to a hundred form I causative verbs can be found while form II and form IV causative verbs run into hundreds, and maybe thousands.

Let us now examine the differences between form II and form IV covert causative verbs. We have stated earlier that in many cases one cannot discern a difference between them. In many other cases, however, the differences can be clearly seen. The following pairs of sentences illustrate such differences, where the verb in the a sentences is a form II causative and in the b sentences a form IV causative:

(31)	1a.	*ᶜallama zaydun ᶜamran al-qur?āna*	'Zayd taught 'Amr the Koran'
	b.	*?aᶜlama zaydun ᶜamran ?anna hindan rajaᶜat ?ilā al-ᶜirāqi*	'Zayd informed 'Amr that Hind went back to Iraq'
	2a.	*ḥassanat al-dawlatu al-barāmija al-taᶜlīmiyyata*	'The state improved the educational programs'
	b.	*yuḥsinu zaydun al-?almāniyyata*	'Zayd masters the German language'
	3a.	*ṣallaḥa al-rādyū*	'He repaired the radio'
	b.	*?aṣlaḥū al-niẓāma al-siyāsiyya*	'They reformed the political system'
	4a.	*ṯawwarahum*	'He revolutionized them'
	b.	*?aṯārahum*	'He irritated them'

The form II verbs in the above sentences indicate an action repeatedly performed with considerable force or intensity and one generally assumes that the act is done deliberately and persistently. The form IV verbs, on the other hand, do not necessarily indicate persistent action. Thus informing someone of something does not require persistency while teaching someone something requires persistency and repeated action. While the verb in (2a) requires a conscious effort on the part of the agent, the verb in (2b) is stative: the state of knowing a language does not require an effort once the individual has mastered that language. Furthermore a form IV verb in certain instances does not have to indicate deliberate action, thus an individual may irritate someone without really meaning to or without even knowing that he is doing so. The following sentence illustrates the point:

(32) *?afsada min ḥayṯu yurīdu al-?iṣlāḥa* — 'He caused mischief where he meant to make amends'

sentence (33) with *fassada* replacing *?afsada* is ungrammatical

(33) **fassada min ḥayṯu yurīdu al-?iṣlāḥa*

Thus intensity or persistency seems to be a feature distinguishing between form II and form IV causative verbs. This is not surprising, since causation is not the only function of form II FaMMaLa verbs; they include such verbs as *kassara* 'to break into many pieces,' *qaṭṭa^{c}a* 'to cut into many pieces,' *ḍarraba* 'to beat violently,' *qattala* 'to massacre' and *ṭawwafa* 'to go around repeatedly.' Such examples suggest that form II verbs are intensive or repetitive in function. Historically one can clearly argue that intensity was the distinguishing feature of form II verb. As a matter of fact there are instances of intensive intransitive verbs in CA which have changed into causative two-place verbs in MSA. The following pairs of sentences illustrate this syntactic and semantic change in form II verbs:

(34)	1a.	CA:	*mawwatat al-?iblu*	'The camels died in large numbers'
	b.	MSA:	*mawwata zaydun al-?ibla*	'Zayd caused the camels to die'
	2a.	CA:	*wa rawwaḥa ri^{c}yānun wa nawwama summaru* (Ibn Abī Rabī'ah, Dīwān: 123)	'And the shepherds went back home and the companions in nightly entertainment slept heavily'
	b.	MSA:	*nawwamat al-?ummu ṭiflahā*	'The mother put her child to sleep'
	3a.	CA:	*barrakat al-?iblu*	'The camels kneeled down in large numbers'
	b.	MSA:	*barraka zaydun al-?ibla*	'Zayd made the camels kneel down'
	4a.	CA:	*bakkat hindun*	'Hind wept much'
	b.	MSA:	*bakkā zaydun hindan*	'Zayd made Hind weep'

The causatives signification is common to form II and form IV verbs, the apparent difference historically being that it is original in form IV, derived in form II. Interestingy, form II has taken over the function of form IV in many contemporary Arabic dialects. Synchronically, where there are two causative verbs a form II verb and a form IV verb derived from the same base verb, the form II verb indicates intentionality, intensity and/or persistency whereas the form IV verb doesn't.

Let us consider at this point the difference between prepositionally derived causative verbs and the other types of covert causatives. Consider the following sentences:

(35)	1a.	*ḏahabat hindun*	'Hind went (away)'
	b.	*ḏahaba zaydun bi hindin*	'Zayd took Hind (away)'
	c.	*?aḏhaba zaydun hindan*	'Zayd made Hind go (away)'

2a.	*xarajat hindun*	'Hind went out'
b.	*xaraja zaydun bi hindin*	'Zayd took Hind out'
c.	*?axraja zaydun hindan*	'Zayd got Hind out'

The verb in the a sentences is a simple nonderived form I verb; it is a prepositionally derived causative verb in the b sentences and a form IV causative verb in the c sentences. The b and c sentences are similar in that the nonagentive noun phrases are affected by the action identified by the verb in the b as well as in the c sentences. The two types of sentences differ in that whereas the agent in the b sentences performs the action identified by the verb in the a sentences, the agent in the c sentences doesn't; the idea of accompaniment is implicit in the b sentences but not in the c sentences. Thus accompaniment expressed by prepositionally derived causatives distinguishes these causative verbs from the other types. Moreover these causatives are derivable only from form I simple verbs which express movement or motion. Prepositionally derived causatives are reminiscent of the comitative constructions discussed in Chapter II, though the two types of constructions differ as can be seen from the following pair of sentences:

(36)	a.	*jā?a zaydun bi ᶜamrin*	'Zayd brought 'Amr'
	b.	*jā?a zaydun wa ᶜamran*	'Zayd came with 'Amr'

The verb is causative in a, not in b. The genitive noun phrase is affected by the agent's action, the accusative noun phrase in b is not affected by the agent's action. In short, the only point in common between the two constructions is accompaniment.

Many form I nonderived transitive verbs indicate causation semantically in the same manner as the causative verbs discussed above; that is, such verbs indicate the bringing about of a state or a process. Form II verbs are derivable from such form I transitive verbs. However these form II verbs are intensive, not causative, verbs as can be seen from the following sentences:

(37)	1a.	*qatalahum*	'He killed them'
	b.	*qattalahum*	'He massacred them'
	2a.	*kasara al-zujāja*	'He broke the glass'
	b.	*kassara al-zujāja*	'He broke the glass into many pieces'

It is important to note that no causative verb is derivable from form I transitive verbs from which an intensive form II verb is derivable. We consider that the causation indicated by such transitive form I verbs is inherent in the verb itself and that this causation is a part of the lexicon. Thus according to the identification of causative verbs given in this chapter, verbs like those in (37) are not syntactically causative because there is no indication that they are derivable, either morphologically or prepositionally, from simpler verbs. The grammatical similarity between these verbs and causative verbs will be discussed and formalized in the next chapter.

The following conclusions have been reached in this section:

(i) It is not possible to derive more than one causative verb from every causativizable verb in the language.

(ii) The difference between a form I causative and a form IV causative, which are derived from the same simple verb, is that while the former indicates the bringing about of a state the latter indicates the bringing about of a process.

Form I causatives are derivable from stative or inchoative base verbs but not from active base verbs.

(iii) Where there are two causative verbs, a form II verb and a form IV verb, derived from the same base verb, the form II verb indicates intentionality, intensity and/or persistency whereas the form IV verb doesn't. Historically many form II causatives originated from form II intensive intransitives.

(iv) Prepositionally derived causatives express accompaniment while others don't. They are derivable only from form I base verbs which express movement or motion.

(v) It is not always possible to make a distinction between two covert causatives derived from the same simple verb.

4.2.4 Syntactic Derivation of Covert Causative Constructions

Many covert causative verbs can be paraphrased by the verb *ja*^{c}*ala* 'to make (causative)' and an intransitive verb. The b sentences are paraphrases of the a sentences below:

(38)	1a.	*?ajlasa zaydun hindan*	'Zayd sat Hind down'
	b.	*ja*^{c}*ala zaydun hindan tajlisu*	'Zayd made Hind sit down'
	2a.	*?axraja zaydun hindan min al-ġurfati*	'Zayd got Hind out of the room'
	b.	*ja*^{c}*ala zaydun hindan taxruju min al-ġurfati*	'Zayd made Hind go out of the room'

This being the case, the following deep structure for sentence 1a above may be posited:

(39)

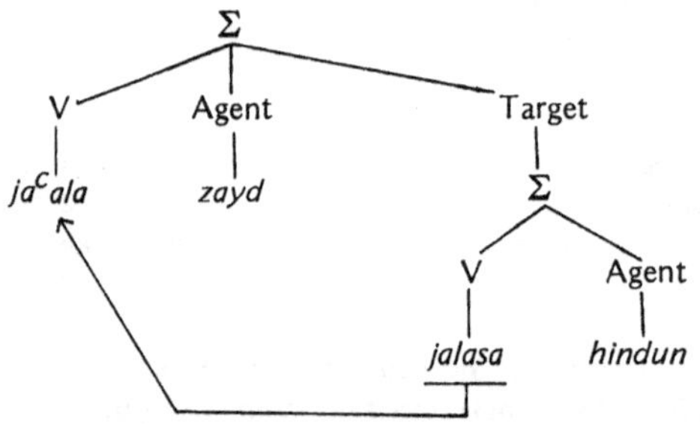

The lower form I intransitive verb *jalasa* undergoes predicate raising as shown by the arrow. A lexicalization transformation incorporates *jalasa* in *ja*^{c}*ala* to give *?ajlasa*. The Agent of the lower sentence becomes an accusative object of the higher sentence and after all relevant transformations are applied, we get sentence 1a of (38) above.

This derivation, however, is not correct for the following reasons:

(i) Whereas a covert causative verb derived from an active form I base verb may be paraphrased by *ja*^{c}*ala* and that base verb, a covert causative verb derived from a stative and/or inchoative form I base verb may not be paraphrased by *ja*^{c}*ala* and that base verb. The ungrammaticalness of the b sentences below illustrates the point:

(40)	1a.	*qaṣṣarat hindun ṯawbahā*	'Hind shortened her dress'
	b.	**ja^calat hindun ṯawbahā yaqṣuru*	'Hind made her dress be short'
	2a.	*?amāta zaydun wālidahu*	'Zayd caused his father to die'
	b.	**ja^cala zaydun wālidahu yamūtu*	'Zayd made his father die'

(ii) If the accusative object of the covert causative verb derived from a form I active verb is inanimate, then the causative verb may not be paraphrased by *ja*^{c}*ala* plus a base verb. Thus,

(41)	1a.	*?axraja zaydun al-ṭāwilata min al-ġurfati*	'Zayd got the table out of the room'
	b.	**ja^{c}ala zaydun al-ṭāwilata taxruju min al-ġurfati*	'Zayd made the table go out of the room'
	2a.	*?anzaltu al-kitāba ^{c}an al-raffi*	'I brought the book down from the shelf'
	b.	**ja^{c}altu al-kitāba yanzilu ^{c}an al-raffi*	'I made the book go down from the shelf'

(iii) The occurrence of certain manner adverbials in causative sentences like (38) makes sentences like (38b), but not sentences like (38a), ambiguous. Compare the a and b sentences below:

(42)	a.	*?axraja zaydun hindan min al-ġurfati bi sur^{c}atin*	'Zayd got Hind out of the room quickly'
	b.	*ja^{c}ala zaydun hindan taxruju min al-ġurfati bi sur^{c}atin*	'Zayd made Hind go out of the room quickly'

The manner adverbial *bi sur*^{c}*atin* 'quickly' may refer to either Zayd's or Hind's activity in b; it may refer only to Zayd's activity in a.

One may argue that the matrix verb in (39) is not the Arabic verb *ja*^{c}*ala* but rather a semantic predicate SABBABA 'CAUSE' which has no surface realization. Thus the above objections to the derivation of covert causative constructions from deep structures like (39) would no longer be valid. It was shown in the last section that there are, in Arabic, causative verbs that indicate the bringing about of a state as well as causative verbs that indicate the bringing about of a process. Sentences (38a) and their paraphrases (38b) suggest that the verbs in (38a) indicate the bringing about of an activity. The following sentences illustrate the three types of causative verbs which are morphologically derived from stative, inchoative and active verbs, respectively:

(43)	a.	*ḥazana zaydun ^{c}amran*	'Zayd caused 'Amr to be sad'
	b.	*?aḏāba zaydun al-šam^{c}ata*	'Zayd melted the candle'
	c.	*?ajlasa zaydun ^{c}amran*	'Zayd sat 'Amr down'

The state, process, and activity suggested by the verbs in (43) can clearly be seen in the following sentences which contain the base verbs from which the verbs in (43) are derived:

(44)	a.	*ḥazina ^{c}amrun*	''Amr was sad'
	b.	*ḏābat al-šam^{c}atu*	'The candle melted'
	c.	*jalasa ^{c}amrun*	''Amr sat down'

The case frames of the verbs in (44) are (45), respectively:

(45) a. [——— Target]
b. [——— Patient]
c. [——— Agent]

It may very well be claimed that the case roles of the subject noun phrases in (44) are the same as the case roles of the object noun phrases in (43). The case frames of the verbs in (43) would be (46):

(46) a. [——— Agent Target]
b. [——— Agent Patient]
c. [——— Agent Agent]

But notice that the case frame (46c) violates Fillmore's principle of one-instance-per-clause. Therefore, if we consider that the noun phrase *'Amr* has the same case role in (43c) and (44c) and if we want to save Fillmore's principle, which is considered a valid principle in this book, then we must analyze (43c) as being clausally complex. In other words, Fillmore's principle compels us not to analyze *?ajlasa* in (43c) as a single discontinuous verb. But if *?ajlasa* is considered a decomposable verb, there is no reason not to consider *ḥazana* and *?aḏāba* also decomposable since their semantic relationship to the verbs from which they are morphologically derived is equivalent to the semantic relationship of *?ajlasa* to the verb from which it is morphologically derived as can be seen from (43) and (44) above. In accordance with this analysis the following deep structures (considerably simplified) may be postulated for the sentences in (43), respectively:

(47) a. *ḥazana zaydun ᶜamran* 'Zayd caused 'Amr to be sad'

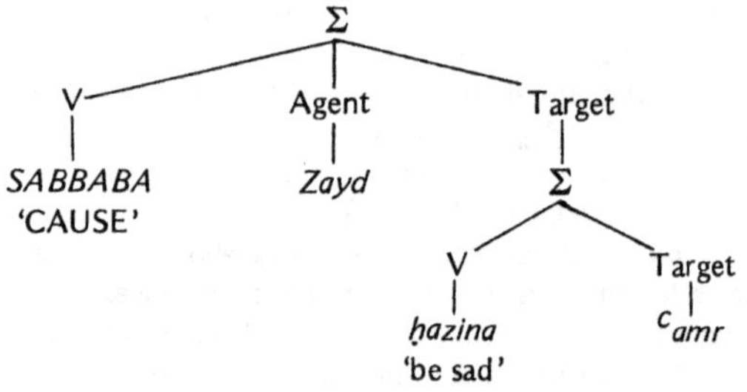

SABBABA 'CAUSE' is a semantic predicate which commands the stative verb *hazina* 'to be sad.'

b. *?aḏāba zaydun al-šamᶜata* 'Zayd melted the candle'

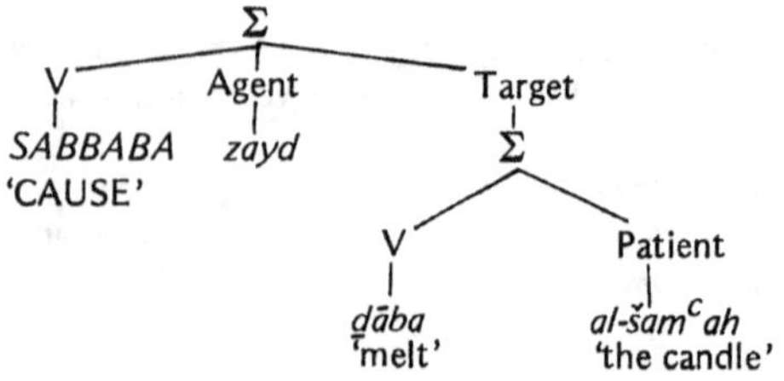

The semantic predicate *SABBABA* 'CAUSE' commands the inchoative verb *ḏāba* 'to melt.'

c. *?ajlasa zaydun* ^{c}*amran* 'Zayd sat 'Amr down'

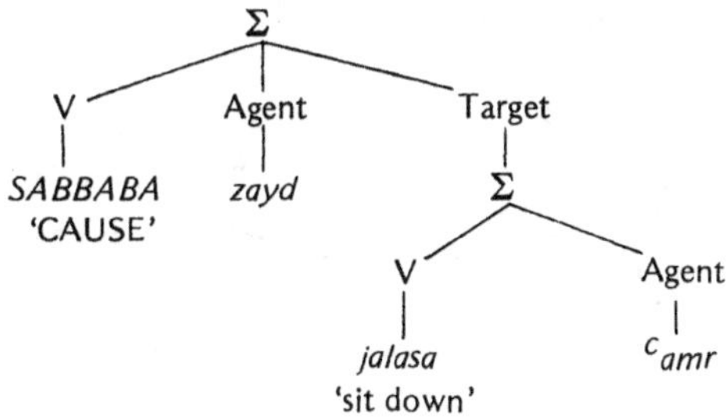

The semantic predicate *SABBABA* 'CAUSE' commands the active verb *jalasa* 'sit down.'

Predicate raising, lexicalization, and the application of all necessary transformations gives sentences (43).

It is important to note at this point that we were forced to postulate the deep structures (47) because the case frame of the active causative verb *?ajlasa* 'to sit down' of sentence (43) was claimed to be (46c), i.e., [____ Agent Agent]. This case frame implies agency on the part of the accusative objects in the following sentences (where (43c) is rewritten as (48a)):

(48)	a.	*?ajlasa zaydun* ^{c}*amran*	'Zayd sat 'Amr down'
	b.	*?aḥḍara zaydun* ^{c}*amran*	'Zayd brought 'Amr'
	c.	*?axraja zaydun* ^{c}*amran*	'Zayd got 'Amr out'

We have shown earlier in this section (cf. (ii)) that sentences (48) may not be paraphrased by the overt causative constructions corresponding to them when the accusative objects are inanimate. The animate objects in (48) can be replaced by inanimate objects as can be seen from the following sentences:

(48)	a.	*?ajlasa zaydun al-dumyata*	'Zayd sat the marionnette down'
	b.	*?aḥḍara zaydun al-biḍā*^{c}*ata*	'Zayd brought the merchandise'
	c.	*?axraja zaydun al-ṭāwilata*	'Zayd took the table out'

It is obvious that no agency or activity can be attributed to the accusative objects in (49). That agency or activity may be attributed to the accusative objects in (48) is a pragmatic accident and is syntactically irrelevant. In point of fact, the role of the accusative objects in (48) is no different from that of the ones in (49). Sentence (48c), for example, implies that Zayd physically carried or pushed 'Amr out. The object noun phrases in (48) and (49) are affected by the action identified by the verb and their case role is no different from the case role of the noun phrase in a sentence like *saqaṭa al-jidāru* 'The wall fell.' Therefore the case frame of verbs like those in (48) and (49) is not [____ Agent Agent] but [____ Agent Target].

In accordance with the facts presented above, covert causative constructions are not clausally complex but rather simplex sentences in the deep structure. The covert causative verb is decomposable but not into <u>*ja^{c}ala*</u> plus a base verb, or a semantic predicate <u>*SABBABA*</u> plus a base verb; it is rather decomposable into a feature (+ causative) which belongs to the Q component plus a base causativizable verb which belongs to the P component. The deep structures of sentences (43) are not (47) but rather (50).

(50) a. *ḥazana zaydun ^{c}amran* 'Zayd caused 'Amr to be sad'

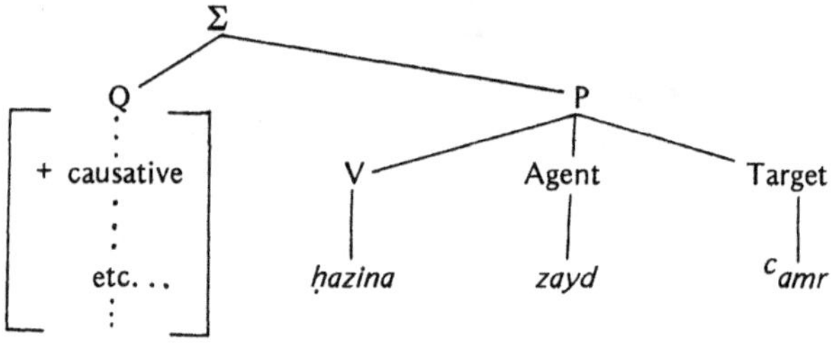

b. *?aḏāba zaydun al-šam^{c}ata* 'Zayd melted the candle'

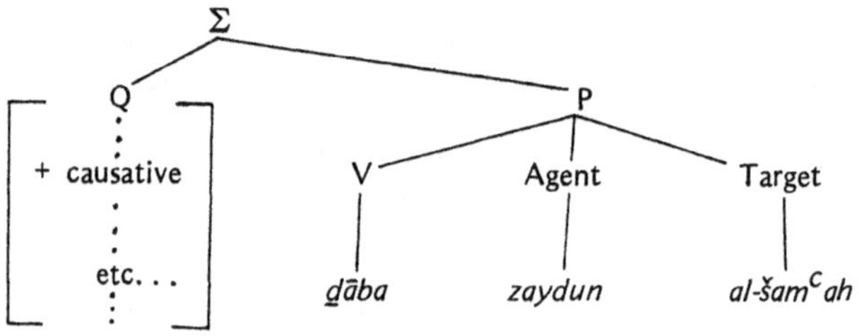

c. *?ajlasa zaydun ^{c}amran* 'Zayd sat 'Amr down'

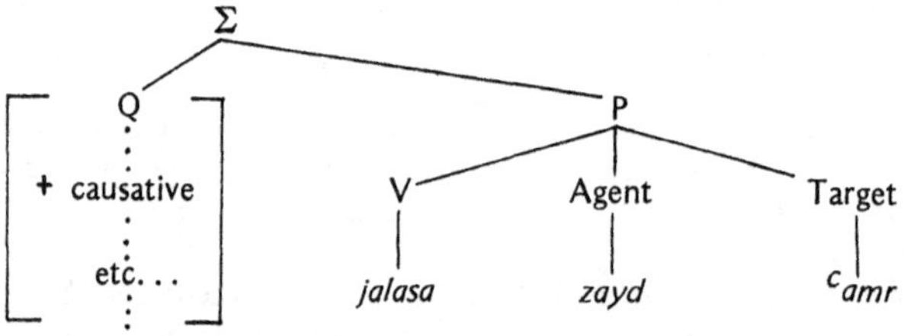

A causative transformation incorporates the feature (+ causative) into the base verb to give the covert causative verb, and after all the necessary transformations are applied we get sentences (43).

The following points have been made in this section:

(i) Covert causative constructions are not derivable from the overt causative constructions corresponding to them and cannot be derived from a semantic predicate plus a base verb.

(ii) Covert causative constructions are not clausally complex but rather simplex sentences in the deep structure.

(iii) Covert causative verbs are decomposable into a base verb which belongs to the P component and a feature (+ causative) which belongs to the Q component and are the result of a causative transformation which incorporates the causative feature into the base verb.

4.3 Overt Causatives

Overt or periphrastic causative constructions are clausally complex constructions in which a clause is embedded on the surface as the complement of a hypercausative verb which is the matrix verb in such overt causative constructions (henceforth O.C.C.). The term "hypercausative" refers to matrix causative verbs like *ja^{c}ala* 'to make causative,' *taraka* 'to let,' *samaḥa* 'to allow,' *?arġama ^{c}alā* 'to force,' *tasabbaba fī* 'to cause,' etc. . . In this section we will examine the differences between O.C.C. and covert causative constructions (henceforth C.C.C), the properties of hypercausatives, and the syntactic behavior and semantic range of O.C.C.

4.3.1 Differences between O.C.C. and C.C.C.

In section 4.2.4 we gave three reasons for not paraphrasing C.C.C. by the O.C.C. corresponding to them (cf. 4.2.4 (i), (ii), and (iii). Here now are several more:

(iv) Certain noun phrases that may be subjects of the hypercausative verb in an O.C.C. may not be subjects of the covert causative verb in a C.C.C.:

(51) a. *ja^{c}ala al-maṭaru al-ṭifla yanzilu ^{c}an al-šajarati* — 'Rain made the child go down from the tree'

b. **?anzala al-maṭaru al-ṭifla ^{c}an al-šajarati* — 'Rain made the child go down from the tree'

(v) Whereas covert causative verbs may take Instruments, hypercausative verbs may not

(52) a. *?anzalat al-ṭifla ^{c}an al-šajarati bi yadayhā* — 'She brought the child down from the tree with her hands'

b. **ja^{c}alat al-ṭifla yanzilu ^{c}an al-šajarati bi yadayhā* — 'She made the child go down from the tree with her hands'

(vi) Under certain circumstances there is no covert paraphrase for an O.C.C. This occurs when the hypercausative verb and the embedded verb have different adverbials. The following pair of sentences illustrates the point:

(53) a. *?arġama zaydun yawma al-sabti ^{c}amran, ^{c}alā ?an yaḏhaba yawma al-?aḥadi* — 'On Saturday Zayd forced 'Amr to go (away) on Sunday'

b. **?aḏhaba zaydun yawma al-sabti ^{c}amran yawma al-?aḥadi* — 'On Saturday Zayd made 'Amr go (away) on Sunday'

Sentences (53) show that in O.C.C. the hypercausative verb and the lower verb must be analyzed as two distinct verbs, while in C.C.C. the covert causative verb must be analyzed as a single discontinuous verb. The above data suggests that C.C.C. are compatible only with simultaneous, direct causation. If an embedded verb and a hypercausative verb have different adverbials, the causation is not simultaneous and direct, and the covert causative verb is blocked syntactically and semantically. O.C.C., on the other hand, may or may not indicate simultaneous direct causation. The direct causation indicated by C.C.C. requires that the verb refer to one, and only one, causer involved in the bringing about of a state or a process. For example, the sentence *?aḏāba zaydun al-šamᶜata* 'Zayd melted the candle' may not be interpreted to imply that the coming about of the melting of the candle is a result of Zayd's asking someone else to perform the act. In contrast to C.C.C., O.C.C. are unsepecified with respect to directness of causation. Consider the following sentences:

(54) a. *?aḍḥaka zaydun hindan* } 'Zayd made Hind laugh'
b. *jaᶜala zaydun hindan taḍḥaku* }

Sentence a implies that Zayd directly did something funny which made Hind laugh. Sentence b may imply the same thing but it also may imply that Zayd, for example, has sent someone else to Hind to make her laugh.

(vii) Whereas most transitive verbs and all covert causative verbs may not be causativized covertly (cf. section 4.2.2), they may be overtly. Any verb in the language may be embedded in an O.C.C. The following, where the embedded verb is transitive in a, covert causative in b, are illustrative sentences:

(55) a. *jaᶜala zaydun ᶜamran yaqtulu bakran* 'Zayd made 'Amr kill Bakr'
b. *jaᶜala zaydun ᶜamran yujlisu bakran* 'Zayd made 'Amr sit Bakr down'

There are no C.C.C. corresponding to sentences like (55) in Arabic. Each of the sentences in (55) indicates an explicit chain of causation: Zayd causes 'Amr to do something and 'Amr causes Bakr to undergo or suffer something. The causation relationship that holds between Zayd and 'Amr is unspecified with respect to directness of action; the one that holds between 'Amr and Bakr indicates direct action, and the one that holds between Zayd and Bakr indicates indirect action. This means that, in an O.C.C. which contains one and only one hypercausative verb, specified indirect causation is discernible only when the embedded verb is a transitive or a covert causative verb.

(viii) Not only transitive and covert causative verbs may be embedded in an O.C.C., but also hypercausative verbs. An O.C.C. may be multiply complex as can be seen from the following sentence:

(56) *?arġama zaydun ᶜamran ᶜalā ?an yuqniᶜa bakran bi ?an yatruka hindan tafᶜalu mā tašā?u* 'Zayd forced 'Amr to persuade Bakr to leave Hind to do whatever she likes'

Specified indirect causation is indicated by (56) and there is no C.C.C. that corresponds to (56) in the language.

(ix) Whereas C.C.C. may not be interpreted intransitively, many O.C.C. may. The b sentences are paraphrases of the a sentences in the following:

(57) 1a.	*ja^{c}ala al-maṭaru al-ṭifla yanzilu ^{c}an al-šajarati*	'The rain made the child go down from the tree'
b.	*nazala al-ṭiflu ^{c}an al-šajarati bi sababi al-maṭari*	'The child went down from the tree because of rain'
2a.	*ja^{c}alanī al-?irtifā^{c}u al-kabīru fī darajati al-ḥarārati ?ataṣabbabu ^{c}araqan*	'The great rise in temperature made me sweat heavily'
b.	*taṣabbabtu ^{c}araqan bi sababi al-?irtifā^{c}i al-kabīri fī darajati al-ḥarārati*	'I sweated heavily because of the great rise in temperature'

Sentences (57a) are pseudo-O.C.C. They must be derived from deep structures underlying sentences like (57b). As we stated in section 4.1, such constructions will not be dealt with in this book.

4.3.2 Hypercausatives

Hypercausatives are causative verbs that occur as matrix verbs in O.C.C. and that require a sentential complement on the surface. The underlined verbs in the following periphrastic causative sentences are representative of the hypercausatives in Arabic:

(58) a.	*ja^{c}ala zaydun ^{c}amran yaxruju min al-ġurfati*	'Zayd made 'Amr go out of the room'
b.	*taraka zaydun ^{c}amran yaḏhabu*	'Zayd let 'Amr go'
c.	*?ajbaranī ^{c}alā ?an ?aqbala bi šurūṭihi*	'He compelled me to accept his conditions'
d.	*?iḍṭarra al-waḍ^{c}u al-siyāsiyyu ^{c}amran ^{c}alā ?an yuġādira al-bilāda*	'The political situation obliged 'Amr to leave the country'
e.	*?arġamahā ^{c}alā ?an tabī^{c}a sayyāratahā*	'He forced her to sell her car'
f.	*?aġrāhā bi ?an tusammima zawjahā*	'He tempted her to poison her husband'
g.	*makkana zaydun ?uxtahu min ?an tusaddida duyūnahā*	'Zayd enabled his sister to pay back her debts'
h.	*xawwala al-ra?īsu muḥāmiyahu bi ?an yatakallama bi ismihi*	'The president granted his lawyer the power to speak in his name'
i.	*samaḥa zaydun li ^{c}amrin bi ?an yaḥḍura al-?ijtimā^{c}a*	'Zayd allowed 'Amr to attend the meeting'
j.	*?aqna^{c}ahum bi ?an yadrusū al-^{c}arabiyyata*	'He persuaded them to study Arabic'

Two types of causation are discernible in these sentences. In the first five the hypercausative verb indicates the occurrence of an activity identified by the embedded verb. We understand from sentence a, for example, that " 'Amr's going out of the room" DID take place. In the second five sentences the hypercausative verb does not necessarily indicate the occurrence of the activity identified by the embedded verb. In sentence f, for example, there is nothing that tells us whether "she poisoned her husband" or not. In spite of the fact that all of the embedded verbs in (58) are active, the hypercausative verbs in the first five sentences indicate the bringing about of an activity while in the second five sentences they indicate the bringing about of a state. The object noun phrase of the matrix sentence in the first five sentences did perform something. Although the object noun phrase in the second five sentences did not necessarily perform anything, it, however, came to be in a state or in a position which enables it to do or perform something. In all of sentences (58) the object noun phrase of the matrix sentence is "affected" by the action indicated by the hypercausative verb.

O.C.C. like (58) should be distinguished from noncausative constructions like (59) similar to them in surface structure.

(59) a. *?arāda zaydun minhā ?an tabīᶜa sayyāratahā* — 'Zayd wanted her to sell her car'

b. *ṭalabū min zaydin ?an yusāᶜidahā* — 'They asked Zayd to help her'

c. *tamannā zaydun ᶜalā hindin ?an tatazawwajahu* — 'Zayd wished Hind to marry him'

d. *rajā zaydun ᶜamran ?an yusāmiḥahu* — 'Zayd begged 'Amr to forgive him'

e. *?ittafaqa maᶜahum ᶜalā ?an yaqbala al-waẓīfati ?allatī ᶜaraḍūhā ᶜalayhi* — 'He agree with them to accept the job that they offered him'

Whereas the object noun phrase in each of the sentences of (58) is definitely "affected" by the action identified by the hypercausative verb, the object noun phrase in sentences (59) is not necessarily affected by the action identified by the matrix verb (the term object here refers to either the direct object or to the object of a preposition). Another difference between (58) and (59) is that the case role of the object noun phrase in (58) is Target, while it is Source in (59a, b, c, d), and Comitative in (59e). Thus the underlined verbs in (59) are not hypercausative verbs.

A very important syntactic difference between the first two sentences and the last eight sentences of (58) is that the former are nonpassivizable while the latter are. The nonpassivizability of (58a, b) is odd, and it provides a counterexample to the case system proposed in Chapter II and to the claims about passivizability made in Chapter III. A portion of the case frame of the hypercausative verb in (58a) is [_____ Agent Target . . .]. Verbs with such a case frame were argued to be passivizable in Chapter III. Surface structurally the noun phrase *ᶜamran* is a direct accusatives object in (58a, b) and it would be most natural for it to be able to become the subject of a passive verb. In spite of all of this, the passive counterparts of (58a, b) are ungrammatical as shown in (60), respectively:

(60) a. **juᶜila ᶜamrun yaxruju min al-ġurfati* — ' 'Amr was made to go out of the room'

b. *?turika ᶜamrun yaḏhabu* — ' 'Amr was let to go'

Let us now examine the differences between sentences (58a, b) (henceforth A-hypercausatives) and sentences (58c-j) henceforth B-hypercausatives). The embedded verb is in the indicative mood in A-hypercausative constructions, but in the subjunctive mood in B-hypercausative constructions. It may be noticed that the subjunctive particle *?an* occurs in all the B-hypercausative sentences of (58) while it does not occur in the A-hypercausative ones. Subjunctive complements are nominalizable in Arabic while the sentential complements in sentences like (58a, b) are not. This can be seen from the following sentences corresponding to (58a) and (58c), respectively:

(61)	a.	**ja^{c}ala zaydun ^{c}amran al-xurūja min al-ġurfati*	'Zayd made 'Amr go out of the room'
	b.	*?ajbaranī ^{c}alā al-qubūli bi šurūṭihi*	'He compelled me to accept his conditions'

In addition, the embedded verb in A- but not in B-hypercausative constructions can be transformed into an active participle as shown in (62):

(62)	*ja^{c}ala zaydun ^{c}amran xārijan min al-ġurfati*	'Zayd made 'Amr go out of the room'

The hypercausative verb taraka is not very common in Arabic; whenever it is used it is mostly in the imperative in the form of da^c as in da^{c}hu yaḏhab 'let him go.' The hypercausative verb ja^{c}ala is much more common. In the remaining part of this section we will restrict the discussion of the A-hypercausatives to the verb ja^{c}ala.

In addition to the syntactic differences presented above between ja^{c}ala and the B-hypercausatives, there are semantic differences. All the B-hypercausative verbs given in (58) indicate a specific semantic feature in addition to causation. The hypercausative verbs in (58c, e) indicate force or coercion; in (58d), necessitation; in (58f), abetting; in (58g, h), power; in (58i), permission; and in (58j), inducement or persuasion. The verb ja^{c}ala, on the other hand, may indicate, in addition to causation, something else which is not specified. Thus the semantic feature accompanying causation in (58a) is vague; it can be force, coercion, abetting, power, inducement etc. The verb ja^{c}ala is also unspecified with respect to the type of Agent it may take. The most common use of the verb ?ajbara 'to compel' is with a human Agent only, and that of the verb ?iḍṭarra 'to oblige' is with an abstract noun as Agent. ja^{c}ala takes, naturally, both types of Agent.

A hypercausative verb that corresponds semantically to ja^{c}ala is sabbaba 'to cause.' Like it, sabbaba is vague with respect to the semantic feature that accompanies causation. Both verbs are nonpassivizable. One difference between them is that whereas ja^{c}ala may not take a sentential object in its nominalized form, sabbaba may only take one in its nonnominalized form:

(63)	1a.	*ja^{c}ala zaydun hindan tuġādiru al-bilāda*	'Zayd made Hind leave the country'
	b.	**ja^{c}ala zaydun muġādarata hindin al-bilāda*	'Zayd made Hind's leaving the country'
	2a.	**sabbaba zaydun hindan tuġādiru al-bilāda*	'Zayd caused Hind to leave the country'
	b.	*sabbaba zaydun muġādarata hindin al-bilāda*	'Zayd caused Hind's leaving the country'

Another difference between the two verbs is that whereas *ja^cala* may indicate an activity, *sabbaba* is a stative verb. Sentence (63. 2b) may be paraphrased by any of the following four sentences:

(64)	a.	*tasabbaba zaydun fī ?an ġādarat hindun al-bilāda*	'Zayd came to be the cause of Hind's leaving the country'
	b.	*tasabbaba zaydun fī mugādarati hindin al-bilāda*	'Zayd came to be the cause of Hind's leaving the country'
	c.	*kāna zaydun al-sababa fī ?an ġādarat hindun al-bilāda*	'Zayd was the cause of Hind's leaving the country'
	d.	*kāna zaydun al-sababa fī mugādarati hindin al-bilāda*	'Zayd was the cause of Hind's leaving the country'

Sentences c and d in (64) clearly indicate "pure" causation. The nature of causation in them is absolutely unspecified. These sentences do not imply that Zayd intentionally caused Hind to leave the country; as a matter of fact they do not imply that Zayd necessarily did or didn't do anything. In accordance with the analysis proposed for *kāna* 'to be' in section 3.4.1.2 the verb in (64c and d) is the surface noun phrase *al-sababa* 'the cause,' which is obviously stative. Since sentences (64a and b) and (63. 2b) are synonymous with (64c and d), the verbs *sabbaba* and *tasabbaba fī*, like (*kāna*) *al-sababa* (*fī*), are stative. Sentences (63.2b) and (64) may be interpreted intransitively as in (65) below:

(65)	*ġādarat hindun al-bilāda bi sababi zaydin*	'Hind left the country because of Zayd'

Since the deep structure of (65) underlies sentences (63.2b) and (64), the hypercausative *sabbaba* is not the matrix verb of an O.C.C. but of a pseudo-O.C.C.

The above analysis is highly tentative. The nature of O.C.C. and hypercausative verbs requires further study and examination.

In conclusion, we have established in this section (4. 3) that:

(i) Overt causative constructions are not paraphrases of covert causative constructions. The former may indicate indirect causation and can express a chain of causation (through successive embedding), but the latter may not.

(ii) Hypercausative verbs have a wide semantic range and differ syntactically from each other. A problem that remains unresolved is the nonpassivizability of O.C.C. whose hypercausative verb is *ja^cala* 'to make causative' or *taraka* 'to let.'

NOTES

1. Very few intransitive verbs seem to have no corresponding causatives. Examples are *nabula* 'to be noble' and *ġazura* 'to be abundant.'

5 Transitivity, ergativity, and the derivation of passives

5.1 Introduction

In Chapter I the traditional definition of transitivity was claimed to be inadequate for the description of passivization in Arabic. In Chapter II the classification of Arabic verbs into transitive and intransitive was discarded in favor of a classification of verbs into passivizable and nonpassivizable and passivizability was explained in terms of the case frame of the verb. In spite of the usefulness and adequacy of that analysis, no alternative has so far been suggested for the useful but inadequate notion of transitivity. In this chapter the following major questions will be dealt with:

(i) The notion of transitivity will be evaluated and a modified definition of it will be proposed; the Arabic verbal system will be examined in terms of transitivity as well as ergativity relationships that hold between the elements of a proposition.

(ii) A proposal for the derivation of passive constructions will be made, and

(iii) Reflexive constructions will be discussed and an account for their resistance to passivization will be given.

5.2 Transitivity and Ergativity

5.2.1 Transitivity

The comments made about transitivity in Chapter I may give the impression that the traditional definition of transitivity has no semantic basis. Syntactically, a transitive verb is a verb that takes an object and an intransitive verb is a verb that does not. John Lyons (1968: 350) makes the following statement about the traditional semantic definition of transitivity: "The traditional 'notional' view of transitivity suggests that the effects of the action expressed by the verb 'pass over' from the 'agent' (or 'actor') to the 'patient' (or 'goal')." The terms used by the early Arab grammarians for verb, subject, and object are *fiᶜl*, *fāᶜil*, and *mafᶜūl bihi*, i.e., Action, Actor, and Acted upon, respectively, which are obviously semantic terms not to be equated with verb, subject and object. According to the Arab grammarians, a transitive verb or rather a transitive action is an action that passes over the actor to an acted upon. Thus a transitive verb requires an actor and a goal while an intransitive verb requires an actor only which means that the actor is obligatory and the goal is optional in Arabic sentences. The syntactic behavior and semantic import of a large number of Arabic verbs give credence to this traditional definition and to the validity of a transitive pattern of clause organization. The following are illustrative sentences:

(1)	a.	*ḏahaba zaydun*	'Zayd went away'
	b.	*ḍaraba zaydun ᶜamran*	'Zayd beat 'Amr'

The verb is intransitive in a, transitive in b; both verbs express an action; and semantically and pragmatically the subject which takes the nominative case ending *-un* is actor in both sentences, and the object which takes the accusative case ending *-an* is goal in b.

The problem with this definition of transitivity is not that it did not have a semantic basis but rather that it was motivated solely by surface structure considerations. Thus in Arabic grammars *al-fāᶜil* 'The Actor' is the noun phrase that has the nominative case and *al-mafᶜūl bihi* 'The Acted upon (or goal)' is the noun phrase that has the accusative case. The semantic structure of Arabic sentences does not always reflect what is semantically presupposed by their surface structure. There is a large number of counterexamples to what is semantically predicted by the transitivity pattern of sentence organization. The following sentences illustrate the point:

(2)	a.	*māta zaydun*	'Zayd died'
	b.	*yaᶜrifu zaydun al-ʔinjlīziyyata*	'Zayd knows English'

The verb is intransitive in a, transitive in b, but neither verb expresses action; the subject in both sentences is not actor; and the object in b is not goal. Consider now the following sentences:

(3)	a.	*yuḥibbu zaydun hindan*	'Zayd loves Hind'
	b.	*yakrahu zaydun hindan*	'Zayd hates Hind'
	c.	*yaḥtarimu zaydun hindan*	'Zayd respects Hind'
	d.	*yaḥtaqiru zaydun hindan*	'Zayd scorns Hind'
	e.	*šāhada zaydun hindan*	'Zayd saw Hind'
	f.	*samiᶜtu ṣawtan jamīlan*	'I heard a beautiful voice'

Here the verb does not indicate action, the subject is not actor though the object may be thought of as a goal, and it is evident that there is no extension of action from an actor to a goal.

In light of the above inadequacies of the traditional notion of transitivity it is suggested here that its semantic definition be modified in such a way that not every transitive verb be required to indicate action. The verbs in (3) indicate experiences rather than actions, but the concept of extension is discernible in these sentences; thus the verb in (3a, b, c, d) indicates an experience extending from an experiencer or undergoer to a goal. It will be noticed that while the subject is necessarily affected, the object is not; the important thing, however, is that the extension of the experience is from the subject to the object and not vice versa. The same can be claimed about sentences (3e, f); in spite of the fact that scientifically the object in these sentences is the source or causer and the subject is affected, what we are concerned with here is the experience of seeing or hearing not the travel of light rays or sound waves. Thus transitivity can be made to indicate the extension of not only an action but also of an experience from one element to another.

Another inadequacy of the notion of transitivity, even as redefined above, is that it fails to account for certain intuitively discernible relationships in the Arabic verbal system.

Consider the following pair of sentences:

(4)	a.	*ʔinkasara al-zujāju*	'The glass broke'
	b.	*kasara zaydun al-zujāja*	'Zayd broke the glass'

On the surface the difference between these two sentences is the same as that between the sentences of (1): the verb in (1a) and (4a) is intransitive, does not have an object, and its subject has the nominative case ending *u(n)*, while the verb in (1b) and (4b) is transitive, has a subject which has the nominative case ending *un*, and an object which has the accusative case ending *a(n)*. A more careful consideration of sentences (4) whose case frames are [______ Patient] and [_____ Agent Patient], respectively, shows that the verb in a is morphologically derived from that in b, and that the only difference between them is the presence of the Agent in b and its absence in a. Except for this difference, the meaning expressed by the two verbs is the same: the semantic relationship between the verb and *al-zujāj* 'the glass' in both sentences is the same in spite of the fact that *al-zujāj* has the nominative case ending in a and the accusative case ending in b. This intuitively discernible semantic relationship between the two verbs in (4) is blurred by an insistence on *al-mafᶜūl* 'the acted upon' being optional and *al-fāᶜil* 'the actor' obligatory.

The facts presented in this section show that transitivity even as redefined does not adequately account for the syntactic and semantic characteristics of the Arabic verb and its relation to sentence organization. To provide an adequate account one has to look elsewhere for an answer.

5.2.2 Ergativity

The relationship that holds between sentences like (4) on the deep structure level finds surface realization in ergative languages like Basque, Eskimo, Georgian, and Samoan which most linguists take as languages in which the object of the transitive verb and the subject of the intransitive verb have the same case marker; this case marker, which is often the nominative, is distinguished from that of the subject of a transitive verb which is called the ergative. The following illustrative Basque sentences are taken from John Anderson (1968:9):

(5)	a.	aita-k	ogia	jan du	'The father has eaten the bread'
		'father'	'bread'	'has eaten'	
	b.	aita	ethorri		'The father has gone'
		'father'	'has gone'		
	c.	ogia	ona	da	'The bread is good'
		'bread'	'good'	'be'	

The object in a and the subjects in b and c have the same (null) case marker. The subject in a has the ergative (-k) case marker.

John Lyons (1968) and M. A. K. Halliday (1967–68) reject such definitions of ergative languages. According to them, the surface structure of ergative languages should not be described in terms of transitivity; rather a language like Eskimo or Basque, for example, has an ergativity system of clause organization in the surface structure which semantically presupposes the existence of causation, causer, and affected (the last two terms are borrowed from Halliday whose main arguments and those of Lyons are adopted here). Thus what is equivalent to a transitive verb, call it an ergative verb, requires a causer and an affected while a nonergative verb requires an affected only, i.e., the causer is obligatory and the affected is optional in sentences of ergative languages. Again the semantic structure of sentences of ergative languages does not always reflect what is semantically predicted by the ergativity pattern of sentences as shown by the following sentences from Basque and Eskimo respectively:

(6)	a.	aita 'father'	ethorri 'has gone'		'The father has gone'
	b.	qimmi-q 'dog'	agna-p 'woman'	takubaa 'see'	'The woman sees the dog'

The 'subject' (nominative) in a is not affected. The 'subject' (ergative 'agna-p') in b is not causer, and the 'object' (nominative 'qimmi-q') is not affected.

We have seen from sentences of (4) above that an ergativity relationship holds between the two sentences on the level of the deep structure. This ergativity relationship holds between the majority of pairs of verbs that are traditionally classified into transitive and intransitive. Such verbs are morphologically related: either the transitive is derived from the intransitive as in *māta* 'to die' ⟶ *?amāta* 'to cause to die,' or the intransitive is derived from the transitive as in *qaṭa*^{c}*a* 'to cut' ⟶ *?inqaṭa*^{c}*a* 'to get cut.' Consider the following sentences, where sentences (4) are rewritten as (7.1):

(7)	1a.	*?inkasara al-zujāju*	'The glass broke'
	b.	*kasara zaydun al-zujāja*	'Zayd broke the glass'
	2a.	*?infataḥa al-bābu*	'The door opened'
	b.	*fataḥa zaydun al-bāba*	'Zayd opened the door'
	3a.	*?intašara al-xabaru*	'The piece of news spread'
	b.	*našarat al-jarīdatu al-xabara*	'The newspaper spread the piece of news'
	4a.	*mātat hindun*	'Hind died'
	b.	*?amāta zaydun hindan*	'Zayd caused Hind to die'
	5a.	*d̲ābat al-šam*^{c}*atu*	'The candle melted'
	b.	*?ad̲āba zaydun al-šam*^{c}*ata*	'Zayd melted the candle'
	6a.	*ḥazinat hindun*	'Hind became sad'
	b.	*?aḥzana zaydun hindan*	'Zayd made Hind sad'

Although surface structurally the relationship is a transitivity relationship between the verbs in a and those in b, semantically or deep-structurally it is an ergativity relationship. The semantic difference between a and b is describable in terms of the presence or absence of the causer rather than in terms of the precence or absence of the goal. The affected is obligatory in all sentences of (7); the causer is optional; it occurs in the b sentences but not in the a ones. Thus the deep structure of Arabic sentences like those in (7) can be better described in terms of ergativity than in terms of transitivity, that is, in terms of cause and effect rather than in terms of action and goal.

One might get the impression from the above discussion that there is no validity to the actor-goal analysis and that we are discarding the concept of transitivity in favor of the concept of ergativity; we have shown above, however, that neither the transitivity pattern nor the ergativity pattern can alone account for the sentence organization in the deep structure of ergative as well as transitive languages. To illustrate the point let us consider the following simple sentence:

(8)	*d̲ahaba zaydun*	'Zayd went away'

Arabic presupposes that Zayd is actor in this sentence while Eskimo presupposes that it is affected. The normal interpretation of this sentence is that Zayd "did something" and in answer to a question like *māḏā faᶜala zaydun?* 'what did Zayd do?' sentence (8) would be an appropriate answer. But sentence (8) could be also used to describe a situation in which Zayd is a very sick man who flew unconscious on a plane from Beirut to Paris for medical treatment, and in answer to a question like *māḏā jarā li zaydin?* 'what happened to Zayd?' sentence (8) would be an appropriate answer. Consider now sentence (9):

(9) *waqaᶜa zaydun* 'Zayd fell'

Arabic presupposes that Zayd is actor in this sentence and Eskimo affected. The normal interpretation of the sentence is that Zayd is affected. But if Zayd is playing a role on the stage whereby he falls, an agentive interpretation would be appropriate. Thus what cannot be accounted for in terms of transitivity can be accounted for in terms of ergativity and vice versa. It must not be understood from the above that every Arabic one place verb is interpretable as either actor or affected. Some one place verbs in Arabic will hardly admit of an agentive interpretation, as can be seen from the following sentences:

(10) a. *māta zaydun* 'Zayd died'
b. *yaʔisa zaydun* 'Zayd became desperate'
c. *mariḍa zaydun* 'Zayd became sick'
d. *saqaṭa al-ḥāʔiṭu* 'The wall fell'
e. *ʔinqaṭaᶜa al-ḥablu* 'The rope got cut'

Other one place verbs will hardly admit a nonagentive interpretation as can be seen from the following sentences:

(11) a. *sabaḥa zaydun* 'Zayd swam'
b. *mašā zaydun* 'Zayd walked'
c. *qafaza al-waladu* 'The boy jumped'
d. *laᶜibat al-bintu* 'The girl played'
e. *ṭārat al-ṭāʔiratu* 'The airplane flew'

(Concerning sentence e, the reader may recall that in Chapter II we defined agency in terms of causation and activity rather than in terms of intentionality.)

The overlap of transitivity and ergativity can be illustrated also by examining the verbs that are known traditionally as transitive. Consider the following sentence:

(12) *qatala zaydun ᶜamran* 'Zayd killed 'Amr'

The verb in this sentence indicates "causation" as well as "extension of action," the subject *zaydun* is causer as well as actor; and the object *ᶜamran* is affected as well as goal. In other words, sentence (12) is describable in terms of transitivity as well as in terms of ergativity. Therefore both transitivity and ergativity are needed to describe Arabic sentences.

5.2.3 A Verb Typology in Terms of Transitivity and Ergativity

In this section the traditional classification of Arabic verbs into transitive and intransitive and into active and passive will be discarded in favor of a classification of

Arabic verbs in light of transitivity as well as ergativity relationships that hold between the elements of a proposition.

Consider the following sentences:

(13)	a.	*kasara zaydun al-zujāja*	'Zayd broke the window'
	b.	*kusira al-zujāju*	'The window was broken'
	c.	*?inkasara al-zujāju*	'The window broke'

The verbs in both b and c look like one place verbs: in both sentences, there is a subject noun phrase which has the case role Patient, is in the nominative case, and has the nominative case ending -u; and there is no accusative object. On the other hand, the verb in a is a two place verb, has an accusative object that has the accusative case ending *-an*, and has a nominative subject that has the nominative case ending *-un*. Thus on the basis of this data alone, one would be tempted to classify the verbs in (13) into two groups, the *kasara* group and the *kusira* and *?inkasara* group. As a matter of fact, such a grouping has been proposed by some modern Arab grammarians who wanted to "liberalize" the Arabic language and "save it from the unnecessary and useless complications imposed on it by the old Arab grammarians." Mahdī al-Makhzūmī (1964: 47), for example, suggests that the subjects in b and c both be considered *fāᶜil* 'actor' and that the distinction made by the early Arab grammarians between them be ignored.

But let us now examine the differences between b and c. A brief survey of the terminology used by the medieval Arab grammarians would be useful here. They called the passive verb *al-fiᶜl al-majhūl fāᶜiluhu* 'The action of which the actor is unknown' or *fiᶜl mā lam yusamma fāᶜiluhu* 'The action whose actor has not been named.' They called the subject of the passive *nā?ib al-fāᶜil* or *qā?im maqām al-fāᶜil* 'supplying the place of the actor'; Sībawayhi (1:10) calls it simply *al-mafᶜūl* 'the acted upon'; according to him the subject in sentences like a above is a "nominativized actor" and the subject in sentences like b is a "nominativized 'acted upon.' " Thus according to these grammarians, the verb in b has an actor while the verb in c does not. This is in agreement with the analysis proposed here, where the passive verb in b indicates external causation while the verb in c does not; that is, the passive embodies the notion of a causer in spite of the fact that this causer does not occur on the surface, while the verb in c does not embody the notion of a causer grammatically, and it is immaterial whether or not an external causer is required in the real world. Thus the subject in b is affected by an external causer that is distinct from itself while the subject in c, though affected, is not affected by an external causer that is distinct from itself. It will be seen that in sentence a also the object is affected by an external causer which is distinct from itself but which in this case is present in the sentence, namely the noun phrase *zayd*. Therefore, a classification of verbs should group verbs like the ones in (13a and b) in one group and verbs like the verb in (13c) in another group. In terms of the ergativity system discussed above, the subject in (13a) is causer and the object is affected, the subject in (13b) is affected and the causer is implicit, and the subject in (13c) is affected and there is no causer. In feature terms we may adopt the following proposal made by Halliday (1968: 185): "There is an opposition of features middle/nonmiddle such that the nonmiddle is interpretable as embodying external causation, the existence of a causer that is not identical with, or at least is treated as discrete from, the affected." In accordance with this feature specification the verbs in sentences (13a and b) above have the feature: (– Middle) while the verb in sentence (13c) has the feature (+ Middle).

The semantic relationships presupposed by an ergativity system of sentence organization finds evidence in the morphological distribution of the verb in Arabic. Thus a transitivization morphological process exists side by side with a detransitivization process, that is, from a primary form I intransitive verb a transitive verb may be morphologically derived, and from a primary form I transitive verb an intransitive verb may morphologically be derived. Thus in the following sentences:

(14) 1a.	*jalasa ^{c}amrun*	' 'Amr sat down
b.	*?ajlasa zaydun ^{c}amran*	'Zayd made 'Amr sit down'
2a.	*fataḥa zaydun al-bāba*	'Zayd opened the door
b.	*?infataḥa al-bābu*	'The door opened'

the transitive verb is derived in 1, primary in 2 while the intransitive verb is primary in 1, derived in 2.

In accordance with the above discussion we label morphologically nonderived transitive verbs as transitive and morphologically derived transitive verbs as causative; we also label morphologically nonderived intransitive verbs as intransitive and morphologically dervied intransitive verbs as reflexive. Sentences (15) and (16) illustrate this classification:

(15) (i) Transitive

a.	*kasara zaydun al-zujāja*	'Zayd broke the glass'
b.	*qaṭa^{c}a zaydun al-ḥabla*	'Zayd cut the rope'
c.	*xada^{c}a zaydun ^{c}amran*	'Zayd cheated 'Amr'
d.	*^{c}aḏḏaba zaydun hindan*	'Zayd tortured Hind'

(ii) Reflexive

a.	*?inkasara al-zujāju*	'The glass broke'
b.	*?inqaṭa^{c}a al-ḥablu*	'The rope got cut'
c.	*?inxada^{c}a ^{c}amrun*	' 'Amr was cheated'
d.	*ta^{c}aḏḏabat hindun*	'Hind got tortured'

(The English translations in b, c and d should not be interpreted as implying external causation; they should be interpreted inchoatively in order to reflect the meaning of the corresponding Arabic sentences.)

(16) (i) Intransitive

a.	*māta ^{c}amrun*	' 'Amr died'
b.	*ḥazina ^{c}amrun*	' 'Amr was sad'
c.	*ḏābat al-šam^{c}atu*	'The candle melted'
d.	*jalasat hindun*	'Hind sat down'

(ii) Causative

a.	*?amāta zaydun ^{c}amran*	'Zayd caused 'Amr to die'
b.	*ḥazana zaydun ^{c}amran*	'Zayd caused 'Amr to be sad'
c.	*ḏawwaba zaydun al-šam^{c}ata*	'Zayd melted the candle'
d.	*?ajlasa zaydun hindan*	'Zayd sat Hind down'

In terms of Halliday's features middle/nonmiddle, intransitive and reflexive verbs are (+ middle), and transitive and causative verbs are (– middle).

It will be noted that in accordance with the theoretical framework followed in this book, all these syntactic elements of the Arabic verbal system are syntactic features in the Q component. This would entail a hierarchy of features in that component: Halliday's (± middle) are superfeatures that dominate the features (± transitive), (± intransitive), (± causative), and (± reflexive). Passive verbs are (– Middle), by definition, because they indicate external causation or action; they are thus either (+ causative) or (+ transitive).

5.2.4 Transitivity, Ergativity and the Case Roles

The analysis of the Arabic verbal system, in terms of transitivity and ergativity, proposed in this chapter complements the analysis of the Arabic verbal system, in terms of the case frame of the verb, proposed in Chapter III. The ergativity term "causer" and the transitivity term "actor" can be replaced by the case role Agent proposed and discussed in Chapter II. The ergativity term "affected" can be replaced by the case role Patient and the transitivity term "goal" can be replaced by the case role Target, both of which were proposed and discussed in Chapter II. The modification in the definition of transitivity proposed here is of great importance and is essential. The transitive and/or ergative relationships in the verbal system of any language are not describable in terms of actor/goal and causer/affected only, but also in terms of affected/goal as we have seen from sentences (3) above. This important fact was established in Chapter III, where it was proposed that passivizable verbs did not only have case frames like [_____Agent Target] and [____ Agent Patient] but also [____ Patient Target].

5.3. Syntactic Derivation of Passives

Let us examine now the effects of the above analysis and proposals on the process of passivization. In Chapter III the following case frames of passivizable verbs were given:

(17) a. [________Agent Patient]
b. [________Agent Target]
c. [________Patient Target]

In an active sentence whose verb has the case frame (17a) or (17b) the Agent is specified, while in a passive sentence with the same case frame the Agent is unspecified. In an active sentence whose verb has the case frame (17c) the Patient is specified, and in a passive sentence with the same case frame it is not. In other words the passive is not transformationally derived from the active. The deep structure of sentences (18a) and (18b) below would roughly be (19a) and (19b) respectively:

(18) a. *qatala zaydun ^{c}amran* 'Zayd killed 'Amr'
b. *qutila ^{c}amrun* ' 'Amr was killed'

(19) a.

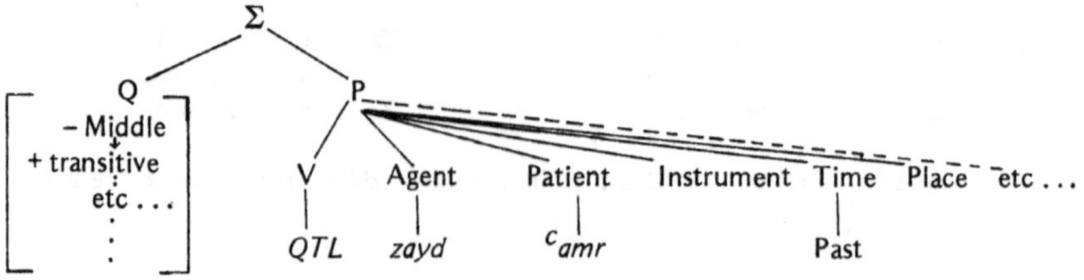

(19) b.

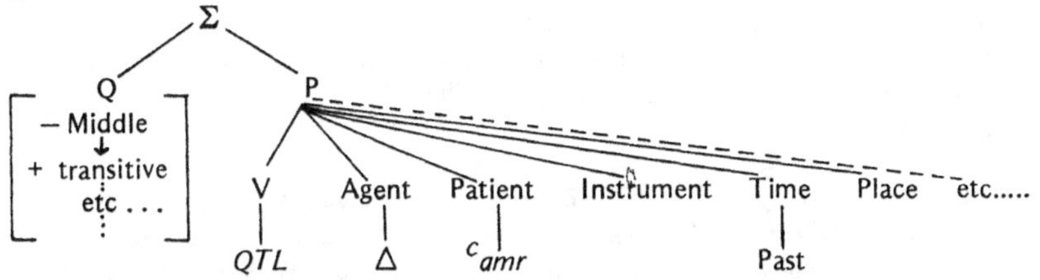

As mentioned before, the verb *qatala* is implemental; therefore in the presence of an animate agent an Instrument role is needed. There is also a time and a place for the action indicated by sentences like (18); the branch labelled "etc. . ." stands for other unspecified roles. Thus in the deep structure all the necessary case roles are represented by nodes that do not branch. On the way to the surface structure these nodes and the branches that connect them with P get deleted. The node Time is specified only vaguely with respect to "Past." Lexicalization transformations incorporate the tense (i.e., Past) and the features [– Middle] and (+ transitive] into the verb which is represented by the root *QTL* under the V node. After the tense is incorporated into the verb, the Time node and its branches get deleted. In accordance with the hierarchy among the elements of the P component, the Agent is the most eligible candidate for becoming the subject of the verb. Thus it becomes subject and gets assigned the nominative case ending *-un* by the rule of subjectivization (cf. Chapter III). Another rule, call it objectivization, assigns *ᶜamr* the surface case ending *-an*. Other agreement transformations give the correct form of the verb. The above rules give the surface structure (18b).

In the deep structure (19b) the Agent is unspecified. The term "unspecified" is not used here in the sense used by Chomsky, Hasegawa or others. It does not necessarily refer only to "someone" or "something"; it dominates a dummy Δ which may refer to any member of a set of noun phrases that may be the Agent in any active sentence whose verb is the active verb *qatala*. The dummy Agent may be treated by the speaker as fully recoverable information. Thus if someone utters the sentences *qutila ᶜamrun* 'Amr was killed' and the hearer asks the question *man qatalahu?* 'who killed him?; the speaker may answer if he wishes *qatalahu zaydun* 'Zayd killed him.' Just as the incorporation of the unspecified time (i.e., tense) in the verb results in a surface form of the verb that indicates time, the incorporation of the unspecified Agent (i.e., Δ) in the verb results in the surface form of the verb that indicates Passivity, that is, unspecified external agency. Thus passivization in Arabic is the result of the incorporation of the unspecified Agent in the verb. Following such incorporation the Agent node and its branches are deleted. In the absence of the Agent from the P component the case hierarchy enables the Patient to become the subject of the verb. The subjectivization rule assigns the nominative case ending to the Patient *ᶜamr*. Application of all other necessary rules gives (18b).

5.4 Three Place Nonmiddle Verbs

All the nonmiddle verbs considered so far in this chapter have been verbs that involve two participants-Agent/Patient, Agent/Target, and Patient/Target. Many nonmiddle verbs are three place verbs; they take a nominative subject and two accusative objects and thus involve three participants. Two place nonmiddle verbs were divided in this chapter into two classes: transitive and causative. It was stated that two place transitive verbs were not morphologically derived from intransitive verbs, but that two place causative verbs were morphologically derived from intransitive verbs. In the same manner three place nonmiddle verbs may be divided into two groups: transitive and causative. The transitive verbs are morphologically nonderived, but the causative verbs are morphologically derived from two place transitives. The following sentences illustrate three place transitive verbs:

(20)	a.	*saqā zaydun ᶜamran mā?an*	'Zayd gave 'Amr water to drink'
	b.	*?aṭᶜama zaydun ᶜamran xubzan*	'Zayd fed 'Amr bread'
	c.	*manaḥat al-jāmiᶜatu hindan jā?izatan*	'The university awarded Hind a prize'

The following sentences illustrate transitive two place verbs and the corresponding three place causative verbs derived from them morphologically:

(21)	1a.	*darasa ᶜamrun al-tārīxa*	''Amr studied history'
	b.	*darrasa zaydun ᶜamran al-tārīxa*	'Zayd taught 'Amr history'
	2a.	*zāra al-wazīru al-qāhirata*	'The minister visited Cairo'
	b.	*?azāra al-ra?īsu al-wazīra al-qāhirata*	'The president made the minister visit Cairo'
	3a.	*ġazā ?abū qatādatin baṭna ?iḍamin*	'Abū Qatādah invaded the Iḍam tribe'
	b.	*?aġzā al-rasūlu ?abā qatādatin baṭna ?iḍamin*	'The prophet made Abū Qatādah invade the Iḍam tribe

The above sentences are passivizable and either of the two accusatives objects of each of the sentences of (20) and (21a) may be the subject of the passive verb. The case frame of the verbs in (20) is [_____Agent Patient Target]; the case frame of the verb in (21.1b) is [_____Agent Patient Range]; and the case frame of the verbs in (21.2b and 21.3b) is [_____Agent Patient Target]. Two place transitive verbs whose case frame is [_______ Patient Target] may also be causativized as can be seen from the following pair of sentences:

(22)	a.	*samiᶜa ᶜamrun ?uġniyatan jamīlatan*	''Amr heard a beautiful song'
	b.	*?asmaᶜa zaydun ᶜamran ?uġniyatan jamīlatan*	'Zayd made 'Amr hear a beautiful song'

The case frame of the verb in (22b) is [_____Agent Patient Target]. The case frames of the verbs in (20), (21b) and (22b) can be summarized by (23):

(23)	a.	[__________	Agent	Patient	Target]
	b.	[__________	Agent	Patient	Range]

In the passive sentences corresponding to the above three-place active sentences the Agent is unspecified. After the unspecified Agent is incorporated in the verb, as was explained earlier in this chapter, the Patient comes to be in a position which enables it to be the subject of the passive verb. In order for the Target or the Range to become subject of the passive, a transformation that interchanges the Agent with the Patient or Range must be applied before the incorporation of the unspecified Agent in the verb (i.e., before passivization).

In sentences whose verb is a three-place nonmiddle verb, either of the nonagentive noun phrases or both may be unspecified in the deep structure as shown below:

(24)	a.	*?udarrisu zaydan al-faransiyyata*	'I teach Zayd French'
	b.	*?udarrisu al-faransiyyata*	'I teach French'
	c.	*?udarrisu zaydan*	'I teach Zayd'
	d.	*?udarrisu fī jāmi^{c}ati hārfard*	'I teach at Harvard University'

The verb in all of these sentences has the same case frame.

5.5 Reflexives

5.5.1 Two-Place Reflexive Verbs

We have shown in this chapter that what we have labeled reflexive verbs are derived morphologically from two-place transitive verbs. Though not numerous, there are two-place verbs that may be derived from three-place causatives as in the following sentences:

(25)	1a.	*^{c}allama zaydun ^{c}amran al-qur?āna*	'Zayd taught 'Amr the Koran'
	b.	*ta^{c}allama ^{c}amrun al-qur?āna*	' 'Amr learned the Koran'
	2a.	*d̲akkara zaydun ^{c}amran bi hindin*	'Zayd reminded 'Amr of Hind'
	b.	*tad̲akkara ^{c}amrun hindan*	' 'Amr remembered Hind'

The case frames of sentences (25) are (26) below:

(26)	1a.	[	Agent Patient Range]
	b.	[	Patient Range]
	2a.	[	Agent Patient Target]
	b.	[	Patient Target]

The relationship between the verb and the Patient in (25b) is a reflexive relationship, while that between the verb and the Range or Target is a transitive one. The transitivity relationship is traceable to the nonderived transitive verbs from which the verbs in (25a) are morphologically derived as can be seen in the following sentences:

(27)	a.	*^{c}alima ^{c}amrun al-qur?āna*	' 'Amr knew the Koran'
	b.	*d̲akara ^{c}amrun hindan*	' 'Amr mentioned Hind'

The verbs of (25) are passivizable, as predicted from their case frames (26). Thus the verbs in (25b) provide examples of reflexive verbs which are not middle verbs. This means that a distinction between reflexive and middle is sometimes necessary in spite of the fact that in most cases reflexive verbs are middle.

5.5.2 Reflexivity

With most verbs that require an animate subject (Agent or Patient) the reflexive is overtly expressed by means of a reflexive pronoun. Such reflexive constructions may be called overt reflexives and are illustrated in the following sentences:

(28)	a.	*qatala zaydun nafsahu*	'Zayd killed himself'
	b.	*lāmat hindun nafsahā*	'Hind blamed herself'
	c.	*kariha zaydun nafsahu*	'Zayd hated himself'

Overt reflexives are not possible where the subject is inanimate as can be seen from (29).

(29)	a.	**kasara al-zujāju nafsahu*	'The glass broke itself'
	b.	**fataḥa al-bābu nafsahu*	'The door opened itself'
	c.	**jammada al-mā?u nafsahu*	'The water froze itself'

Covert reflexives equivalent to sentences (29) but not to sentences (28) are possible, as can be seen from (30) and (31) below:

(30)	a.	**?inqatala zaydun*	'Zayd got killed'
	b.	**?inlāmat hindun*	'Hind got blamed'
	c.	**?inkaraha zaydun*	'Zayd got hated'

(31)	a.	*?inkasara al-zujāju*	'The glass broke'
	b.	*?infataḥa al-bābu*	'The door opened'
	c.	*tajammada al-mā?u*	'The water froze'

Let us examine now the difference between the following two sentences:

(32)	a.	*?inkasara al-zujāju*	'The glass broke'
	b.	*qatala zaydun nafsahu*	'Zayd killed himself'

Both of these sentences indicate that there is no external agency involved in the bringing about of the event (whether or not an external agent is required in the real world, for (32a), is immaterial). The absence of external causation explains the ungrammaticalness of passive constructions corresponding to (32). The difference between the two sentences is that there is no agency involved on the part of the Patient (*al-zujāju* 'the glass') in (32a) while agency is involved on the part of the patient (*nafsahu* 'himself') in (32b) where the Agent is identical with the Patient. Overt reflexives therefore are the real reflexives, while covert reflexives are more inchoatives than reflexives. The common denominator between the two types is the absence of external agency, which distinguishes them from nonmiddle active or passive constructions.

The verbs like those in (28) must indicate agency; this agency could be either external or internal and it finds expression in nonmiddle active or passive constructions, or in overt reflexive sentences, respectively, as can be seen in the following sentences:

(33)	a.	*qatala zaydun ^{c}amran* *'Zayd killed 'Amr'*	External Agency
	b.	*qutila ^{c}amrun* *''Amr was killed'*	

c. *qatala zaydun nafsahu* — Internal Agency
'Zayd killed himself'

On the other hand, verbs like those in (29) may indicate external agency but they may not indicate internal agency, as in the following sentences:

(34) a. *kasara zaydun al-zujāja* — External Agency
'Zayd broke the glass'
b. *kusira al-zujāju*
'The glass was broken'
c. **kasara al-zujāju nafsahu* — Internal Agency
'The glass broke itself'

Verbs like those in (31) do not indicate either external or internal agency; they simply do not indicate agency and are thus inchoative verbs. No inchoative may be derived from qatala 'to kill,' for example, because killing cannot come about without the intervention of an Agent which is a concrete person, animal, or thing, and which can be identical with the Patient in overt reflexives. Hence the ungrammaticalness of (30). Structurally, the reflexivity of covert reflexives (i.e., inchoatives) is represented as a syntactic feature in the Q component but that of overt reflexives is represented in the P component. Thus the verbs in sentences like (28) above are transitive and their case frames are [_____ Agent Patient], [_____ Agent Target], and [_____ Patient Target], respectively. The relationship between the two case roles in each of the sentences of (28) is that they refer to the same entity. Thus the underlying form of sentence (28a), for example, would roughly be something like (35) in the P component:

(35) *qatala* $zayd_i$ $zayd_i$ — 'Zayd$_i$ killed Zayd$_i$'

Sentence (35) clearly indicates that there is no external agency; hence there is no passive sentence corresponding to (35), since passivization requires at least two nonidentical participants, the first of which being unspecified, the second specified. In (35) the two noun phrases can only be either both unspecified or both specified. The nonpassivizability of (35) (i.e., 28a) has nothing to do with the syntactic features of the verb; it is a characteristic of the whole proposition.

It should be noted that the subject (i.e., Agent or Patient) of overt reflexives, in addition to being animate noun phrases, can be noun phrases like ᶜā?ilah 'family,' hizb 'political party,' ?ummah 'nation,' munaẓẓamah 'organization' etc. . . as in the following sentences:

(36) *ḥalla al-ḥizbu nafsahu* — 'The political party dissolved itself'

One should not infer from the above discussion that all Arabic verbs are only either covert or overt reflexives; certain verbs are both, as can be seen from the following sentences:

(37) 1a. *xadaᶜa zaydun nafsahu* — 'Zayd cheated himself'
b. *?inxadaᶜa zaydun* — 'Zayd got cheated'
2a. *ᶜaḏḏabat hindun nafsahā* — 'Hind tortured herself'
b. *taᶜaḏḏabat hindun* — 'Hind got tortured'

3a.	*ḥalla al-ḥizbu nafsahu*	'The political party dissolved itself'
b.	*?inḥalla al-ḥizbu*	'The political party got dissolved'

Now consider the following sentences:

(38)	a.	*qatala zaydun$_i$ ibnahu$_i$*	'Zayd$_i$ killed his$_i$ son'
	b.	*mašaṭat hindun$_i$ ša^{c}rahā$_i$*	'Hind$_i$ combed her$_i$ hair'

The suffix pronouns refer to the subjects in (38). Sentences (39) below look as if they are the passive constructions corresponding to sentences (38), respectively:

(39)	a.	*qutila ibnu zaydin*	'Zayd's son was killed'
	b.	*mušiṭa ša^{c}ru hindin*	'Hind's hair was combed'

The unspecified Agents in (39), however, cannot be interpreted in such a way as to refer to the Agents, *zayd* and *hind*, in (38). The case frame of the verbs in sentences (38) and (39) is [_____Agent Patient]. The Patient is a noun phrase that contains in it a noun phrase identical to the Agent noun phrase in (38), which explains why passivization for these sentences is blocked.

Identity of noun phrases in the P component explains the nonpassivizability of other types of constructions in the language. Consider the following sentence:

(40)	*?arāda zaydun min ^{c}amrin ?an yastaqīla*	'Zayd wanted 'Amr to resign'

The case frame of the matrix verb of this sentence is [_____Patient Source Target], where *zayd* has the case role Patient, *^{c}amr* Source, and the complement *?an yastaqīla* Target. Although the [_____ Patient Source . . .] portion of the case frame in question is resistant to passivization, the [_____Patient . . . Target] portion is not; hence the grammaticalness of (41) below, which is the passive construction corresponding to (40).

(41)	*?urīda min ^{c}amrin ?an yastaqīla*	'It was wanted from 'Amr that he resign'

Now consider the following sentence:

(42)	*?arāda zaydun ?an yastaqīla*	'Zayd wanted to resign'

The case frame of the matrix verb in (42) looks on the surface like [_____Patient Target], which would predict that a sentence like (42) is passivizable, but it is clear from (43) below, which looks like the passive construction corresponding to (44), that the unspecified agent must not refer to the subject of the embedded sentence.

(43)	*?urīda ?an yastaqīla zaydun*	'It was wanted that Zayd resign'

The above case frame is not the correct one for the matrix verb in (42); the deep structure of (42) is roughly (44):

(44)

?arāda	*zayd* $_i$	*(min)*	*zayd* $_i$	*(?an)*	*yastaqīla*	*zayd* $_i$
'want'	'Zayd $_i$	'from'	'Zayd $_i$'	'that'	'resign'	'Zayd $_i$'

The case frame of the matrix verb in (44) is [____ Patient Source Target], where the first *zayd* is Patient, the second *zayd* is Source and the complement sentence *?an yastaqīla zayd* is Target. Although the portion [____ Patient . . . . . Target] of the case frame in question allows passivization, the fact that it contains a noun phrase which is identical to the Patient of the matrix sentence necessarily blocks it.

In the same manner it can be shown that a sentence like (45) below is nonpassivizable:

(45) *?urīdu ?an ?aḏhaba* 'I want to go'

It follows that passivization is affected not only by the syntactic features and case frame of the verb but also by the syntactic and semantic relations between the nonverbal elements of the P component.

The following conclusions have been reached in this chapter:

(i) The traditional definition of transitivity is modified to indicate not only the extension of an action from an Agent to a Target or Patient but also the extension of an experience from a Patient to a Target.

(ii) Arabic verbs are classified not only on the basis of a transitivity system of clause organization but also on the basis of an ergativity system of clause organization.

(iii) The common denominator between active and passive sentences is that both of them indicate external agency which is explicit in active sentences, unspecified in passive sentences.

(iv) The passive transformation involves the incorporation of the unspecified Agent (or Patient) in the verb which as a result takes the passive form

and

(v) Reflexive constructions do not have passive counterparts because they do not indicate external agency: overt reflexives indicate internal agency while covert reflexives indicate no agency.

6 Conclusion

This book has been an attempt at describing the process of passivization in Arabic and its relation to causation and transitivity. It represents the first major syntactic study of Arabic published so far within the framework of the case grammar theory of syntax. In accordance with this framework the Arabic sentence has a Q component (which is a categorial element through which verbal qualifiers such as Interrogative, Negative, Causative, Reflexive, etc., affecting the entire sentence, are introduced into sentences) and a P component (which consists of a verb and one or more deep structure cases or case roles such as Agent, Patient, Target, Goal, etc., each associated with the verb in a particular case relationship). Twelve deep structure cases in the latter component are posited and a hierarchy among them is assumed to exist (Chapter II).

The following are the major points that have been made in this work:

(i) The traditional syntactic definition of transitivity as a basis for passivization is inadequate and counterexamples to the claim that transitivity triggers passivization are presented (cf. 1.1). The traditional semantic definition of transitivity has also been shown to be inadequate and is modified to include not only the extension of an action from an Agent to a Target or Patient but also the extension of an experience from a Patient to a Target (cf. 5.1). But it is passivizability rather than transitivity which determines passivization. Passivizability is defined semantically in terms of the case frame of each individual verb in the language. Verbs with the following case frames are passivizable in Arabic:

[———Agent Patient]
[———Agent Target]
[———Patient Target]
[———Agent $\text{Range}_{\text{count, nongeneric}}$] (cf. 3.4.2)

(ii) The notion of passivizability has proven very useful in solving some outstanding problems related to passivization:

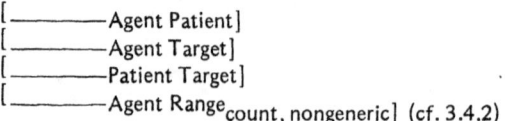

(a) The nonpassivizability of verbs like kallafa 'to cost' and wazana 'to $\text{weigh}_{\text{itr}}$' and šābaha 'to resemble', which have always been considered exceptions to passivization in various syntactic analyses of English, is easily and naturally accounted for in terms of their case frames. The case frame of verbs like the first two [____Target Range], and that of verbs like the third [____ Target Goal], are those of nonpassivizable verbs (c.f., 3.4.1.3 and 3.4.1.4).

(b) Verbs whose case frame is [____ Agent $\text{Range}_{\text{generic}}$]' [____Agent Time], or [____ Agent Place] are passivizable in CA but not in MSA. A targetization rule transforms the $\text{Range}_{\text{generic}}$' Time, or Place, in these case frames, into a Target, thus making them a case frame of passivizable verbs, namely [____Agent Target]. This is an instance of syntactic historical change in the grammar of Arabic: the targetization rule, which is a rule of CA, has been lost in MSA (cf. 3.4.3).

(c) Sentences whose matrix verbs are verbs of Certainty and Doubt are clausally complex. Their case frame is [____Patient Target]. Sentences like:

ᶜalimtu ʔaxāka karīman	'I knew your brother to be generous'

were claimed to be derived from structures like the following by subject raising:

ᶜalimtu $[_{\Sigma}$ *ʔaxūka karīmun* $_{\Sigma}]$

(where the embedded sentence is assigned the Target case role). More investigation, however, is needed to prove or disprove the validity of such a subject raising analysis (cf. 3.4.2.9).

(iii) Arabic passive constructions are agentless on the surface structure level, and there is no genuine agentive particle in Arabic equivalent to English by or French par. Such passive sentences as *qutila zaydun ᶜalā yadi ᶜaduwwihi* 'Zayd was killed at the hand of his enemy' which "indirectly" express the agent and which, incidentally, are widely attested in CA and the Koran and are not modern innovations, as some Arabists claim, are not surface structure full passives with agents and do not syntactically and/or semantically correspond, for example, to English or French full passives.

On the deep structure level, however, Arabic passive constructions are not agentless; rather, the agent is unspecified. This agent may be an Agent or a Patient depending on whether the verb is an active or an inchoative verb.

(iv) Passivizable as well as passive verbs are labelled nonmiddle verbs in contrast to nonpassivizable verbs which are labelled Middle verbs. Nonmiddle verbs indicate external agency which is explicit in active sentences but implicit or unspecified in passive ones; middle verbs do not. Nonmiddle verbs have the feature (-middle) in the Q component and are of two types: transitive and causative; transitives are basic form I verbs, while causatives are morphologically or prepositionally derived verbs. The feature (—middle) is a superfeature that dominates the feature (+ causative) or (+ transitive) in the Q component. Middle verbs have the feature (+ middle) in the Q component and are of two types: intransitive and reflexive; the former are basic form I verbs, while the latter are morphologically derived verbs. The feature (+ middle) is a superfeature that dominates the feature (+ intransitive) or (+ reflexive) in the Q component. These superfeatures have tentatively been posited in this wok; further study and investigation are needed to justify such a hierarchy in the Q component.

This verb classification is based upon an analysis of Arabic in terms of not only transitivity but ergativity as well. On the deep structure level Arabic exhibits an ergativity system as well as a transitivity system of clause organization. Transitivity predicts extension of action or experience from an actor or an experiencer to a goal; ergativity predicts causation involving a causer and an affected. Both ergativity and transitivity are necessary to describe the Arabic verbal system.

(v) Causatives are of two types: overt and covert. In the former, a clause is embedded on the surface as the complement of a matrix verb like *jaᶜala* 'to make (causative),' *ʔarġama* 'to force' etc. Covert causative verbs consist of four classes, three morphologically derived, one prepositionally derived (cf. Chapter IV). In general, intransitive, stative transitive, and inchoative transitive verbs are causativizable, active transitive verbs are not. However, in CA but not in MSA, some active transitives like *zāra* 'to visit' and *ġazā* 'to invade' are causativizable, which means that causativization in CA was more productive than it is in MSA. This is an instance of syntactic difference between the two varieties of Arabic. Another instance of syntactic development is the case of an intensive intransitive morphologically derived verb like *mawwata* 'to die in large numbers' in CA, which has become a causative two place verb *mawwata* 'to cause to die' in MSA. These instances of historical syntactic development have to be further investigated so that linguistically significant generalizations can be made.

Covert causatives are not syntactically derivable from overt causatives or from constructions in which the causative verb is a pro-verb or a semantic predicate. They are derived by a transformation which incorporates the causative feature from the Q component into the verb.

(vi) The passive transformation is a natural rule which simply involves the incorporation of the unspecified agent (Agent or Patient) in the verb which, as a result, takes the passive form. This rule provides the most appropriate and simplest account for the process of passivization in Arabic (cf. Chapter V). A very important finding in my study is the clear and unambiguous separation of the passivization process from the formation of the subject of the passive verb. The latter has nothing to do with the former or more precisely with the passive transformation. In point of fact it is no different from the formation of the subject of the nonpassive verb. A subjectivization rule simply assigns the nominative case to the noun phrase closest to the verb regardless of whether that verb is passive or active, provided that the noun phrase is not separated from the verb by a preposition. If it is and there is no other noun phrase that can become subject of the passive, the verb is assigned an impersonal subject, i.e., it is in the 3 m.s.

Bibliography

A. ARABIC REFERENCES

Al-Qur'ān al-Karīm. Beirut: al-Maktab al-Islāmī, 1386 H. /1966 A.D.

Abd al-Ḥamīd, Muḥammad Muḥyī al-Dīn, ed. (1956). *Awḍaḥ al-Masālik ilā Alfiyyat Ibn Mālik.* Cairo: al-Nasr Press.

————. (1967). *Sharḥ Ibn 'Aqīl.* Cairo: Al-Maktabah al-Tijāriyyah al-Kubrā.

Al-Astarābādhī, Raḍiyy al-Dīn. *Sharḥ Kāfiyat Ibn al-Ḥājib.* Cairo.

————. *Sharh Shāfiyat Ibn al-Ḥājib.* Edited by Muḥammad Nūr al-Ḥasan, Muḥammad al-Zafzāf, and Muḥammad Muḥyī al-Dīn Abd al-Ḥamīd. Cairo: Hijāzi Press.

Al-Ghalāyīnī, Muṣṭafā. (1963). *Jāmi' al-Durūs al-'Arabiyyah.* Beirut: al-Maktabah al-'Aṣriyyah.

Al-Ḥadīthī, Khadījah. (1965). *Abniyat al-Ṣarf fī Kitāb Sībawayhi.* Baghdad: Al-Nahḍah Bookshop.

Ḥasan, 'Abbās. (1971). *Al-Naḥw al-Wāfī.* Cairo: Dār al-Ma'ārif.

Ibn Fāirs, Aḥmad. (1951). *Mu' jam Maqāyīs al-Lughah.* Cairo: Dār Ihyā' al-Kutub al-'Arabiyyah, 1371 H.

Ibn Hishām, Abū Muḥammad. *Mughnī al-Labīb 'an Kutub al-A 'ārīb.* Edited by Muḥammad Muḥyī al-Dīn Abd al-Ḥamīd. Cairo: al-Maktabah al-Tijāriyyah al-Kubrā.

————. (1965). *Sharh Shudhur al-Dhahab.* Cairo: al-Sa'adah Press.

Ibn Jinnī, Abū al-Fatḥ. (1954). *Al-Munṣif. Sharḥ Ibn Jinnī li Kitāb al-Taṣrīf li al-Imām al-Māzinī.* Edited by Ibrāhīm Muṣṭafā and Abd Allah Amīn. Cairo: Muṣṭafā al-Bābī al-Ḥalabī.

Ibn al-Qūṭiyyah, Abū Bakr. (1894). *Kitāb al-Af'āl.* Edited by Ignazio Guidi. Leiden: E.J. Brill.

Ibn al-Sarrāj, Abū Bakr Muḥammad. (1965). *Al-Mūjaz fī al-Naḥw.* Edited by Muṣṭafa al-Shuwaymī and Bin Sālim Dāmirjī. Beirut: Badrān Press.

Ibn Ya'īsh, Muwaffaq al-Dīn. *Sharḥ al-Mufaṣṣal.* Cairo: Al-Munīriyyah Press.

Al-Makhzūmī, Mahdī. (1964). *Fī al-Naḥw al-'Arabī.* Beirut: Al-Maktabah al-'Aṣriyyah.

Al-Mutanabbī, Abū al-Ṭayyib. (1964). *Al-'Arf al-Tayyib fī Sharḥ Dīwān Abī al-Ṭayyib.* Edited by Nāṣīf al-Yāzijī. Beirut: Ṣādir Press and Beirut Press.

Sībawayhi, Abū Bishr. (1881 & 1889). *Kitāb Sībawayhi.* 2 Vols. Edited by Hartwig Derenbourg. Paris. Reprinted, Hildesheim, New York: Georg Olms Verlag.

Al-Ṭabarī, Abū Ja'far. (1962). *Tārīkh al-Ṭabarī.* Vol. 3. Edited by Muḥammad Abū al-Faḍl Ibrāhīm. Cairo: Dār al-Ma'ārif.

Al-Zamakhsharī, Jār Allah. (1879). *Al-Mufaṣṣal fī al-Naḥw.* Edited by J.P. Broch. Christianiae: Libraria P. T. Mallingii.

B. GENERAL REFERENCES

Abdel-Hamid, Ahmed Kamal El-Din. (1972). *A Transfer Grammar of English and Arabic.* Ph.D. dissertation. Austin: The University of Texas.

Abu Absi, Samir. (1972). *Passive-Reflexive Verbs in Lebanese.* Ph.D. dissertation. Bloomington: Indiana University.

Ali, Abdullah Yusuf, translator. (1946). *The Holy Qur'ān.* New York: Hafner Publishing Company.

Anderson, John. (1968). *"Ergative and Nominative in English,"* Journal of Linguistics, 4/1, 1–32.

Babcock, Sandra Scharff. (1972). *"Paraphrastic Causatives,"* Foundations of Language, 8/1, 30–43.

Bach, Emmon, and Harms, Robert T., eds. (1968). *Universals in Linguistic Theory.* New York: Holt, Rinehart and Winston, Inc.

Bakalla, M.H. (1975). *Bibliography of Arabic Linguistics.* London: Mansell.

Bates, Roberta Reed. (1969). *A Study in the Acquisition of Language.* Ph.D. dissertation. Austin: The University of Texas.

Bolinger, Dwight. (1977) *"Transitivity and Spatiality: The Passive of Prepositional Verbs."* In Adam Makkai, *et al* (eds.) Linguistics at the Crossroads. Padova/Pine Bluff: Jupiter Press.

Chafe, Wallace. (1970). *Meaning and the Structure of Language.* Chicago: The University of Chicago Press.

Chomsky, Noam. (1957). *Syntactic Structures.* The Hague: Mouton.

————. (1965). *Aspects of the Theory of Syntax.* Cambridge, Mass.: The MIT Press.

————. (1972). *Studies on Semantics in Generative Grammar.* The Hague: Mouton.

Chouémi, Moustapha. (1966). *Le Verbe dans le Coran.* Paris: Librairie C. Klincksieck.

Cowan, J. Milton, ed. (1966). *Hans Wehr's A Dictionary of Modern Written Arabic.* Ithaca, N.Y.: Cornell University Press.

Cruse, D.A. (1972). *"A Note on English Causatives,"* Linguistic Inquiry, 3/4, 520–28.

Dowty, David R. (1972a). *Studies in the Logic of Verb Aspect and Time Reference in English.* Ph.D. dissertation. Austin: The University of Texas.

————. (1972b). *"On the Syntax and Semantics of the Atomic Predicate Cause,"* Papers from the 8th Meeting of the Chicago Linguistic Society, 62–74.

Fillmore, Charles. (1968). *"The Case for Case."* In Universals in Linguistic Theory, 1–88. Edited by Emmon Bach and Robert T. Harms. New York: Holt, Rinehart and Winston, Inc.

————. (1969). *"Toward a Modern Theory of Case."* In Modern Studies in English: Readings in Transformational Grammar, 361–75. Edited by David A. Reibel and Sanford A. Schane. Englewood Cliffs, New Jersey: Prentice-Hall, Inc.

————. (1970). *"The Grammar of Hitting and Breaking."* In Readings in Transformational Grammar, 120–33. Edited by Roderick A. Jacobs and Peter S. Rosenbaum. Waltham, Mass.: Ginn and Company.

————. (1971). *"Some Problems for Case Grammar,"* Report of the 22nd Annual Round Table Meeting on Linguistics and Language Studies, No. 24, 35–56, Edited by O'Brien.

Fillmore, Charles J., and Langendoen, D. Terence, eds. (1971). *Studies in Linguistic Semantics.* New York: Holt, Rinehart and Winston, Inc.

Fleisch, Henri. (1968). *Esquisse d'une structure linguistique.* Beyrouth: Dar El-Machreq Edeteurs.

Fodor, J.A. (1970). *"Three Reasons for not Deriving 'kill' from 'Cause to Die'."* Linguistic Inquiry, 1/4, 429–38.

Freidin, Robert. (1974). *"On the Analysis of Passives,"* Reproduced by Indiana University Linguistics Club.

Geis, Jonnie E. *"Subject Complementation with Causative Verbs."* Institute for Research on Exceptional Children. University of Illinois.

Greenberg, Joseph H. (1961). *"Some Universals of Grammar with Particular Reference to the Order of Meaningful Elements."* In Universals of Language, 73–113. Edited by Joseph H. Greenberg. Second edition, 1968. Cambridge, Mass., and London, England: The MIT Press.

Hall, Barbara. (1965). *"Subject and Object in Modern English."* Ph.D. dissertation. Cambridge, Mass.: MIT.

Halliday, M.A.K. (1967–8). *"Notes on Transitivity and Theme in English,"* Journal of Linguistics, 3/1 (April 1967), 37–81; 3/2 (October 1967), 199–244; 4/2 (October 1968), 179–215.

Hasegawa, Kinsuke. (1968). *"The Passive Construction in English,"* Language, 44, 230–43.

Howell, Mortimer Sloper. (1880). *Grammar of the Classical Arabic.* Allahabad.

Huddleston, Rodney. (1970). *"Some Remarks on Case Grammar,"* Linguistic Inquiry, 1/4, 501–10.

Jacobs, Roderick A., and Rosenbaum, Peter S. (1970). *Readings in English Transformational Grammar.* Waltham, Mass.: Ginn and Company.

Jespersen, Otto. (1927). *A Modern English Grammar on Historical Principles.* Heidelberg: Carl Winters Universitatsbuch and Lung.

————. (1933). *Essentials of English Grammar.* New York: Henry Holt and Company.

Kac, Michael B. (1972). *Action and Result: Two Aspects of Predication in English."* In Syntax and Semantics, vol. 1, 117–24. Edited by John P. Kimball. New York and London: Seminar Press.

————. (1972). *"Reply to McCawley."* In Syntax and Semantics, vol. 1. Edited by John P. Kimball. New York and London: Seminar Press.

Kastovsky, Dieter. (1973). *"Causatives,"* Foundations of Language, 10/2, 255–315.

Killean, Mary Carolyn Garver. (1965). *The Deep Structure of the Noun Phrase in Modern Written Arabic.* Ph.D. dissertation. Ann Arbor: University of Michigan.

Kimball, John P. ed. (1972). *Syntax and Semantics.* New York and London: Seminar Press.

Lakoff, George. (1968). *"Instrumental Adverbs and the Concept of Deep Structures,"* Foundations of Language, 4/1, 5–29.

————. (1970). *Irregularity in Syntax.* New York: Holt, Rinehart and Winston, Inc.

Lakoff, George, and Peters, Stanley. (1969). *"Phrasal Conjunction and Symmetric Predicates."* In Modern Studies in English: Readings in Transformational Grammar, 113–42. Edited by David A. Reibel and Sanford A. Schane. Englewood Cliffs, New Jersey: Prentice-Hall, Inc.

Lakoff, George, and Ross, John Robert. (1972). *"A Note on Anaphoric Islands and Causatives,"* Linguistic Inquiry, 3/1, 121–5.

Lakoff, Robin. (1971) *"Passive Resistance."* In Papers from the 7th Regional Meeting, Chicago Linguistic Society, 149–62.

Lee, David A. (1973). *"Stative and Case Grammar,"* Foundations of Language, 10/4, 545–68.

Lee, Gregory. (1971). *"Subjects and Agents."* Working Papers in Linguistics, No. 7, L1–L118.

Lehmann, W.P. (1973). *"A Structural Principle of Language and its Implications,"*

Language, 49/1, 48–66.
Lewkowicz, N.M.K. (1967). *A Transformational Approach to the Syntax of Arabic Participles.* Ph.D. dissertation. Ann Arbor, MI: University of Michigan.
Lyons, John. (1968). *Introduction to Theoretical Linguistics.* Cambridge: Cambridge University Press.
McCawley, James D. (1970). *"English as a VSO Language,"* Language, 46/2, 287–99.
———————. (1971). *"Prelexical Syntax,"* Report of the 22nd Annual Round Table Meeting on Linguistics and Language Studies, No. 24, 19–33. Edited by O'Brien.
———————. (1972). *"Kac and Shibatani on the Grammar of Killing."* In Syntax and Semantics, vol. 1. Edited by John P. Kimball. New York and London: Seminar Press.
———————. (1973) *"Syntactic and Logical Arguments for Semantic Structures."* In Osamu Fujimura (ed.), *Three Dimensions of Linguistic Research*, 259–376. Tokyo: TEC.
Partee, Barbara Hall. (1971). *"On the Requirement that Transformations Preserve Meaning."* In Studies in Linguistic Semantics, 1–21. Edited by Charles J. Fillmore and D. Terence Langendoen. New York: Holt, Rinehart and Winston, Inc.
Postal, Paul M. (1971). *Cross-Over Phenomena.* New York: Holt, Rinehart and Winston, Inc.
Reibel, David A., and Schane, Sanford A., eds. (1969). *Modern Studies in English: Readings in Transformational Grammar.* Englewood Cliffs, New Jersey: Prentice-Hall.
Robson, Roy Anthony. (1972). *On the Generation of Passive Constructions in English.* Ph.D. dissertation. Austin: The University of Texas.
Rogers Jr., Andrew Daylon. (1974). *Physical Perception Verbs in English: A Study in Lexical Relatedness.* Ph.D. dissertation. Los Angeles: UCLA.
Saad, George N. (1974). *"Causatives and Passives in Arabic,"* An Nashra: Journal of the American Association of Teachers of Arabic, 7/1, 22–31.
Shibatani, Masayoshi. (1972). *"Three Reasons for Not Deriving 'Kill' from 'Cause to Die' in Japanese."* In Syntax and Semantics, vol. 1, 125–37. Edited by J.P. Kimball. New York and London: Seminar Press.
Sinha, Anjani K. (1972). *"The Passive Construction in English and Hindi."* Paper read at 47th Annual Meeting, Linguistic Society of America.
Smith, Carlota S. (1978) *"Jespersen's 'Move and Change' Class and Causative Verbs in English."* In Mohammad Ali Jazayeri; Edgar C. Polome; Werner Winter (eds.), *Linguistic and Literary Studies in Honor of Archibald A. Hill*, Vol. II Descriptive Linguistics, 101–9. The Hague: Mouton.
———————. (1972). *"On Causative Verbs and Derived Nominals in English,"* Linguistic Inquiry, 3/1, 136–8.
Snow, James. (1965). *A Grammar of Modern Written Arabic Clauses.* Ph.D. dissertation. Ann Arbor, MI: University of Michigan.
Southard, O. Bruch. (1971). *"Tagalog, English and Topicalization."* Working Papers in Linguistics, No. 10, 212–20.
Van Olphen, Herman. (1970). *The Structure of the Hindi Verb Phrase.* Ph.D. dissertation. Austin: The University of Texas.
Wright, William, ed. and trans. (1967). *A Grammar of the Arabic Language.* 3rd edition. Cambridge: Cambridge University Press.
Zwicky, Arnold M., and Sadock, Jerrold. (1975). *"Ambiguity Tests and How to Fail Them."* In John P. Kimball (ed.), *Syntax and Semantic*, vol. IV, 1–36. New York & London: Academic Press.

Glossary of technical terms: English-Arabic

accusative case	حالة المفعوليّة ، الحالة الإعرابيّة لنصب الأسماء والصفات
accusative of accompaniment	المفعول معه
accusative of cause	المفعول لأجله (الدالّ على السَّبَبيَّة)
accusative of distance	المفعول المطلق الدالّ على المسافة
accusative of duration	المفعول فيه الدالّ على الدَّيمومة (المُدَّة)
accusative of place	ظَرفُ المكان
accusative of purpose	المفعول لِأجله
accusative of specification	التَمييزُ
accusative of time	ظَرفُ الزَمانِ
active construction	تركيب الفعل المَبنِيِّ لِلمَعلوم (المعلومُ فاعِلُه)
active participle	اِسمُ الفاعِل
active verb	الفِعلُ المَبنِيُّ للمعلوم (أو المذكورُ فاعِلُه)
adjective	الصِفَة
Agent	العامِلُ ؛ حالة الفاعل المعنويّ النحويّة في البِنيَة العَميقَة
agent	الفاعِل في تركيب الفِعل المَبنِيِّ لِلمَجهول (لا مُقابِل لَه في العَربيّة)
aspect	وِجهة الحَدَث (للأفعال)
base verb	الفعل المجرّد أو الفعل الأساسيّ
Beneficiary	حالة المُستَفيد النحويّة في البِنيَة العَميقَة
case	الحالة (في النحو) ؛ حالة إعراب الاسم أو الصِفَة
case ending	الحركة الإعرابيّة لِلأسماء والصفات
case frame	الإطار النحويّ لِلفعل (أيُّ ما يرافق الفعل من حالات نحويّة في البِنيَة العَميقَة)

case grammar	قواعد الحالات النحويّة في البنية العميقة
case role	الحالة النحويّة العميقة ؛ الحالة النحويّة الباطنة
causation	السَبَبِيَّة أو التَسبيب (أو التَعدِيَة)
causative verb	الفعل المُتَعَدّي ؛ فعل الجَعل أو التَسبيب
causativizability	إمكانيّة تحوّل الفعل إلىٰ فعلٍ جَعلٍ
causativization	تحويل الفعل إلىٰ فعلٍ جَعلٍ
causer	المُسَبِّبُ
cognate accusative	المفعول المُطلَق
cognitive verb	فعل الإدراك الفكريّ
Comitative	حالة المَعِيّة ؛ حالة المفعول معه المعنويّ النحويّة في البنية العميقة
complex sentence	الجُملَة المُعَقَّدَة (أو المُرَكَّبَة)
congruence	المُطابَقَة ؛ التَطابق النَحويّ أو التَوافق النَحويّ
copula	الفعل الرابط
covert causative construction	تركيب فعل التسبيب المُقَدَّر (أو الخفِيّ)
covert causative verb	فعل التسبيب المُقَدَّر (أو الخَفِيّ)
deep structure	البِنيَةُ العميقة (أو الباطِنَةُ)
deep structure case	الحالة النحويّة للبنية العميقة
defective verb	الفعل الناقص
detransitivization	إزالة التَعدِيَة
direct causation	التسبيب المباشر ؛ التَعدِيَة
direct object	المفعول به المُباشِر
emotive verb	الفعل الإنفعاليّ (الدالّ على العاطِفة)
emphasis particle	أداة التوكيد ؛ حرفُ التحقيق
ergative language	اللغة الفاعِليّة أو اللُغَةُ الإرگتيّةُ (أي اللُغَة الّتي يكون فيها الفاعل فَضلَة والمفعول عُمدَة صرفيّا)
external agency	الفاعلية الخارجية (أي الفاعليّة المُضمَرة في صيغة الفعل المبنيّ للفاعل المجهول)
first object	المفعول به الأوّل
full passive	تركيب الفعل المبنيّ للفاعل المجهول المذكور فاعله (لا مُقابِل له في اللغة العربيّة)

genitive case	حالة الجـرّ
hypercausative verb	فِعل الجَعل الرئيسيّ في الجملة المركّـبة من فعل جَعل رئيسيّ وفعلٍ تابِع
Idafa construction	الإضـافـَـة
impersonal passive	الِفعل المبنيّ للمجهول الّذي لا نائبَ فاعل صريحا له ؛ الفعل اللاشخصي
implemental verb	فِعل العِـلاج (حسب تعريف ابن يعيش)
inalienable implement	الآ لـة المـُلازِمَـة (كاليد والرجل والقَدَم)
inchoation	الصَيرورَة
inchoative verb	فِعل الصَيرورَة
indicative mood	الصيغَة الإخبارِيَّة ؛ الحالة الإعرابِيَّة لِرفع الأفعال
indirect causation	التَعدِيَة غير المباشرة ؛ التَسبيب غير المباشر
instrument	الآ لَة
Instrument case	الحالة النَحويّة لِلآ لة في البِنية العَميقَة
interrogation	الِاستِـفهام
interrogative particle	أداة (حرفُ) الِاستِـفهام
intransitive verb	الِفعل اللازِم
jussive mood	صيغَة الجَزم ؛ حالة الجَزم
locative verb	الِفعل المَكانِيّ (أَي الِفعل الّذي يَتَطَلَّبُ مكانا أَو موضِعا لِحُدوثِه مثل فعل " وضع ")
Manner	الحالة النَحويّة لِصِفَة الِفعل في البِنيَة العَميقَة
manner adverbial	نَعتُ الفعل الوَصفِيّ أَو صِفَة الفعل الوَصفِيَّة
mood	صيغة (الأفعال) ؛ حالة اعراب الفعل
negation	النَـفيُ
negation particle	أداة النَـفي
nominal modifier	المـُعَـدِّلة الِاسمِيَّة ؛ الوَصفُ الِاسمِيُّ
nominative case	حالة الرَفع ؛ الحالة الإعرابيّة لرفع الأسماء والصفات

nonpassivizable verb	الفِعل اللامَبنِيّ للمَجهول (أي الّذي لا يمكن بناؤه للمجهول)
noun phrase	التَعبيرَة الإسمِيَّة
object	المفعول بِهِ
object of a preposition	المَجرور
overt causative construction	تركيب فعل التَعدِيَة (أو التسبيب) الظاهر
overt causative verb	فعل التَعدِيَة (أو التسبيب) الظاهر (أو الصريح)
particle of accompaniment	أَداة المَعِيَّة
passive construction	تركيب الفعل المبنيّ للمجهول
passive participle	اِسم المفعول
passive transformation	التحويل إلى الفعل المبنيّ للمجهول ؛ القاعدة التحويلية لاشتقاق تركيب الفعل المجهول فاعله
passive verb	الفعل المبنيّ للمجهول ؛ الفعل المبنيّ للفاعل المجهول ؛ الفعل المبني للمفعول
passivizable verb	الفعل الّذي يمكن بناؤه للمجهول
passivization	الإشتقاق النَحويّ لتركيب الفعل المبنيّ للمجهول
Patient	الحالة النحويّة للمفعول به المُتأَثِّر بحَدَث الفعل في البنية العميقة
physical perception verb	فعلُ الإدراك الحِسِّيّ
Place	حالة المَكان النَحوِيَّة في البنية العميقة
postpositional language	اللُغة الّتي يَلي فيها الجارُّ المجرورَ (كاليابانيّة)
predicate	الخَبَر
prepositional language	اللُغة الّتي يَلي فيها المجرورُ الجارَّ (كالعربيّة)
prepositional phrase	شِبهُ الجُملَةِ
prepositionally derived causative verb	فعل الجَعل أو التسبيب المتعدّي بحرف الجر
pronominalization	التَضمير ؛ الإضمار
preposition	حَرفُ الجَرّ
P component (= proposition component)	
proposition component	العُنصُر الإنشائيّ أو العُنصُر الخَبَريّ
Q component (= qualifier component)	
qualifier component	العُنصُر الوَصفِيّ أو المُكَوّن الوَصفِيّ

Range	التَعديّة ؛ حالة المَدىٰ النَحويَّة أو حالة المَجال النَحويَّة في البنية العميقة (يقابل هذه الحالة المفعول المطلق في البنية السطحية)
reflexive construction	تركيب فعل المُطاوَعَة ؛ تركيب الفعل الانعِكاسِيّ أو تركيب الفعل العاكِس
reflexive pronoun	الضَمير العاكِس أو الضَمير الانعِكاسِيّ
reflexive verb	فعل المُطاوَعَة ؛ الفعل العاكِس أو الانعكاسِيّ
reflexivity	المُطاوَعَة ؛ الانعِكاس
reflexivization	الِاستِطواع ؛ العَكس ؛ العَكسِيّة
remove verb	فعل السَلب
requestitive verb	فعل الطَلَب
resultative verb	الفعل الإنتاجيّ أو الفعل الإنشائيّ
second object	المفعول به الثاني
sentence qualifier	مُعَدِّل الجُملَة ؛ ناعت الجُملَة أو واصف الجُملَة
simplex sentence	الجُملَة البسيطة ، الجُملَة غير المُرَكَّبَة
Source	المَصدَريَّة (النَحويَّة) ؛ حالة مَصدَر الحَدَث النَحويَّة في البنية العميقة
Stative adjective	صِفَة (أو نَعت) الدَوام أو نَعت الكَينونَة
Stative verb	فعل الكَينونَة
Stativity	الكَينونَة
subject	المُسنَدُ اليه ؛ المُبتَدَأ أو الفاعل في البنية السَطحِيّة
subjectivization	الإسنادُ (السطحيّ) ؛ إشتقاق الفاعل أو المبتدأ في البنية السطحية على أساس قاعدة تحويلية
subjunctive mood	صيغة المضارع المنصوب ؛ الحالة الإعرابيّة لنَصب الأفعال
subjunctive particle	أداة النَصب
surface structure	البنية السَطحِيّة (أو الظاهرَة) ؛ التركيب السطحيّ
surface structure case	الحالة الإعرابيّة للاسم أو الصفة في البنية السطحيّة
Target	الحالة النحويّة للمفعول به الّذي يقع عليه حَدَث الفعل (سواء تأثّر بهذا الحدث أم لم يتاثر) . وهذه الحالة من الحالات النحويّة في البنية العميقة
tense	الزمَن ؛ زَمَن الفعل
Time	الزَمَنِيّة ، حالة الزمان النحويّة في البنية العميقة
topic	المَوضوع ؛ المُسنَد اليه ؛ المُبتَدَأ
topicalization	الِاستِبداء (أي إشتقاق المبتدأ في البنية السطحيّة علىٰ أساس قاعدة تحويلية)

transformation	التَّحويل ، قاعِدة تَحويليَّة
transformational grammar	النَّحوُ التَّحويليُّ
transitive verb	الفعل المُتَعَدّي
transitivization	التَّعدِيَةُ
transitivity	التَعَدّي
unspecified agent	الفاعل المعنَويّ غير المُخَصَّص
verb of acquiring	فعل المِلكِيَّة
verb of causation	فعل السَبَبِيَّة
verb of certainty	فعل اليَقين
verb of doubt	فعل الظَنّ أو فعل الشَكّ
verb of transforming	فعل التَحويل
verb phrase	التَعبيرَة الفِعلِيَّة (لا مُقابِل لها في العرَبِيَّة)
verbal modifier	مُعَدِّل الفعل ؛ ناعت الفعل أو واصف الفعل
verbal noun	المَصدَرُ
verbal qualifier (= verbal modifier)	
word order	ترتيب الكلمات في الجملة ؛ نَظمُ الكَلام

General index

A–hypercausative 81ff, 85f
Abdel-Hamid, A.K. 36
Abu Absi, S. 33f
accompaniment 25, 75f
accompaniment, particle of 25
accusative 25, 27, 56, 76, 95ff
accusative, cognate 23, 32, 34, 43f, 60f
accusative case 11, 13, 16, 43f, 45, 68, 88ff
accusative of accompaniment 25
accusative of cause 27,
accusative of distance 28, 31, 61
accusative of duration 28, 31, 61
accusative of place 31,
accusative of purpose 27,
accusative of specification 27,
accusative of time 31
acquiring, verb of 55f
active construction 1, 31, 37, 98ff
active participle 43f, 54, 85
active verb 7, 43f, 47, 52f, 62, 68f, 91ff, 103
actor 71, 87ff, 94ff
adjectival expression 8,
adjective 42, 43, 50, 65
adjective, stative 3,
adverbial, manner 43f, 77ff
affected 8, 60f, 71, 84, 88ff, 94ff
affix 8, 9, 15, 16, 32, 69, 100ff
agency 3, 19, 20, 26, 79, 91ff, 98ff
agency, external 19, 22, 35, 98ff
Agent 14, 17, 18, 19, 20, 26, 29, 34, 39f, 48f, 51f, 61ff, 70f, 76ff, 85, 94ff
agent 1, 3, 16, 34f, 95ff
agent, unspecified 20, 35, 63, 85, 95ff
Agentive 17, 18, 26, 36, 38
agentive particle 35f, 38, 103
Agreement transformation 33f, 95
alienable implement 18f, 49f
ambiguity 54, 77
Anderson, J. 89
animate agent 17, 18, 49f, 95ff
appointative verb 55
Arabic, Classical 3,
Arabic, Lebanese 33f
Arabic, Modern Literary 3,
Arabic, Modern Standard 3, 32
Arabic, Modern Written 3,
Arabic script 30,
Aspect 16,
al-Astrābādhī 55, 72f
auxiliary 9, 14,

B–hypercausative 85f
base verb 73ff
Basque 89, 90
Benefactive 39, 56
Beneficiary 25, 29,
bleeding 41

case, accusative 11, 16, 45, 68
case, deep structure 13, 20, 22, 48, 52ff
case, nominative 1, 11, 16, 45, 69f
case, surface structure 13, 25,
case ending 11, 25, 29,
case frame 39, 48, 78ff, 94ff
case grammar 13, 17, 19, 20, 27, 28, 30, 102
case marker 89ff
case role 13, 14, 15, 18, 19, 20ff, 27, 37f, 94ff
categorial entities 8-9, 13, 102
causation 9, 56, 65ff, 82ff, 89, 91ff
causation, direct 82ff
causation, indirect 82ff
Causative 14, 49, 69f, 95ff

causative, cover 65
causative, morphologically derived 66ff
causative, overt 65ff, 81ff
causative, periphrastic 65ff
causative, prepositionally derived 67ff
causative construction 65ff
causativizability 70
causativizable verb 68f, 80
causativization 68f, 71f
cause, accusative of 27,
causer 71, 82, 88, 94ff
certainty, verb of 56f, 103
certainty and doubt, verbs of 56f, 103
Chafe, W. 20, 44
Chomsky, Noam 8, 10, 95
Classical Arabic 3, 32,
clitic particle 16
cognate accusative 23, 32, 34, 43f, 60f
cognate noun 60
cognate object 34, 64
cognitive verb 53ff, 69f
colloquial Arabic 3, 4
Comitative 25f, 29, 40, 84
comitative construction 26, 75
comparison 47,
comparison, standard of 46f, 48,
compensatory pronominalization 58
complementizer insertion transformation 58
complementizer placement 58f
complex sentence 56, 80f
congruence marker 15,
conjunct 51
conjunction 26
construct, possessive 11,
construction, active 1, 31, 37, 98ff
construction, causative 65ff
construction, comitative 26, 75
construction, cover causative 81ff
construction, Idafa 11,
construction, passive, 12, 18, 31, 32, 36f, 60, 61, 87ff, 95ff
construction, reflexive 87ff
construction, relative 8,
co-occurrence restrictions 35
copula 42f
copying transformation 11, 58
count noun 23, 60
counter examples 10, 49, 59, 61f, 84, 88, 102
covert causative 65ff, 74f
covert causative construction 76f, 79ff
covert causative verb 74ff, 80ff
covert reflexive 98ff
cross-over movement 32

declarative sentence 9
declare verb 59f
decomposable verb 78ff
deep structure 13, 16, 18, 20, 21, 28, 35ff, 76ff, 90ff
deep structure case 13, 17, 20, 22, 27, 48, 52ff
defective verb 41ff,
definite article 4,
deletion rule 34, 41f,
denominative 67
derivative, verbal 54
derived causative verb 66ff, 74f
derived form 4, 66f
descriptive adequacy 34
desiderative 14,
detransitivization 93ff
detransitivized verb 59
direct causation 82f
direct object 1, 38, 41, 68f, 70
discontinuous verb 56, 78, 81f
distance, accusative of 28, 31, 61
doubly transitive verb 71
doubt, verb of 56f, 103
duration, accusative of 28, 31, 61

early Arab grammarians 11, 31, 42f, 56f
early Arab rhetoricians 46, 47, 48, 56, 87, 92
Egyptian Arabic 4
embedded sentence 16, 57, 58, 65, 81f, 100, 103
emotive verb 53ff
emphasis particle 58
ending, accusative case 11, 31, 42f, 63
ending, case 11, 25, 29,
ending, genitive case 16, 29, 31, 41
ending, nominative case
English 1, 2, 8, 10, 18, 19, 26, 34, 36, 37, 38, 44, 49, 102, 103
equative verb 49f
equational sentence 57
ergative 87ff
ergative language 89

ergative verb 89ff
ergativity 87ff
ergativity relationship 87ff
Eskimo 89, 90, 91
expose verb 59f
expression, adjectival 8,
expression, genitival 8,
extension of action 91ff, 104
extension of experience 99ff, 104
extension of meaning 60f
external agency 19, 22, 35, 98ff

Fillmore 11, 16, 17ff., 20, 25, 28, 32, 41, 46, 47, 52, 56, 78f
first object 31
form, case 16
frame, case 39, 48, 78ff
French 2, 20, 36, 38, 103
full passive 35, 37, 103

gemination, consonant 8,
gender 15, 33,
generic noun 60
genetivization 29, 64
genitival expression 8,
genitive 13, 16, 25, 43f, 50, 60, 68f
genitive case ending 16, 29, 31, 41
Georgian 89
German 19,
Goal 14, 24, 25, 27, 29, 39f, 48, 94ff
goal 48, 87ff, 94ff
grammar, case 13, 17, 19, 102
grammar, transformational 8, 49,
grammaticalness 17, 18, 43, 100
Greenberg, J. 8, 9-10,

Halliday, M.A.K. 20, 22, 45f, 89, 92, 93f
Hasegawa, K. 95
hierarchy (linguistic) 14, 15, 16, 28f, 40, 93, 95, 102, 103
historical change 60, 71, 74, 103
homophonous 51
hypercausative verb 81ff
hypercausative-A 81ff, 85f
hypercausative-B

Ibn Abī Rabī'ah, 'Umar 74
Ibn Aḥmad, al-Khalīl 72, 73
Ibn al-Ḥājib 55
Ibn Ya'īsh 43, 49, 60f, 64

iḍāfa construction 11,
imperative 85
impersonal passive 2, 32, 34, 104
impingement verb 49f
implement, alienable 18f, 49f
implement, inalienable 18f, 49f
implemental verb 49f, 95ff
inalienable implement 18f, 49f
inanimate 17, 20, 49f, 77ff
inchoative verb 44, 51ff, 68ff, 79, 98ff
indefinite 10, 60
indicative mood 85f
indirect causation 82ff
inflection 43f
inflectional language 8
informats 3, 18
Instrument 17, 19, 21, 27, 29f, 38, 40f, 49f, 51f, 81f, 95ff
instrument 18, 21, 50f
Intensive 9, 14, 74, 104
Intentionality 19, 20, 74, 91ff
internal agency 98ff
internal vowel 1, 73
internal vowel modification 66f
interrogation 9,
Interrogative 14, 15, 102
interrogative particle 14
interrogative pronoun 14
interrogative sentence 9
intransitive verb 1, 2, 33, 41f, 68f, 87ff
intuition, native 3, 73, 88f
Iraqi Arabic 20

Japanese 13,
jussive mood 15,

kāraka 16
kartā 16
Killean, M.C.G. 8, 10,
Koran (Qur'ān), Holy 36ff, 73, 103

language, agglutinative 8
language, ergative 89
language, inflectional 8
language, OV 13
language, postpositional 9
language, prepositional 9
language, SVO 8, 10, 11
language, VO 8, 9
language, VSO 8, 9, 10, 11

Lebanese Arabic 33f,
Lehmann, W.P. 8, 14, 15
Lehmann's placement principle 14, 15
Lewkowicz, N.M.K. 8, 10, 33,
lexicalizable 51
lexicalization transformation 76, 79, 95ff
lexicon 3, 75
Libyan Arabic 20
Literary Arabic, Modern 3,
locative verb 58f
logic 10
Lyons, J. 87, 89

Makhzūmī, M. 92
Manner 24f, 29, 40
manner adverbial 43f, 77ff
marker, congruence 15
marker, modality 14, 15
marker, mood 15
matrix verb 77f, 81, 83f, 86, 100ff
meaning preserving 1, 61
means adverbial 38
metaphor 61
middle verb 92f, 97ff
modal qualifier 15,
modality 14, 15, 16, 51f
modality marker 14
Modern Literary Arabic 3,
Modern Standard Arabic 3, 32,
Modern Written Arabic 3,
modifier, nominal 8
modifier, syntactic 8,
modifier, verbal 9
mood 16
mood, indicative 85f
mood, jussive 15
mood, subjunctive 15, 85f
mood marker 15
morphological derivation 4, 51, 66ff, 77ff, 89, 93ff, 103f
morphological distribution 54, 92
morphological structure 4, 8
morphologically derived causative 66ff
morphology 8,
al-Mutanabbī 47, 71

necessative 14,
negation 9, 16
negation particle 14
Negative 14, 15, 102

nominal modifier 8,
nominal sentence 57
nominative 11, 16, 29, 31
nominative case 1, 11, 31, 45, 62, 69f, 88ff
nominative case ending 11, 31, 42f, 63
nominativization 11, 92ff
noncausativizable verb 68f
noncount noun 23, 60
nontransitive (verb) 42
noncount noun 23, 60
nonergative verb 89ff
nonimplemental verb 49f
nonmiddle verb 92f, 95ff
nonpassivizable verb 39, 41f, 46, 48, 52f, 99ff
noun, verbal 42f, 60f, 70
noun phrase 10, 11, 17, 18, 22, 24ff, 27, 29, 34f, 43f, 52f, 61ff, 70, 84, 90ff
number 15, 33

OV language 13,
OVS language 10
object 1, 8, 9, 10, 11, 19, 20, 22f, 43, 45, 52f, 60f, 76, 84
object, cognate 34, 64
object, direct 2, 38, 41
object, first 31
object, second 31
objectivization 29, 95
observational adequacy 34
one-place verb 39f, 41, 48, 51f, 91ff
order, word 8, 9, 16
overt causative 81ff
overt causative construction 79
overt reflexive 98ff

P component 13, 28, 40, 62, 80, 95ff, 99f, 102ff
Panini 16
participle, active 13, 16, 43f, 54, 85
participle, passive 3, 43f
particle, agentive 2, 36, 103
particle, emphasis 58
particle, interrogative 14
particle, negation 14
particle of accompaniment 25
passive, agentless 2, 35
passive, full 35, 37, 103
passive, impersonal 2, 32, 34

passive construction 1, 12, 18, 31, 36f, 60, 61, 87ff, 98ff
passive participle 3, 36, 43f
passive transformation 1-2, 32,
passive verb 7, 31, 48f, 55, 59, 84, 91ff
passivity 95ff
passivizability 12, 33, 38, 60f, 84, 102
passivizable verb 33, 39, 43, 48, 49f, 52f, 55f, 58, 94ff, 97ff
passivization 1, 3, 31, 33, 38ff, 55f, 95ff
past tense 3,
Path 28,
Patient 14, 21f., 26, 28, 29, 39, 51f, 70f
periphrastic causative 65ff
periphrastic qualifier 15,
Persian 20,
Person, third 2,
Phonology 3,
phrase, noun 10, 11, 17, 18, 22, 27, 52f, 70
phrase, prepositional 32, 42
phrase, verb 10, 11, 14,
phrase structure rules 11, 13, 16, 33
physical perception verb 51f, 69f
Place 24, 28, 39, 61
place, accusative of 31
placement, complementizer 58f
possessive construct 11
postposition 9, 16
postpositional language 9,
potential
predicate 10, 42f, 76
predicate, semantic 77f, 79ff, 104
predicate raising 76f, 79f
preposition 2, 16, 19, 20, 25, 29, 36, 42, 62, 64, 65, 70, 104
prepositional language 9
prepositional phrase 32, 42
prepositionally derived causative 67ff, 74ff, 104
primary topicalization 11, 34
pronominalization 11, 58
pronoun, interrogative 14
pronoun, reflexive 98ff
proposition 13, 16, 87ff, 99ff
pseudotransitive verb 70
purpose, accusative of 27

Q component 13-5, 28, 44, 48, 56, 62, 80, 94ff, 99f, 102ff
quadri literal root 12
qualifier 13
qualifier, modal 15
qualifier, periphrastic 15
qualifier, sentence 14, 15
qualifier, verbal 13, 15, 102
quality Range 45f
quantity Range 45f
question particle 9

raising 58, 103
raising, predicate
Range 22f, 40f, 45, 59f, 70f, 94ff
Range, quality 45f
Range, quantity 45f
reciprocal 48ff, 52f
reciprocity 9, 48
referent 58
Reflexive 14, 97ff, 102
reflexive, covert 98ff
reflexive, overt 98ff
reflexive construction 87ff, 101ff
reflexive pronoun 98ff
reflexive verb 93ff, 97ff
Reflexivity 99ff
reflexivization 9,
relationship, ergativity
relationship, transitivity 70f
relative construction 8
remove verb 59f
requestitive verb 62f
resultative verb 53f, 67
role, case 13, 14, 18, 19, 20, 48, 94ff
root 4, 23, 44, 67, 95

SVO language 8, 10, 11, 33
SVSO language 11
Samoan 89
Sanskrit 16
second object 31
secondary topicalization 11, 34
semantic constraints 4,
semantic properties 1, 12, 68, 72f
semantic relationship 72ff, 88ff, 92ff, 101ff
sentence, active 1, 2, 16, 20, 32
sentence, complex 56, 80
sentence, passive 1, 2, 16, 20, 32, 57
sentence, simplex 65ff, 80
sentence complement 27, 32, 83, 85

sentence qualifier 14, 15
Sībawayhi 44, 48, 72, 92
simple form 4,
simplex sentence 65ff, 79ff
Snow, J. 8, 10, 32,
sociolinguistic function 3,
Source 23f., 27, 28f, 38, 39, 84, 88
specification, accusative of 27,
Standard Arabic, Modern 3,
standard of comparison 46f, 48,
stative adjective 3,
stative verb 3, 40, 46f, 48, 51f, 68f, 80ff
structure, deep 13, 16, 18, 20, 21, 28, 35ff
structure, surface 13, 16, 28, 84, 88ff
style 3,
subject 1, 10, 11, 18, 20, 31, 45, 95ff
subjectivization 29, 61ff, 95
subjunctive 14, 15, 85
subjunctive mood 15, 85f
subjunctive particle 85
suppletion 16
surface structure 13, 16, 23, 25, 27, 28, 42ff, 84, 88ff
surface structure case 13, 25, 27, 95ff
surpass verb 59f
synonymous 47f, 57, 62, 72, 86
syntactic change 4, 60, 74, 103, 104
syntactic constraints 4,
Syntactic properties 1, 12, 45, 68, 72f
Syrian Arabic 4

al-Ṭabarī, 71
Target 14, 22, 26, 28, 29, 39, 48, 51f, 56f, 76ff, 84, 94ff
Target-deletion 41
Targetization 61ff, 103
tense 3, 15, 16, 44
three-place verbs 55ff, 71, 95ff
Time 15, 24, 28, 29, 40, 44, 61
time, accusative of 31
time adverbial 44
topic 10
topicalization 11, 29, 40
topicalization, primary 11, 34,
topicalization, secondary 11, 34
traditional approach 1
transformation 1, 11, 13, 28f, 38ff, 76, 80
transformation, complementizer insertion 58
transformation, passive 1, 32
transformation, truncation 1,
transformational grammar 8, 32, 49
transforming, verb of 55ff
transitive verb 1, 38, 41, 45, 49f, 69f, 87ff, 95ff
transitivity 1, 3, 12, 33, 38, 41, 45, 87ff
transitivity relatonship 87ff
triliteral root 4
Turkish 13
two-place verbs 42, 45f, 48, 74, 95ff
typology 8, 34

underlying form 2, 62,
underlying structure 16, 18
ungrammaticalness 18, 33, 46, 74, 76, 98, 99
universal base 8
universals, linguistic 8, 9-10
unspecified agent 20, 34, 63, 85, 95

VO language 8, 9, 13,
VOS language 10
VSO language 8, 9, 10, 11, 32f
verb, active 7, 47, 52f, 68
verb, appointative 55
verb, base 73ff
verb, causative 8, 12, 56ff, 65ff
verb, causativizable 68f, 80
verb, cognitive 53ff, 69f
verb, covert causative 80ff
verb, declare 59f
verb, decomposable 78ff
verb, defective 41ff
verb, derived causative 66ff
verb, detransitivized 69
verb, discontinuous 56
verb, emotive 53ff
verb, equative 49f
verb, ergative 89ff
verb, expose 59f
verb, hypercausative 81ff
verb, impingement 49
verb, implemental 49f
verb, inchoative 51f, 68f
verb, intransitive 1, 33, 38, 41, 68f, 87ff
verb, locative 58f
verb, middle 92f, 97ff
verb, noncausativizable 68f
verb, nonergative 89ff
verb, nonimplemental 49f

verb, nonmiddle 92f, 95ff
verb, nonpassivizable 39, 42f
verb, one-place 29, 41f, 48, 51f
verb, passive 7, 31, 49, 55, 59, 84
verb, passivizable 33, 39, 43, 49f, 58, 94ff, 97ff
verb, physical perception 51f, 59f
verb, pseudotransitive 70
verb, reciprocal 8, 48f
verb, reflexive 93ff, 97ff
verb, remove 59f
verb, requestitive 92f
verb, resultative 53f
verb, stative 3, 40, 46f, 49, 51f, 68f,
verb, surpass 59f,
verb, transitive 1, 33, 38, 41, 45, 49f, 69f, 87ff
verb, three-place 55ff, 71
verb, two-place 42, 45f, 48, 74
verb classification 4,
verb form 4
verb of acquiring 55f
verb of certainty 56f, 103
verb of certainty and doubt 56f, 103
verb of doubt 56f, 103
verb of transforming 23, 55ff
verb phrase 10, 11, 14
verbal derivative 3, 54
verbal modifier 9
verbal noun 42f, 60f, 70
verbal qualifier 13, 15
Vibhakti 16
voice 33
vowel lengthening 8

Wehr, Hans 38
word order 8, 16
writing system, Arabic 4
Written Arabic, Modern 3

For Product Safety Concerns and Information please contact our EU representative GPSR@taylorandfrancis.com
Taylor & Francis Verlag GmbH, Kaufingerstraße 24, 80331 München, Germany

www.ingramcontent.com/pod-product-compliance
Lightning Source LLC
Chambersburg PA
CBHW052129300426
44116CB00010B/1826
* 9 7 8 1 1 3 8 9 8 6 0 4 6 *

دراسة التعدية والسببية والبناء للمجهول
دراسة نحوية - دلالية للفعل في اللغة العربية الفصحى

مكتبة اللسانيات العربية
رئيس التحرير : د. محمد حسن باكلا
جامعة الملك سعود (جامعة الرياض سابقا)
الرياض ـ المملكة العربية السعودية

الكتاب الرابع

دراسة التعدية والسببية والبناء للمجهول
دراسة نحوية ـ دلالية للفعل في اللغة العربية الفصحى

تأليف

جورج نعمه سعد
جامعة امهرست ـ الولايات المتحدة الامريكية

مؤسسة كيغان بول العالمية
لندن ـ هنلي ـ بوسطن
١٤٠٢ هـ / ١٩٨٢ م

بسم الله الرحمن الرحيم

تقديم

على الرغم من الجهود الكبيرة المشرّفة التي بذلها العلماء العرب المسلمون الأوائل في ميدان النحو أو دراسة نظم الكلام وتركيبه ،فانّ هناك موضوعات وقضايا شتّى لم تدرس دراسة فاحصة بعد . ومع تطور الدراسات اللغوية واللسانية في عصرنا ، بدأ يظهر كثير من الفراغات التي تحتاج إلى ملء ،وعديد من القضايا التي تتطلب إعادة نظر أو صقل أو تغيير جزئي أو جذري . ولعل هذه هي سنة الحياة القائمة على التغير والتطور والنمو ، إذ أنّ الثبات ليس إلا للّه وحده .

هذا الكتاب

يعدّ هذا الكتاب الأول من نوعه في الدراسات اللسانية العربية من عدّة جوانب .

أولا : أن الكتاب ينصبّ على قضيّة نحوية واحدة ، محاولا أن يجلو غوامضها وأن يجد الحلول للمشكلات المعترضة متى ما وجدت، ويقدم هذه الحلول في إطار لغوي متكامل يعتمد على الاستقصاء للحقائق والمشكلات اللغوية ليس فقط في الدراسات العربية الأصيلة القديمة وإنما يغطي أيضا الدراسات الحديثة والمعاصرة في القضايا ذات العلاقة .

ثانيا :يعتمد هذا الكتاب في الأساس على نظرية جديدة ظهرت في أوائل الستينات من هذا القرن الميلادي ، يطلق عليها " نظرية الحالات الإعرابية " . وتقوم هذه النظرية على اكتشاف العلاقات الظاهرة (السطحية) والباطنة (العميقة) في نظام الجملة ، والكشف عن الروابط الأساسية بين اللفظ والمعنى في هذا النظام . وهي دراسة علمية تقوم على أساس من البحث اللغوي الرياضي والمنطق الرياضي وقد طبقت هذه النظرية على لغات كثيرة ومختلفة ، ولها مدرسة أو مدارس مشهورة في الشرق والغرب تقوم بأبحاث كثيرة في الوقت الحاضر من أجل تثبيت قواعد النظرية وصقلها وتوسيع رقعتها في التنظير والتطبيق .

ثالثا : لا يرى هذا الكتاب مانعا من الاستفادة من المدارس الأخرى إلى جانب النظرية العامة التي يعتمدها .فيستفيد الكتاب من مدارس علم اللغة الاجتماعي وعلم اللغة الرياضي ، والمدرسة التحويلية التوليدية ، ونظريات التايبولوجيا اللغوية وعموميات اللغة وما إلى ذلك ويعد هذا العمل إضافة جديدة في مجال نظرية الحالات الإعرابية بالشكل الحالي .

لكل هذه الأمور مجتمعة تظهر أهمية الكتاب في معالجة قضايا التعدية والتعدّي والبناء للمجهول في اللغة العربية . فجاءت هذه الدراسة متكاملة الجوانب دراسة وبحثا . ولعل هذه النظرية المعتمدة ـ كما تدل نتائج البحث ـ أقرب النظريات الحديثة وأكثرها ملاءمة لمعالجة القضايا المدروسة في هذا الكتاب .

يشتمل الكتاب على ستة فصول ، أولها يحتوى على مقدمة تبيّن الهدف من تأليفه وتشرح بعض الأوّليّات التي توصل إليها هذا العمل . أما الفصل الثاني فيرسم الإطار الذي بنيت عليه الدراسة والنظرية التي اتبعها مع بيان أهم الحالات الإعرابية الباطنة التي نحتاج إليها في تحليل الجملة العربية والعمليات التحويلية التي تتطلبها اللغة للتعبير عن هذه الحالات الباطنة العميقة . وأما الفصل الثالث فيتركز على قضايا البناء للمجهول ويقارن بين نظرة علماء العرب المسلمين القدامى وعلماء اللسانيات المحدثين إليها ، مشيرا إلى نقاط القوة والضعف في كلتا النظرتين . ثم ينتقل إلى تبيان الأفعال التي لا يمكن بناؤها للمجهول والأفعال التي يمكن بناؤها للمجهول مع تقديم بعض المشكلات ومحاولة وضع حلول لها .

ويختص الفصل الرابع بأفعال الجعل الظاهرة والمقدّرة. ويعقد الفصل الخامس الحديث حول ظواهر التعدّي والأرجتية والمطاوعة في العربية مبينا الفروق بين الفاعل النحوي والفاعل المعنوي .

والحق يقال إن دراسة التعدّي والتعدية بالرغم من أنها كانت دقيقة وفاحصة لدى علماء العربية القدماء إلاّ أنها كانت

دراسات شبه عابرة وغير مركزة في كثير من الأحيان . بل تجد النظرات الجيدة كحبات العقد المنفرطة هنا وهناك . وخير من يصور هذا الاتجاه في معالجة الموضوع العلامة أبو الفتح عثمان بن جني (ت ٣٩٢ هـ) . ففي كتابه سر صناعة الاعراب (ج ١ ، القاهرة مصطفى البابي الحلبي ، ١٩٥٤ م) في " باب الباء " حين يتحدث عن محل الإعراب للجار والمجرور معاً يتناول موضوع المبني للمجهول ، فيقول (ص ١٤٨) :

" قَضى النحويون على موضع الجار والمجرور إذا أسند الفعل إليهما بأنهما في موضع رفع . وذلك نحو : ما جاءني من رجل ، وما قام من أحد. وكذلك ما لم يسمّ فاعله نحو : سيرَ بزيد ، وعُجِبَ من جعفر ، ونُظِر إلى محمد ، وانصُرِفَ عن زيد ، وانقُطِعَ بالرجل وإنما قضوا في هذه الأشياء في هذه المواضع برفع معانيها من قبل أنها قد كانت مع الفعل المسند إلى فاعله منصوبة المواضع ، نحو : سِرتُ بزيد، وعَجبت من خالد ، ونحو ذلك . فلما لم يُسَمّ الفاعل، قُضِيَ برفعه لقيامه مقام الفاعل " .

وفي كتابه اللُمع في العربية (تحقيق حسين محمد محمد شرف ، القاهرة : عالم الكتب ، ١٩٧٩ م) يقول ابن جني في باب الفاعل (ص ١١٥) :

" اعلم أن الفاعل عند أهل العربية كل اسم ذكرته بعد فعل وأسندت ونسبت ذلك الفعل إلى ذلك الاسم وهو مرفوع بفعله . وحقيقة رفعه بإسناد الفعل إليه . والواجب وغير الواجب في ذلك الاسم سواء. تقول في الواجب : قام زيد . وفي غير الواجب : ما قام زيد ، وهل يقوم زيد ؟. "

وفي الباب الذي يليه (أي باب المفعول الذي جعل الفعل حديثا عنه ، وهو ما لم يُسَمّ فاعله) يقول ابن جني (صص ١١٧ – ١١٩) :

" اعلم أن المفعول به في هذا الباب يرتفع من حيث يرتفع الفاعل ، لأن الفعل قبل كل واحد منهما حديث

عنه ومسند اليه . وذلك قولك : ضُرِبَ زيد ، وشُتِمَ بكر فإن كان الفعل يتعدّى إلى مفعولين أقمت الأول منهما مقام الفاعل ، فرفعته ، وتركت الثاني منصوبا بحاله تقول : أعطيت زيدا درهما . فإن لم تسمّ فاعله قلت : أُعطِيَ زيد درهما . فإن كان الفعل يتعدّى إلى ثلاثة مفعولينَ أقمت الأول منهما مقام الفاعل فرفعته ونصبت المفعولَينِ بعده . تقول : أعلم الله زيدا عمرا خير الناس . فإن لم تُسَمِّ الفاعل قلت : أعلم زيدعمرا خير الناس . فإن لم يكن الفعل متعديا لم يجز إلاّ أن تذكر الفاعل لئلا يكون الفعل حديثا عن غير متحدث عنه . وذلك نحو قولك : قام زيد ، وقعد عمرو ، ولا تقول قيمَ ولا قُعِدَ لما ذكرت لك . فإن اتصل به حرف جر أو ظرف أو مصدر جاز أن تقيم كل واحد منها مقام الفاعل . تقول : سِرت بزيد فرسخين يومين سَيرا شديدا . فإن أقمت الباء وما عملت فيه مقام الفاعل قلت سيرَ بزيد فرسخين يومين سيرا شديدا . فالباء وما عملت فيه في موضع رفع . فإن أقمت المصدر مقام الفاعل قلت : سير بزيد فرسخين يومين سَيرٌ شديدٌ . ترفع الذي تقيمه مقام الفاعل بفعله لا غير . فإن كان هناك مفعول به صريح لم تُقِم مقام الفاعل غيره . تقول : ضَربت زيدا يوم الجمعة ضَربا شديدا . فإن لم تسمّ فاعله قلت : ضُرِبَ زيد يوم الجمعة ضَربا شديدا ترفع زيدا لاغير . "

مثل هذه اللفتات القيمة إلى الموضوع من لدن ابن جني وغيره تناولها الكتاب الذي بين يدي القارىء الآن بشكل مفصل وبطريقة أوضح وبمنهج أحدث . وهذه من المبررات التي وضع من أجلها هذا الكتاب . فيعدّ بهذا لبنة من لبنات بناء صرح الدراسات النحوية الحديثة ، إذ نحن أحوج ما نكون في عصرنا إلى مثل هذه الدراسات القيمة التي تعمد إلى القديم فتشذبه وتهذبه وتعمد الى الحديث فلا ترى غضاضة من الاستفادة من أجوده بقدرما يضيف جديدا ويؤكد حقائق سابقة ، وبقدر ما يضع الدراسات القديمة على محكّ التجربة وعلى ضوء النظريات الحديثة ، وكذلك بقدر ما يعطي دفعة قوية للدراسات القديمة بعدما توعّك بها

السير وثقلت خطاها وتوقف نبض علوم العربية المتدفق لحين من الزمن إلاّ بما كان يردده ويجترّه الخلف أحيانا دون فهم واضح لما يعنيه السلف الصالح . ولعل هذه الدراسة النحوية بداية طيبة لدراسات أخرى تفيد منها العربية ولسانياتها . وإنها لانطلاقة جيدة في موضوع يستحق البحث العميق والدراسة الدقيقة باستمرار .

كلمة عن المؤلف

يعدّ الدكتور جورج نعمه سعد من علماء اللسانيات العرب القلائل المهتمين بدراسة النحو العربي دراسة نقدية ، مقارنة عصرية . وقد نشأ اهتمام المؤلف بهذا الموضوع من خلال إعداده الجامعي كباحث في الوطن العربي وفي الولايات المتحدة الأمريكية .

ولد الدكتور سعد (أبو نبيل) عام ١٩٤٠ م في حيفا بفلسطين وتلقى دراسته الابتدائية والثانوية في المدارس العربية والانجليزية والفرنسية بفلسطين ولبنان . وحصل على درجة الليسانس في اللغة العربية وآدابها من الجامعة اللبنانية عام ١٩٦٦ م . ثم حصل على درجة الليسانس في اللغة الانجليزية وآدابها من الجامعة نفسها عام ١٩٦٩ م . وحصل على الدكتوراه في اللسانيات العربية من جامعة تكساس في أوستن بأمريكا عام ١٩٧٥ م . ويساهم الدكتور سعد بقلمه الثرّ في تنشيط حركة اللسانيات العربية المعاصرة بقسميها النظري والتطبيقي . وتتركز كتاباته على النحو العربي ، والنحو العمومي(العالمي). وقد دفعه الاهتمام بالنحو العربي القديم وبخاصة نحو القرآن الكريم إلى دراسة " الكتاب " لسيبويه والذي لا يزال يعدّ من المراجع الأساسية في النحو العربي في أيامنا هذه . ويعتبر المؤلف من الرواد المعاصرين الذين يشيدون بالنحاة العرب المسلمين الأوائل ونظرياتهم في الولايات المتحدة الأمريكية . وهو من أوائل العرب المحدثين المهتمين بدراسة العلاقات التي تربط اللغة بالحضارة . وقد شارك المؤلف في مؤتمرات عالمية عدة في مجالات النحو والصرف وصناعة المعاجم . وهو عضو فعّال في جمعية دراسات الشرق الأوسط ، ورابطة أساتذة اللغة العربية بأمريكا .

أما عن مساهماته في مجال التربية فقد بدأ المؤلف التدريس عام ١٩٦١ م في المدارس الثانوية بلبنان . ومنذ ذلك الوقت وهو يزاول التدريس إلى جانب البحث والتأليف . فقد عمل محاضرا في جامعة تكساس وأستاذا مساعدا في جامعة الرياض ، ويعمل حاليا أستاذا في جامعة ماساشوستس بأمهرست في شمال شرقي أمريكا . وبالإضافة إلى محاضراته في اللسانيات العربية واللسانيات العامة وتدريسه اللغة العربية كلغة ثانية فقد شارك في تأليف كتب عدة تهدف إلى نشر اللغة العربية على النطاق العالمي . وهو أحد مؤلفي كتاب " مبادىء اللغة العربية المعاصرة " الذي نشرت جامعة متشغان طبعته الثانية المنقحة عام ١٩٧٥ م . كما ساعد الدكتور سعد في تأليف كتاب " اللغة العربية في المرحلة المتوسطة " من السلسلة ذاتها ونشرته جامعة متشغان عام ١٩٧١ م ومن مؤلفات الدكتور سعد كتاب " أصوات العربية وحروفها " وقد نشرته جامعة ماساشوستس عام ١٩٧٩ م ، ومعجم مصطلحات علم اللغة الحديث (بالاشتراك مع عدد من اللغويين العرب) وقد نشرته مكتبة لبنان ومؤسسة لونغمان عام ١٩٨٢ م . وللمؤلف مقالات عدة نشرت في مجلات متخصصة .

والكتاب الذي بين يدي القارىء من الأبحاث الأصيلة التي تضع حجر الأساس في التفسير العلمي للنحو العربي . وهو لا يخدم دارسي اللغة العربية من الطلاب والأساتذة والباحثين فحسب ، وإنما يتعدّى ذلك إلى خدمة الدراسات اللغوية العامة المعاصرة وكذلك العلوم الانسانية الأخرى النسبية والمقاربة .

رئيس التحرير
محمد حسن باكلا
جامعة الملك سعود
" جامعة الرياض سابقا "

مقدّمـــة

يعرض هذا الكتاب لموضوعي التعدّي والتعدية في اللغة العربية الفصحى وعلاقتهما بالاشتقاق الصرفي والنحوي لتراكيب الأفعال المبنيّة للمجهول . والمقصود بالتعدّي هو الصفات النحوية والدلالية الملازمة للأفعال المتعدية . أما المقصود بالتعدية فهو الاشتقاق الصرفي للأفعال المتعدية المزيدة المشتقة من الأفعال المجردة كما في اشتقاق فعل " أَجلَسَ " مثلا من فعل" جَلَسَ"

ويشكّل هذا الكتاب أول محاولة لدراسة جانب هام من جوانب نحواللغة العربية الفصحى دراسة علمية تفصيلية دقيقة ضمن إطار نظري يجد أسسه في نظرية الحالات النحوية التي اشتهرت على يد العالم اللغوى الامريكي تشارلز فِلمور Fillmore ، وفي نظرية وآراء علماء اللغة العرب القدماء وعلى رأسهم سيبويه .

في الفصل الأول أعرّف باللغة التي أنوي بحثها ودراستها في هذا الكتاب . وخلافا لما جرت عليه العادة في الغرب من تمييز بين لغة عربية معاصرة ولغة عربية كلاسيكية ، لا أجد مبررا لمثل هذا التمييز وأعرض للبحث في هذا الكتاب لغة عربية معيارية واحدة هي اللغة العربية الفصحى . ومع أن هنالك فروقا بين مايسمى بالعربية المعاصرة وما يسمى بالعربية الكلاسيكية من حيث أساليب الكتابة والمفردات إلاّ أن هذه الفروق لا تبرر القول بلغتين مستقلتين إذ أنه لا فروق هامة بين اللغتين المزعومتين من حيث الصفات اللغوية الأساسية أي النظام الصوتي والتراكيب النحوية والصيغ الصرفية .

أُثبت في هذا الفصل أيضا أن نظام الجملة الأساسي في اللغة العربية من حيث ترتيب الكلام فيها هو : فعل ـ فاعل ـ مفعول. أما نظم ترتيب الكلام الأخرى مثل فعل ـ مفعول به ـ فاعل ، و مفعول به ـ فعل ـ فاعل مثلا فما هي إلاّ نظم فرعية في هذه اللغة ولا أرى أيّ مبرر للقول بوجود عبارة فعلية Verb Phrase في اللغة العربية كما هو الحال مثلا في اللغة الانكليزية أو الفرنسية ويقابل العبارة الفعلية الموجودة في مثل هذه اللغات جملة فعلية خبرية في اللغة العربية .

في الفصل الثاني أقدّم النظرية اللغوية المتبنّاة في هذا الكتاب كمنطلق للبحث • تقوم هذه النظرية وهي نظرية الحالات النحوية ، على أساس التمييز بين الحالات الظاهرة والحالات الباطنة للعبارة الاسمية Noun Phrase في اللغة العربية • وكان أول من نادى بمثل هذا التمييز اللغوي السنسكريتي القديم بانيني Panini • وتدل على الحالات الظاهرة علامات شكلية موضوعية تختلف من لغة لأخرى • ففي بعض اللغات تُعرَف حالة الاسم الظاهرة من موقع ذلك الاسم في الجملة كما في اللغة الانكليزية مثلا ، وفي بعضها الآخر تُعرَف من خلال حركة الاسم الإعرابية كما في اللغة اللاتينية أو اللغة العربية الفصحى التي فيها ثلاث حالات نحوية ظاهرة هي الرفع والنصب والجر أما الحالة النحوية الباطنة فهي الوظيفة المعنوية للاسم أو العبارة الاسمية • وفي حين يختلف عدد الحالات النحوية الظاهرة من لغة إلى أخرى تفترض هذه النظرية أن يكون عدد الحالات النحوية واحدا في كل اللغات وتتألف الجملة على المستوى الباطن من عنصرين أساسيين هما العنصر الوصفي Qualifier Component والعنصر الإنشائي Proposition Component • ويتكون العنصر الأول من صفات نحوية معنوية مميزة تسبق الفعل وتعطيه خصائص معينة ، ويتكون الثاني من فعل تتبعه حالات نحوية باطنة • فالجملة الاستفهامية " أما قَطَعت المرأة اللحم بسكّين اليوم في البيت ؟ " ، على سبيل المثال ، يكون تركيبها الباطن كما يلي :

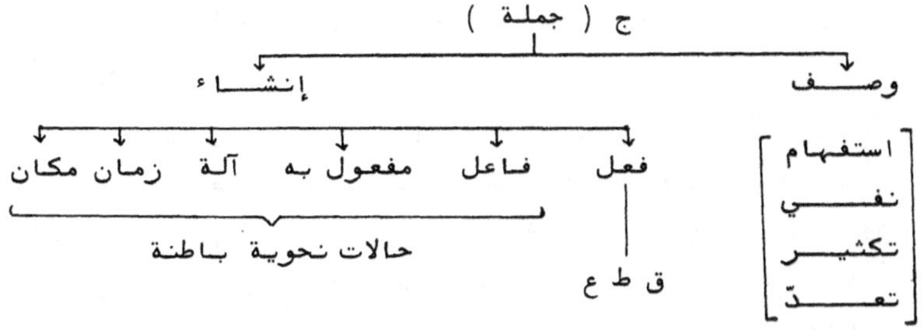

أُحدّد في هذا الفصل اثنتي عشرة حالة نحوية باطنة وأحاول تعريفها تعريفا معنويا وافيا •

يدور البحث في الفصل الثالث حول التراكيب النحوية للفعل المبني للمجهول • أقدّم في هذا الفصل عرضا لمعالجة النحاة

العرب القدماء لهذه التراكيب . وجدير بالذكر أن النحاة العرب اهتموا بناحية لم يدرك أهميتها علماء اللغة الغربيون. فقد حاول هؤلاء النحاة تحديد الفئات اللغوية التي يمكن إقامتها مقام الفاعل عندما يبنى الفعل للمجهول . أما في الغرب فقد جرت العادة على اعتبار المفعول به Direct Object الفئة الوحيدة القابلة للنيابة عن الفاعل . ولعلّ اللغوي اوتو يسبرسن Jespersen من اللغويين الغربيين القلائل الذين تنبهوا لأهمية هذا الموضوع .

أقدّم في هذا الفصل أيضا عرضا للمحاولات التي جرت على أيدى اللغويين الامريكيين التحويليين لتفسير تراكيب الفعل المبني للمجهول في اللغة العربية الفصحى . وقد أهمل هؤلاء اللغويون الطبيعة الصرفية والنحوية للغة العربية وفسّروا تراكيب الفعل المبني للمجهول في اللغة العربية في ضوء التركيب النحوي للغة الانكليزية مما جعل هذا التفسير تفسيرا عشوائيا مصطنعا لا علاقة له بطبيعة تراكيب الفعل المبني للمجهول في اللغة العربية . ولعل أهم ما أتناوله في هذا الفصل هو الطبيعة النحوية والدلالية لتراكيب الفعل المبني للمجهول في اللغة العربية . يصرّ كثير من علماء اللغة العرب والمستعربين على انه يمكن إبراز الفاعل المعنوي في جمل الفعل المبني للمجهول . ويستشهدون لإثبات رأيهم هذا بجمل مثل " قُدِّم مشروع إلى الامم المتحدة من قبل السفير الفرنسي " أو " قُتِل زيد على يد عمرو) ويقولون بأن مثل هذه التراكيب قد أُحدِثت في اللغة العربية بفضل تأثر هذه اللغة بلغات أجنبية مثل الانكليزية والفرنسية . والواقع أن مثل هذه التراكيب ممكنة فقط مع عدد قليل من الأفعال في اللغة العربية ، وأنها تراكيب قديمة موجودة أمثالها حتى في القرآن الكريم . وقد أوردت في هذا الكتاب بعض آيات كريمة تثبت حقيقة أصالة هذه التراكيب ومن هذه الآيات الآية الكريمة " كتاب أحكمت آياته ثم فصلت من لدن حكيم خبير ."(سورة هود الآية الأولى) . وقد بينت أن ما يعتبر فاعلا معنويا في مثل هذه الجمل والآيات ليس في الواقع فاعلا وإنما هو دليل معنوي على المصدر الذي صدر عنه الفعل أو دليل على الآلة المستعملة لغاية ما الخ... (انظر الفصل الثالث القسم الثالث) . وأود أن أشير في هذا الصدد لحقيقة لامجال للخلاف

فيها وهي عدم توفر حرف جر فاعلي في اللغة العربية شبيه بحرف الجر الفاعلي By في اللغة الانكليزية أو Von في اللغة الألمانية على سبيل المثال .

في هذا الفصل أحاول أيضا أن أحدّد الصفات التي تميز الأفعال التي يمكن بناؤها للمجهول عن الأفعال التي لا يمكن بناؤها للمجهول . وأورد أمثلة لأفعال يمكن بناؤها للمجهول مع أنها غير متعدية لا نحويا ولا معنويا ، كما أورد أمثلة لأفعال لا يمكن بناؤها للمجهول رغم كونها متعدية . وأظهر في هذا الفصل أن الأفعال القابلة للبناء للمجهول لا تقتصر فقط على الأفعال الدالة على حدث والتي يسميها ابن يعيش بأفعال العلاج، وإنما تشمل أيضا أفعالا غير دالة على حدث مثل أفعال الحواس وأفعال الدراية الخ ... وأوضح بالنسبة لهذه الأفعال أن فكرة التعدي لا تقتصر على التعدي من فاعل معنوي إلى مفعول به معنوي وإنما تشمل أيضا تعدي التجربة الحسية أو النفسية أو العقلية من مُعانٍ لهذه التجربة إلى كائن أو ظاهرة موجودة خارج نطاق الكائن المُعاني . والأمثلة على هذه الأفعال في اللغة العربية وغيرها من اللغات كثيرة منها الأفعال " سَمِعَ " و " شاهَدَ " و " أَحَبَّ " و " عَرَفَ " الخ ...

خلافا لما قال به معظم علماء اللغة المعاصرين في الشرق والغرب أقول في هذا الفصل: إن انابة المفعول عن الفاعل ليست جزءا من عملية اشتقاق التراكيب المبنية للمجهول وإنما هي نتيجة لذلك الاشتقاق . والدليل على ذلك أن اشتقاق الفعل المبني للمجهول لا يتطلب بالضرورة مفعولا به منصوبا وذلك كما في المثال " ذَهَبَ زَيدٌ بِهِندٍ ⟸ ذُهِبَ بِهِندٍ " . وهنالك لغات كثيرة بالإضافة إلى العربية لا تتطلب بالضرورة نائبا عن الفاعل أما في حال وجود أحد المفاعيل القابلة للانابة عن الفاعل فيقام عندئذ المفعول مقام الفاعل ويحرك بالرفع ، وذلك نتيجة لبناء الفعل للمجهول وذلك كما في المثال" أَكرَمَ زَيدٌ بَكراً ⟸ أُكرِمَ بَكرٌ " .

في الفصل الرابع أُقصر البحث على قسم واحد من الأفعال المعداة (أي المتعدية المزيدة) . يشمل هذا القسم الأفعال الدالة على التسبيب ، أو ما يمكن تسميتها بالأفعال السببية وقد سماها نحاتنا القدماء أفعال الجَعل . وأعرض للطرائق التي

يمكن بموجبها تعدية الفعل اللازم إلى فعل متعدّ إلى واحد وتعدية المتعدي إلى واحد إلى متعدّ إلى اثنين • وأعتبر عملية التعدية هذه عملية صرفية محضة يترتّب عليها تراكيب نحوية ذات ميزات محدّدة • وهنالك ثلاث طرائق صرفية لتعدية الأفعال المجرّدة إلى أفعال سببيّة :

(١) فَعِل ← فَعَلَ مثال : حَزِنَ ← حَزَنَ

(٢) فَعُل ← فَعَّلَ مثال : دَرَسَ ← دَرَّسَ

(٣) فَعُل ← أفعَلَ مثال : ذَهَبَ ← أَذهَبَ

كما أن هنالك طريقة نحوية لتعدية الفعل المجرّد إلى فعل سببيّ وذلك بواسطة حرف الجر الباء كما في المثال " جاءَ بَكرٌ ⟸ جاءَ زَيدٌ بِبَكرٍ " •

يمكن إيجاز ما في هذا الفصل بالقول : إن تراكيب الأفعال السببيّة المشتقة صرفيا هي تراكيب بسيطة غير مركبة • وأحاول في هذا الفصل إثبات هذه الفرضية • وأستطيع القول : إن ما أنادي به في هذا الفصل بالنسبة لتراكيب الأفعال السببيّة المشتقة في اللغة العربية ينطبق على مثل هذه التراكيب في اللغات الأخرى التي يشتق فيها مثل هذه الأفعال اشتقاقا صرفيا • وأوضح في هذا الفصل أن التراكيب السببيّة الفعلية المركبة الوحيدة في اللغة العربية هي التراكيب التي تحتوي على فعلين : فعل رئيسي وفعل تابع كما في الجملة " جَعَلَ زَيدٌ بَكراً يُغادِرُ البلاد " حيث " جَعَلَ " هو الفعل السببيّ الرئيسي و " يُغادِرُ " هو الفعل التابع •

في الفصل الخامس أحاول بحث ظاهرة التعدّي ليس فقط على الصعيد النحوي وإنما أيضا على الصعيد المعنوي • وأظهر أن التركيب النحوي لجمل الأفعال المتعدّية لا يدل دائما دلالة دقيقة على التركيب المعنوي لهذه الجمل • فالفاعل المرفوع في جملة " ذَهَبَ زَيدٌ " مثلا هو فاعل نحوي وفاعل معنوي في الوقت نفسه • أما في جملة " ماتَ زَيدٌ " مثلا فالفاعل المرفوع هو مفعول معنوي رغم كونه فاعلا نحويّا • ونظام الفعل الصرفي العربي يميّز بين فاعلِ فعلٍ لازم هو مفعول من حيث المعنى وفاعل فعلٍ لازمٍ هو فاعل من حيث المعنى • وبواسطة التعدية يمكن رد المفعول المعنوي المرفوع على أنه فاعل نحوي إلى مفعول نحوي كما يمكن رد الفاعل المعنوي المرفوع إلى فاعل نحوي وذلك كما يبدو واضحا من الجمل التالية :

(١) أ ـ ذابَ المِلحُ (٢) أ ـ جَلَسَ زَيدٌ

ب ـ أذابَ زَيدٌ المِلحَ ب ـ جالَسَ زَيدٌ بَكراً

في جملتي رقم (١) " الملح " مفعول معنوي في كلتا الجملتين وفي جملتي رقم (٢) "زيد" فاعل معنوي في كلتا الجملتين ۰ ويرى القارئ بسهولة أن هناك توافقا كاملا بين التركيب النحوي الظاهر والتركيب المعنوي الباطن في رقم (٢) بينما يرى أن هناك تناقضا بين التركيب النحوي الظاهر والتركيب المعنوي الباطن في رقم (١). والواقع أن هناك كثيرا من اللغات التي تعرف باللغات الفاعلية أو الأرجتية التي يعكس تركيبها النحوي الظاهر العلاقات المعنوية الموجودة في جملتي الرقم (١) ۰ من هذه اللغات على سبيل المثال لغة الباسك ولغة الاسكيمو ۰ نجد في هذه اللغات أن فاعل الفعل اللازم ومفعول الفعل المتعدي يتحركان بالحركة الإعرابية ذاتها التي تختلف عن حركة فاعل الفعل المتعدي فلو فُرِضَ للإيضاح أن اللغة العربية لغة فاعلية (أرجتية) على الصعيد النحوي الظاهر لاستُطيعَ تحريك الأسماء المرافقة للأفعال في جمل رقم (١) و (٢) على الوجه التالي :

(٣) أ ـ ذابَ المِلحَ (٤) أ ـ جَلَسَ زيداً

ب ـ أذابَ زَيدٌ المِلحَ ب ـ جالَسَ زَيدٌ بَكراً

أُظهِر في هذا الفصل أن نظام الفعل الصرفي في اللغة العربية يوحي بانه يجب وصف الجمل العربية على الصعيد المعنوي الباطن ليس فقط على أساس مفعولي حيث يُعتبر الفاعل " عُمدَة " ترافق اللازم والمتعدي والمفعول " فَضلَة " ترافق المتعدي فقط ولكن أيضا على أساس فاعلي (أرجتي) حيث يعتبر المفعول عُمدَة ترافق اللازم والمتعدي والفاعل فَضلَة ترافق المتعدي فقط ۰ وما ينطبق على اللغة العربية بموجب هذا التحليل ينطبق على كثير من لغات العالم ۰

أُحاول في هذا الفصل أيضا أن أظهر الفرق المعنوي بين الفعل المبني للمجهول والفعل العاكس Reflexive والمقصود بالفعل العاكس الفعل اللازم المشتق صرفيا مثل " انفَتَحَ " و " انكَسَرَ " و " احتَرَقَ " و " تَعَذَّبَ " ۰ فبينما تتضمن صيغة الفعل المبني للمجهول معنى الفاعلية لا تتضمن مثل هذا المعنى صيغة الفعل العاكس ۰ ففي جملة " كُسِرَ الكَأسُ " مثلا يستفاد أن هنالك فاعلا معنويا (أي كاسِر في هذه الحالة خارج عن نطاق الجملة) ۰

أما في جملة " انكَسَرَ الكَأسُ " مثلاً فلا يستفاد أن هنالك مثل هذا الفاعل المعنوي . والدليل على هذا أن جملة مثل " انكَسَرَ الكَأسُ بِنَفسِهِ " يمكن قبولها أكثر مما يمكن قبول جملة مثل " كُسِرَ الكَأسُ بِنَفسِهِ " . أما تركيب الفعل المبني للمجهول فيفسر في هذا الكتاب ليس على أساس حذف فاعل معلوم ولكن على أساس دمج فاعل غيرمعروف أو محدد أو مخصص ضمن بنية جذر الفعل مما ينتج عنه صيغة الفعل المبني للمجهول (انظر الفصل الخامس القسم الثالث) . في هذا الفصل أيضا وصف تفصيلي للفروق بين ميزات تراكيب الأفعال العاكسة كما في جملة (انكَسَرَ الكَأسُ) وتراكيب الأسماء العاكسة كما في جملة " لامَت هِندٌ نَفسَها " .

يشكل الفصل السادس والأخير موجزا لما تم بحثه في هذا الكتاب .

إن تأثري بنظريات وآراء نحاتنا العرب القدماء لا يخفى على كل من يقرأ هذا الكتاب ولو قراءة عابرة . ورغم الأخطاء والعيوب الكثيرة التي نجدها في تحليل نحاتنا العرب للغة العربية إلاّ أن وصفهم لتركيب هذه اللغة النحوي لا يزال حتى اليوم أشمل وأوفى وأفضل وصف نحوي لهذه اللغة . هذا لا يعني أنه ليس بالإمكان أفضل مما كان ولكن مع الأسف الشديد أيضا هو أن نحاتنا العرب لا يُعتَرَفُ بفضلهم على علم اللغة في الغرب بشكل عام وفي الولايات المتحدة بشكل خاص ويمكنني القول باعتزاز : إن نحاتنا القدماء قد تطرقوا إلى كثير من المشكلات النحوية التي لم يتنبه إليها معظم علماء اللغة الغربيين حتى اليوم . إلى ذكرى هؤلاء اللغويين العرب الذين وفروا لنا تراثا مجيدا في علم اللغة أرفع أسمى آيات التقدير والإجلال .

أود أن أتقدم بالشكر إلى كثير من الإخوان والزملاء الذين كان لنصحهم وآرائهم النقدية البناءة أثر إيجابي كبير على هذا الكتاب . أخص بالشكر الأخ الدكتور المرحوم نجم بزرگان والأخ الدكتور بيتر عبود والدكتور ونفرد ليمان والدكتور كارل باكر والدكتورة سولڤاي فلوگر . إلاّ أن أعمق شكري وأبلغ امتناني يعودان إلى الأخ الدكتور محمد حسن باكلا الذي كان لمساعدته وتشجيعه أكبر الأثر ليس فقط على الكتاب بل وعلى المؤلف أيضا . وغني عن القول أن هؤلاء العلماء ليسوا مسؤولين عن أية أخطاء أو عيوب في هذا الكتاب تلك هي مسؤوليتي وحدي .

أسأل الله أن يكون هذا الجهد المتواضع ذا فائدة لأساتذة اللغة العربية الفصحى وطلابها في عالمنا العربي والإسلامي ، إنه سميع مجيب الدعاء .

جورج نعمه سعد
جامعة ماساشوستس في أمهرست
الولايات المتحدة الأمريكية